AF251667

MESA

"Partners in Progress" by Daniel F. Ruskin

Produced in Cooperation with the Mesa Southwest Museum

Windsor Publications, Inc.
Northridge, California

M E S A

Windsor Publications, Inc.—
    History Books Division
Managing Editor: Karen Story
Design Director: Alexander D'Anca

Staff for *Mesa*
Senior Editor: Susan L. Wells
Manuscript Editor: Marilyn Horn
Editor, Corporate Biographies: Alyson Gould
Production Editor, Corporate Biographies:
    Albert Polito
Senior Proofreader: Susan J. Muhler
Editorial Assistants: Didier Beauvoir, Una
    FitzSimons, Thelma Fleischer, Kim
    Kievman, Michael Nugwynne, Kathy M.
    Peyser, Pat Pittman, Theresa J. Solis
Sales Representative, Corporate Biographies:
    Richard R. Fry
Art Director: Christina Rosepapa
Layout Artist, Corporate Biographies:
    Bonnie Felt
Layout Artist, Editorial: Michael Burg
Designer: Tanya Maiboroda

Library of Congress
Cataloging-in-Publication Data
Mead, Tray C.
    Mesa: beneath the shadows of the
    superstition
    "Partners in Progress, by Daniel F.
    Ruskin" (Ch. 7)
    Bibliography: p.157
    Includes index
    1. Mesa (Ariz.)—History. 2. Mesa (Ariz.)—
Description—Views. 3. Mesa (Ariz.)—
Industries. I. Price, Robert C. II. Mesa
Southwest Museum. III. Title.
F819.M4M34   1988   979.1'73   88-27701
ISBN: 0-89781-254-9

Windsor Publications, Inc.
Elliot Martin, Chairman of the Board
James L. Fish, III Chief Operating Officer

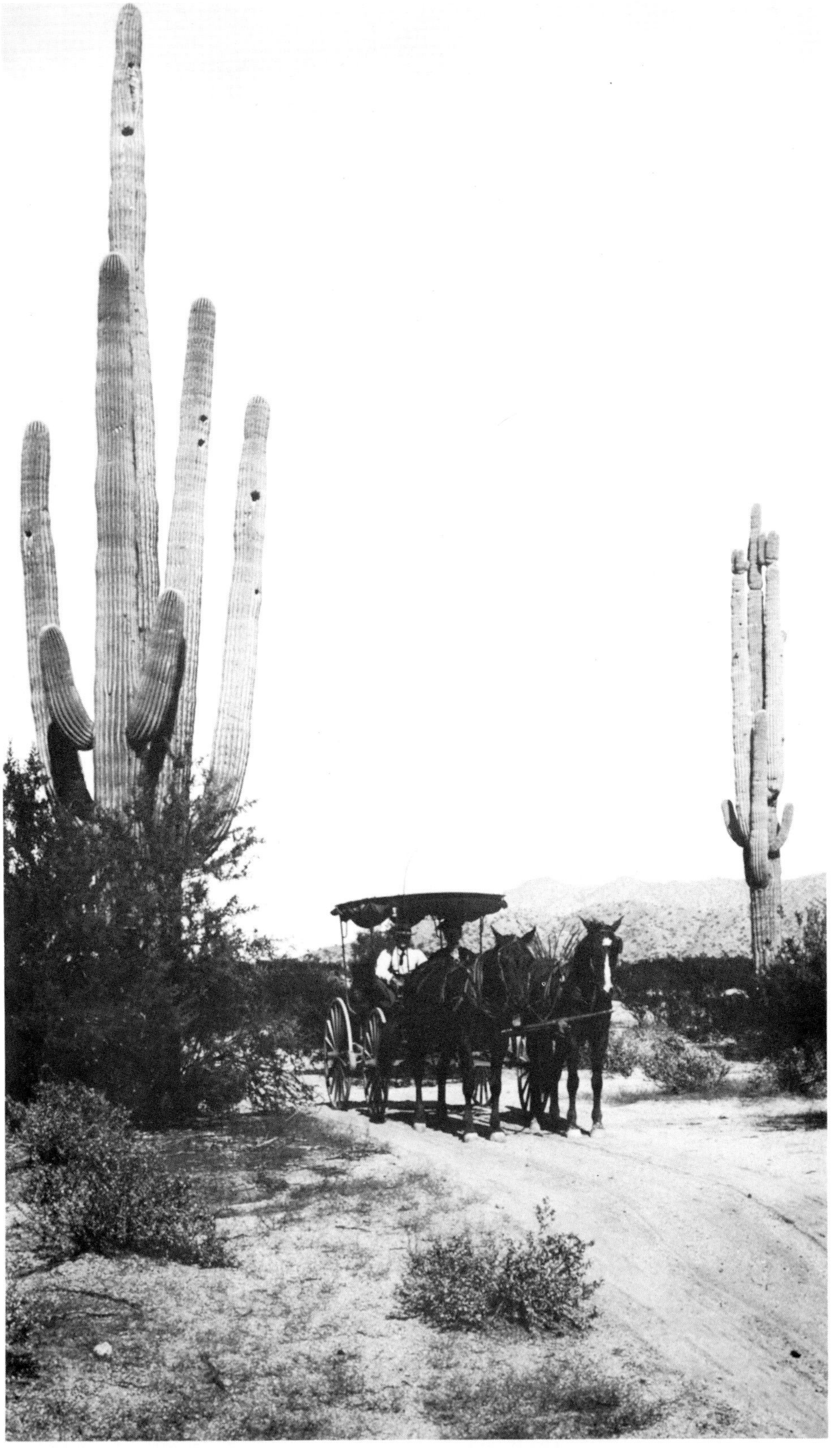

Right: Walter J. Lubken and his driver
paused on the Apache trail near the Superstition Mountains. Lubken was the official government
photographer for the Roosevelt Dam
Project and also maintained a private studio
in Mesa. Courtesy, Norman Mead Collection

Contents

The Arizona state tree, the
Palo Verde, and the state
flower, the saguaro blossom,
are captured in silhouette
against a purple sunset.
Photo by Norman Mead

The authors would like to dedicate this book to the late W. Earl Merrill, loving
caretaker of Mesa's history for nearly 50 years, without whose pioneer research and
early documentation of our city's past this book could not have been written

INTRODUCTION
▼ ▼ ▼

I have always been fascinated by history, which above all else records the accomplishments of *people,* which makes history such an exciting and revealing subject.

I was delighted to learn that Tray C. Mead and Robert C. Price had written a history of my own backyard—Mesa, Arizona. There is a unique spirit to this place that I and my fellow Mesans hold dear. The book's title, *Mesa: Beneath the Shadows of the Superstitions,* has a nice ring to it, and I am confident that its contents will be intriguing to all.

To me, the big challenge faced by Mead and Price was to capture that spirit, and present a picture of Mesa as something different, not just to write a narrative of another American town. When I first scanned a proposed outline of the book, I knew that the authors had succeeded admirably in doing just that. They have found why Mesa has a warm charm and a wide appeal that sets it apart from other places of human habitation.

Mesa's past is much more than the chronology of a sleepy little farm town. It is a diverse history that dates back to 10,000 B.C., when hunters and gatherers were busy on the local scene. Since those long-ago years, Mesa has evolved through many different stages of development, becoming one of the fastest growing cities in the county.

It takes dedicated writers with a love of their community to weave a significant pattern that offers a true picture of the evolution of a thriving town borne of the hardships and adversities of those who went before us. History, to be worthy of its name, must be accurate. The authors have sifted through an enormous amount of material to separate the wheat from the chaff.

Beneath the Shadows of the Superstitions, written in seven illuminating chapters and illustrated and supplemented by a wealth of pictures, effectively makes the long leap from those bygone years to today. Very important to our past is the role of the Hohokam, whose ancient Indian culture dates to 300 B.C. These early inhabitants left us a visible complex of canals into which was diverted water from the Salt River, giving life to the vast arid desert. The saga of reclamation and the building of Roosevelt Dam in more recent times is also an essential part of any history of this region.

To me, perhaps, the most enchanting part of the book describes Mesa's growth into a tourism center, which tells how Mesa was discovered by the rest of the world as a destination point. Beginning in the 1930s, the era of the dude ranch and the singing cowboy put Mesa on the map. Mesa's credits include the filming of many Hollywood Westerns on the historic Apache Trail; the advent of major league baseball spring training; the preparation of the British Royal Air Force cadets at Falcon Field for combat during World War II; and the development of winter accommodations and other attractions for our visitors.

Other histories about our town have made good reading, but I believe that *Beneath the Shadows of the Superstitions* will leave for us and future generations the richest legacy of all!

—Walter Zipf

This Arizona family enjoys an outing in their new Ford touring car in 1910 near the cottonwoods along the Salt River near Mesa. Courtesy, Norman Mead Collection

MESA THROUGH THE YEARS

10,000 B.C.: Early man is believed to have crossed the Bering Strait into America as long as 30,000 years ago. Around 10,000 B.C., the Mesa region is seasonally inhabited by the mammoth hunters, Paleo-Indians who follow and hunt the great, lumbering beasts for food. Using short, stout spears with "Clovis" points, they drive the mammoths into large bogs along the Salt River. The climate is wet and humid in central Arizona.

5,000 B.C.: The mammoths now have become extinct, forcing prehistoric man to utilize different aspects of his environment for survival. The hunters of the Mesa region, who must track smaller game, develop a throwing device called an "atlatl," which increases the power and range of thrown spears. They also depend more on gathering, and feed on the seasonal crops provided by nature, such as saguaro fruit and mesquite beans.

300 B.C.: The Hohokam Indian civilization of central Arizona, including the Mesa region, has developed from the earlier Paleo-Indians, and their Pioneer Period has begun. Agriculturally oriented, the Hohokam live in well-established farming communities, and are quite adept at weaving the cotton that they grow. They also develop a type of pottery unique to the region, with their prototypical red-on-buff styling pattern the most common.

A.D. 600: The Hohokam, now in their Colonial Period, build Mesa Grande, the governmental and religious center for their expanding city, which today lies beneath present-day Mesa. The Mesa Grande ruins remain undisturbed, preserved in northwest Mesa by an act of City Council in 1987. Massive colonization and trade occur during this period, which also sees the development of a prehistoric ball game to satisfy recreational needs. An extensive canal system, unparalleled among prehistoric cultures, is developed to irrigate the arid desert.

1100: The Sedentary Period of the Hohokam begins. The Mesa Grande structure has been greatly expanded, as has the entire Hohokam empire, but growth now slows. Short periods of flood, drought, and famine occur, but overall the period is one of prosperity. The Aztecs are now becoming the dominant culture in central Mexico, and trading between the two cultures is taking place.

1450: The Hohokam's Classic Period, 1100 to

Some of Arizona's most beautiful sunsets are on the desert lands just east of Mesa. Spectacular nightly sunsets are the rule rather than the exception. Photo by Norman Mead

Above: The Hohokam Indians who lived in the Mesa area from 300 B.C. to A.D. 1450 excelled in many art forms. This shallow bowl, which was painted red on a buff background, is typical of those produced during the Classic Period of their empire, around A.D. 1200. Courtesy, Mesa Southwest Museum Collections

Above right: Pictographs, commonly misidentified as hieroglyphics, are abundant in the Superstitions as well as other mountains that ring the Salt River Valley. Many treasure seekers interpret these markings as maps and signs to lost fortunes. A more widely accepted story is that the pictographs are religious and cultural markings depicting significant events in the lives of prehistoric peoples. Courtesy, Norman Mead Collection

Far right: These are some of the best-preserved ruins of the Salado Indians, who vanished from Mesa around A.D. 1500. Many archaeologists believe they were an offshoot blend culture of the Hohokam and the Mogollon to the north. The Salados were expert weavers who also made excellent black-on-white pottery. Photo by Walter J. Lubken, courtesy, Norman Mead Collection

circa 1450, draws to a close. It is a time of transition and mystery. This era sees the development of compound-style living in above-ground, fort-like structures, and the complete abandonment of many previously flourishing communities. Burial practices change as well. All of these occurrences serve notice of significant, and not altogether positive, changes within Hohokam society.

1500 (circa): The Hohokam civilization vanishes. Many theories are proposed to explain this disappearance; none have been proven. The final chapter of the Hohokam culture remains one of the great unanswered questions in modern archaeology. By the mid-sixteenth century, the Apache Indians are established in Arizona, having entered from the northwest territories, providing fuel for arguments linking the Apache to the Hohokam's disappearance.

1539-1540: Spanish exploration of Arizona and the Southwest begins, centering around the search for the "Seven Cities of Cibola," a legendary land of incredible riches, gold-paved streets, and houses lined with pure turquoise. A party led by Father Marcos de Niza travels north, becoming the first group of white men to gaze upon the Casa Grande ruins, a major structure left by the Hohokam, approximately 35 miles south of present-day Mesa. Then he is said to have passed through the valley and Mesa area, leaving his "calling card" behind: a rock bearing the inscription of de Niza's name, which can be found in Phoenix's South Mountain Park and is purported to have come from Marcos de Niza's own hand.

De Niza, carried away with the thrill of his search for these cities of gold, sends back elaborate reports of the riches he *expects* to find. These reports provide the incentive for Francisco Vasquez de Coronado to launch a major expedition into the area in 1540. After five rugged months, Coronado's army reaches its journey's end, finding no such riches. De Niza later dies in disgrace in a Mexican convent.

1699-1700: Father Eusibio Francisco Kino travels extensively throughout central Arizona, exploring the lower Salt River, stopping just short of present-day Mesa. Credited with naming the Salt River, "Rio Salado," Father Kino establishes several missions in what will become Arizona, including San Xavier del Bac in southern Arizona.

From this base he spreads his teachings, including improved farming methods that are readily adopted by the agricultural Indian tribes of the region. He develops an especially strong friendship with the Pima, who provide a strong buffer against the warlike Apache. He also introduces the first cattle, horses, and sheep to the area.

1767: Following rumors of wealthy mines discovered but not reported by the Spanish priests, the Jesuits are expelled from Mexico, and many flee to remote corners of the Spanish Empire, including central Arizona. One popular theory behind the "Lost Dutchman's" gold mine in Mesa's nearby Superstition Mountains is that the gold discovered there was actually Spanish Jesuit treasure.

1774: Juan Bautista de Anza, accompanied by Father Francisco Tomas Garces, Franciscan successor to Father Kino, begins a land-route exploration from Tubac to Yuma. Called "el Camino del Diablo" (or "the Devil's Highway") by de Anza, the route is difficult, but this initial expedition lays the groundwork for the establishment of an overland route from Arizona to California, which will greatly enhance settlers' accessibility to central Arizona.

Above: Silver reales coins such as this 1740 Spanish Colonial silver cob were known in the United States as bits. Each bit was worth 12.5 cents, and eight bits equaled one dollar. Spanish coins were used widely as legal tender in the United States, not only when Arizona was a Spanish territory, but even into this century. Early Mesa merchants frequently accepted Spanish coins in payment of merchandise. Courtesy, Mesa Southwest Museum Collections

Right: Ramon Nonatus is traditionally represented in this santo holding a monstrance. Nonatus was a priest of the Mercedarians of Berriz, whose apostolic mission was the ransoming of Christians captured by Moslems around the twelfth century. Nonatus is perhaps best known for offering himself as hostage after his ransom funds were exhausted. Courtesy, Mesa Southwest Museum Collections

Far right top: This reconstruction of an arrastra—a simple mill—at a tourist attraction demonstrates the methods used by Spanish explorers to pulverize gold and silver ore. Mules or horses pulled the grinding machine. Arrastras can be found throughout Arizona. Courtesy, Norman Mead Collection

Above: Although the desert is often thought to be a barren wasteland, the Superstition Mountains are surrounded by a carpet of desert greenery. Photo by Norman Mead

Right: The blossoms of the cholla cactus add bright red and pink colors to the desert landscape. Photo by Norman Mead

Right: An Indian of Mexico is shown wearing colorful, traditional Aztec headdress. Photo by Norman Mead

Below right: Mesa's large fall Indian Powwow draws thousands of spectators and Indian participants from 10 Western states. This event is held and sponsored by the Mesa Southwest Museum usually in October of each year. Photo by Norman Mead

Below: A tribal woman of noted virtue presides over this Apache Sunrise Ceremony; through massaging, she transfers her virtues and skills to a young Apache woman. The ceremony is performed to help make the young women marriageable. Photo by Norman Mead

1781: After seven years of continued exploration, Father Garces and his large combined military-missionary forces are massacred by Yuma Indians near the present site of Yuma. As a result of this bloody event, Spanish expeditions into the Arizona region are curtailed, and their influence diminished, for nearly 50 years. This allows another hostile tribe, the Apache, to reinforce its control of the Mesa region and much of central Arizona.

1821: Mexico wins its independence from Spain, and the Mesa region is now under its nominal control. Little change occurs; Captain Jose Romero, who commanded the area during the Spanish reign, remains as the commander for Mexico. Two years later Mexico will identify Arizona as a territory called "Nuevo Mexico."

The years between 1821 and 1846 reflect the turbulence of Mexico's national government, and no real strategy is formulated for its frontier provinces. The Apache, momentarily satisfied to be rid of the imperialistic Spanish, are peaceable, but will break out in 1831 with a new series of attacks.

1824: The first American trappers trek across the Mesa region as they trap along the Salt and Gila rivers. Their main objective is beaver pelts, and they gravitate to the south as beaver become scarce in the northern streams. Some trappers realize there is a lucrative market for Indian scalps, with the Mexican government paying 100 pesos for every Apache scalp in a last-ditch effort to eradicate the tribe. In 1837 frontiersman James Kirker will earn an estimated $100,000 from scalp bounties, which contributes to the depopulation of the Arizona area prior to the arrival of the first white settlers. Among the more reputable trappers to enter Arizona are "Old Bill" Williams, a legendary mountain man and hermit; Pauline Weaver, for whom the Superstition Mountain landmark "Weaver's Needle" is named; and James Pattie, who becomes famed for written accounts of his adventures on the Western frontier. Two years later Pattie will camp by himself near Mesa and in doing so avoids a Papago massacre of French trappers.

1846: Twenty-five years of Mexican occupation of Arizona ends soon after President James K. Polk declares war on Mexico, prompted by a Mexican attack on U.S. soldiers in Texas. Lieutenant Colonel Philip Cooke's "Mormon Batallion," a group of 500 members of the Church of Jesus Christ of Latter-day Saints, drives out a Mexican garrison and takes possession of Tucson. The battallion, whose wages are used to finance the Mormon move from New York to Utah, effectively ends the Mexican American War as it relates to Arizona. Many of these soldiers later become early settlers of the Mesa area.

1848: The Mexican War officially ends with the signing of the Treaty of Guadalupe-Hidalgo. A new United States-Mexico border is set at the Gila River, just 20 miles south of what will soon become Mesa. Confusion surrounding the survey of the border will necessitate the Gadsen Purchase of 1853.

1850: Congress officially designates Arizona, including the Mesa area, as part of New Mexico Territory, in an "omnibus bill." The first territorial census of New Mexico Territory lists 6,547 residents.

1853: The Gadsden Purchase adds 45,537 acres south of the Gila River to U.S. territory, repositioning Mesa in the center of the Arizona region. Kit Carson describes the ceded land as "so desolate, desert, and God-forsaken that a wolf could not make a living on it."

1861: Efforts to make peace with the Apache continue. The Apache leader Cochise meets with Second Lieutenant George Bascom at Apache Pass under the white flag of truce. Bascom, fresh out of West Point, betrays the white flag, and, allegedly acting under orders, accuses Cochise of kidnapping and captures him, but Cochise manages to slit a tent and escape. Bascom's efforts result in a new round of Indian wars, and the Superstition Mountains east of Mesa become a stronghold for the Apache during the following 11 years of bloody warfare.

1862: Growing sympathy for the Southern cause culminates in a pronouncement of "Arizona" as part of the Confederate States of America. Lieutenant Colonel John Baylor proclaims himself territorial governor, and in February the Confederate Congress passes a bill creating Arizona Territory, making the Mesa region part of the Confederacy. Marcus McWillie is for-

Four Apache Indian women posed for Mesa photographer Walter J. Lubken. Basket making became a fine art among the Apaches, while pottery, being much less durable, was not developed to any great proficiency. Photo by Walter J. Lubken, courtesy, Norman Mead Collection

Multilevel Indian dwellings at Tonto National Monument are pictured as they appear today. Doorways were extremely small, designed for both defense and heating and cooling conservation. Early Mesa visitors mistakenly concluded from the small doorways that these early Indian people were a race of midgets. Courtesy, Norman Mead Collection

mally seated in the congress as Arizona's delegate. Confederate troops occupy southern Arizona and New Mexico until being driven out in April 1862.

1863: In response to continuing Confederate overtures, the U.S. Congress belatedly passes a bill making Arizona a U.S. territory. In his argument in support of territorial status for Arizona, New Mexico delegate John Watts is quite eloquent: "An Italian sunset never threw its gentle rays over more lovely valleys or heaven-kissing hills, valleys harmonious with the music of a thousand sparkling rills, mountains shining with untold millions of mineral wealth, wooing the hand of capital and labor to possess and use it."

1864: Union Colonel James Henry Carleton assumes "authority of the United States over the people of Arizona." He commissions former mountain man and scout Kit Carson to fight the Mescalero Apache and their tribal brothers, the Navajos. The surrendering Indians are marched more than 300 miles to Bosque Redondo, a reservation established in northeastern New Mexico. By December this camp contains 8,354 Navajos.

Meanwhile, on February 23, the "Bloody Tanks" massacre occurs near the Salt and Verde rivers confluence, north of Mesa. A party formed in Prescott, in search of stolen cattle, meets with hostile Indians, resulting in a skirmish in which two dozen Indians are killed along with one white man, Cyrus Lennon, believed to be the first white man buried in the Salt River Valley, just outside the present city limits of Mesa.

1865: Following the end of the Civil War, attentions turn to the problem of the Apache Indians, who have continued to menace early settlers in the Salt River Valley. The McDowell Crossing and Fort McDowell are established just north of Mesa, now marked by a monument constructed by pioneer Hugh Dana. The crossing greatly facilitates travel and exploration in the east valley region. Situated on the west bank of the Verde River, seven miles above its junction with the Salt, the fort is designed to control the Apache travel routes in the lower Verde valley, and will be manned for the next 25 years. The increased safety owing to the military presence makes the area much more appealing to settlers, providing the initial catalyst for the settlement of Mesa.

1867: Jack Swilling develops the first irrigation system in the valley. Swilling, a Confederate deserter and reputed murderer, takes note of the ancient Hohokam canals in the Salt River Valley, and soon raises $10,000 to begin excavation of these canals. Agriculture flourishes in the valley as a result, and the farming community of Pumpkinville, soon to be renamed "Phoenix," is established.

The success of the Swilling Irrigation Canal Company spawns a host of other canal companies, and by 1890 more than 70,000 acres of land are under cultivation in Arizona. Patrick Hamilton, Arizona's first "press agent," who was commissioned by the legislature to extol the virtues of the state and promote immigration, states correctly, albeit to the detriment of the territory's image as a center for agriculture, that "water . . . is the most precious element for the farmer in Arizona."

1868: William Rowe builds an adobe station to cater to travelers to and from Fort McDowell, on the trail between Phoenix and the McDowell Crossing. This station combines with the settlement of the Charles Whitlow family to become the village of Maryville, named for Whitlow's 12-year-old daughter.

Maryville will survive less than 10 years, as the importance of the McDowell Crossing is greatly diminished by the development of the more convenient Hayden's Ferry river crossing several miles to the west. Cottonwood logs and timber used in Maryville's modest buildings will be recycled by future pioneers in what will soon become the city of Mesa, just across the river.

The Salt River Valley, including the Mesa region, is "sectionalized": surveyed and laid out for township

The Apache Indians suffered many relocations similar to Kit Carson's relocating them in 1864. In 1906 they were once again moved just a few miles out of town at the encampment of Granite Reef, which today borders Mesa's city limits. Courtesy, Norman Mead Collection Collection

development. The surveyors' report describes Mesa and the east valley as follows: "There is considerable grass on the mesa or uplands, and, on the river bottoms, is quite luxuriant . . . Cottonwood timber is found along the banks of the Salt River, with greasewood and sage brush on the mesa, and arrow-weed on the bottom-lands."

1870: Arizona's population totals 9,658. The settlements of Phoenix and Maryville combined total "74 dwellings, 21 families, 192 white males, 48 white females, two colored males, and four colored females," for a total population of 246.

1871: Hayden's Ferry, a reliable crossing over the unpredictable Salt River, is established. Charles Trumbull Hayden, a Connecticut native, establishes a flour mill on the Salt River between Phoenix and Maryville, and the surrounding community that develops also takes the name "Hayden's Ferry." The community undergoes a series of name changes, until an expatriate Englishman, "Lord" Darrel Duppa, suggests the name "Tempe," finding the dusty desert village reminiscent of the Vale of Tempe in Greece.

1872: The first noted reference to the name "Superstitions" for the mountain range to the east of Mesa occurs in the *San Francisco Bulletin,* in an article written by Ben C. Truman in his account of a trip from Prescott to Tucson: "The mountain scenery . . . is grand and superb beyond description . . . in the distance, 140 miles away, is 'Superstition Mountain,' the most romantic elevation in Arizona, where, the legends of the country tell us, exist fabulous deposits of native silver and pure gold . . ."

The Superstitions are also the site for the continuing Apache wars. In one of the most noteworthy battles, a band of 100 Mojave-Apache hiding in an impregnable cave in the north wall of the Salt River Canyon comes under attack by General Crook and his

men. The soldiers unleash a barrage of bullets which ricochet off the cave walls, killing the majority of the Indians; this cave later becomes known as "Skeleton Cave."

1875: The first seeds of Mesa's settlement are planted when a seven-man expedition from Utah, led by Daniel W. Jones, visits the Salt River Valley. Although Jones' original plan bypasses the valley in favor of a route along the Colorado River into Mexico, a telegram from Brigham Young dictates a detour into central Arizona.

The exploration party is surprised by the temperate conditions found upon entering the valley that fall. Jones writes: "While crossing the Mogollon Mountains, the weather was quite cold. As we descended toward the lower valley, the temperature changed very rapidly. We were very much surprised on entering Salt River Valley . . . a fertile looking soil and miles of level plain . . . What made the country look more real was the thrifty little settlement of Phoenix, with its streets already planted with shade trees." This positive report sent to Brigham Young results in further exploration of the area, and will ultimately initiate settlement of Mesa.

While valley development remains in an embryonic state, four farmers discover the Silver King mine in the Superstitions, northeast of Mesa. Due to their inexperience in mining, they lose $12,000 during their first year of operation, and offer the mine to a local merchant as payment on an overdue account—the offer is refused. Over the next nine years, however, the mine produces more than six million dollars' worth of silver.

1876: A party of 84 men, women, and children is gathered in St. George, Utah, in answer to a call from the leaders of the Mormon Church to found a settlement in "the far south." Their destination is not specified; church leaders simply dictate that they settle at a location at which "they feel impressed." Leading the party once again is Daniel Jones, who will guide them toward the Salt River Valley area which so impressed him just a few months earlier. During a meeting with Brigham Young, Jones is asked what kinds of settlers he would like to lead. His response: "Give me men with large families and small means, so that when we get there, they will be too poor to come back, and they will have to stay."

1877: The Jones company of colonists is organized, and on January 17 begins its momentous trek southward. After 58 days of arduous travel, the party reaches the McDowell Crossing. On March 6, a vote is taken on whether to settle on the Salt River or move on; all but one vote to stay, and a community is founded. Over the next few years, it will be known as Utahville, Jonesville, and finally Lehi, named for a prophet in the *Book of Mormon,* before becoming part of Mesa in the early 1900s.

In the new community, called Fort Utah, the first building is a four-wall adobe structure with no roof. Individual families are allotted one room each, over which they build a dirt roof within the fort's walls; they live in these temporary surroundings while building permanent homes in the vicinity. Canal building begins almost immediately upon the pioneers' arrival; a four-mile canal, completed in time for summer planting and accomplished by a mere 20 men with hand shovels, is the first of many in the east valley.

Meanwhile, back in Utah, the call to colonize attracts a second group of settlers, and in September a party that will eventually number 76 sets out for the Salt River Valley. The bulk of this party consists of members of the families of four men: Charles Crismon, Francis Pomeroy, George Sirrine, and Charles Robson. They will become known in Mesa as the "four founding families," and their arrival in 1878 will bring about the first settlement in the region that will become central Mesa.

1878: The second group of Mesa settlers reach the Lehi settlement on February 14. They choose to settle in an area approximately three miles south of the previous settlement, on a slightly higher elevation, a "mesa," contingent on the development of an irrigation system. The Mesa Canal, an eight-mile waterway leading from the Salt River south to the new townsite, is constructed, while the new arrivals set up temporary residence in the Lehi camp. Their new canal follows the path of an ancient Hohokam canal first built some 1,000 years earlier, and is successfully completed in October.

Soon after, William Newell builds the first house on the mesa, surely the Arizona equivalent of a "log cabin": a small structure constructed from saguaro cactus, plastered with mud, covered with a dirt roof. Within two years, 21 other families will join them in the new community, the first step in the repopulation of an area that was a booming Hohokam metropolis just 400 years earlier.

Meanwhile, in the Superstitions, German-born miner Jacob Waltz, having prospected in the area for some six years, is suspected of having discovered a major gold strike. Although he constantly eludes those who attempt to follow him into the mountains, the "Dutchman" sells quantities of gold in Florence and Mesa. Rumors of his riches and hidden mine circulate, triggering subsequent gold rushes into the mountains east of Mesa.

Waltz's death in 1891 leaves this mystery unsolved, and thousands of would-be prospectors will follow his trails east of Mesa for years, even to the present day. The "Lost Dutchman's Mine" eventually becomes known around the world, becoming the subject for Hollywood motion pictures and leading to the mysterious deaths of dozens of fortune hunters.

1879: As additional parties arrive from Utah to the new Mesa settlement, President Hayes signs a new declaration that holds the potential to stop development of the Salt River Valley: he declares the Salt River Valley, including Phoenix, Tempe, and Mesa, as one large Indian reservation.

This rash proclamation is made following the public airing of mistreatment of Pima residents on the Salt River by some white settlers. When military personnel recommend the establishment of reserved land for the Indians, Hayes far exceeds the request. Soon after the uproar of Arizona's white residents reaches Washington, the order is rescinded, and the somewhat smaller Salt River Indian Reservation is established for the Pima, bordering Mesa.

1880: Two very different but important facets of life in Mesa are introduced: honey bees and wine making. Mr. and Mrs. Elijah Pomeroy are credited with bringing the first bees into the Mesa area upon their arrival in December. Their journey from St. George, Utah, takes six weeks, as Elijah periodically removes the hive from the wagon and "takes the bees out for exercise." Merchant B.F. Johnson will start Mesa's first apiary four years later.

The Bagley brothers, Samuel and David, open

Contrary to popular belief, these birds do not bury their heads in the sand to hide from their enemies; they are fierce fighters. The largest known ostrich was eight feet high and weighed 300 pounds. Courtesy, Douglas R. Brown Collection

This mother-and-child photo was taken by Walter J. Lubken at the turn of the century. The cradleboard was a back-pack for transporting Apache babies, who were strapped in so tightly that many Apaches suffered bone deformation. Courtesy, Norman Mead Collection

Mesa's first winery. The *Phoenix Gazette* reports in 1885: "The brandy and wine of Mesa City is pronounced by connoisseurs to be equal to the most excellent of California." The wine industry flourishes, and by 1893 there are three major wineries and one distillery, with production reaching 30,000 gallons of wine and 4,000 gallons of brandy.

The settlement of Stringtown, just west of Mesa, is founded. The community gets its name from the fact that residents are "strung out" down a shady, cottonwood-lined thoroughfare, now located one and a half miles east of the Mesa-Tempe border.

1881: Mesa's first post office, under the name of "Hayden," is established, serving a population of about 300. Fannie VanCott Macdonald is the first postmaster. Although the town's name of Mesa is already gaining popularity, another Arizona settlement called Mesaville precludes "official" use of that name. The community's official name will become Mesa after the demise of Mesaville eight years later.

1882: The area's first lumber home is built in Stringtown, and Mesa's first wooden schoolhouse is built. It is uncertain whether the "little red schoolhouse" is actually built from redwood or is simply painted red. The school will remain in use until 1906, when it is replaced by the larger Alma School, from which one of Mesa's major thoroughfares will take

its name. Lumber is scarce in the Salt River Valley, and expensive. Writes one scribe: "The great bodies of the pine forests of Arizona are as yet untouched by the woodman's axe, and must remain so to a great extent until railroads open up the country."

1883: The attempted robbery of a Chinese peddler sets off Mesa's first criminal manhunt. A posse of 75 Mesans, led by Deputy Sheriff Charles Robson, tracks down a band of outlaws which includes "Curley Bill" Brocuis and "Three-Fingered Jack" Williams. The posse confronts the outlaws near the Salt River, but lacking a warrant, cannot arrest them. After obtaining a warrant, the posse trails the gang north to Pleasant Valley, but the outlaws escape.

"White-collar" crime is also prevalent, much of it based on a clause in the Gadsden Purchase agreement that honors Arizona land grants that were given under Spanish rule some 100 years prior. James Reavis files a claim to over 10 million acres in central Arizona, including Mesa and Phoenix—the notorious "Peralta Land Grant." He produces an endless supply of faded documents, wills, and pictures of the Peralta family, to whose grant he had allegedly fallen heir. After 10 years of investigation, Reavis is found guilty of fraud and bribery, and is sentenced to six years in prison.

Mesa citizens petition the Maricopa County

Board of Supervisors, requesting incorporation of settlement as a village, and on July 15, "Mesa City" is incorporated. Soon after, however, the municipality's population is reduced significantly by a smallpox epidemic, which kills 44, and forces the townspeople to develop the city's first cemetery.

1884: Polygamists come under fire as Congress passes the Edmunds Act, which stiffens the penalties for polygamy and steps up enforcement. Phoenix newspapers espouse a liberal "live and let live" philosophy, but federal officers stage raids on Mormon communities throughout the West, and many Mesans spend time in the Yuma Territorial Prison. Anti-Mormon sentiments run strong during this period.

The development of the community continues, however. The village council officially gives names to the streets within Mesa's square mile; and the Zenos Co-op is built, which will serve as a gathering place and major downtown mercantile for years to come.

1886: Mesans join with other Arizona citizens in an appeal to Governor Zulich to stop Geronimo, whom they claim is responsible for the deaths of 100 Arizona men, women, and children. The Apache chief finally surrenders to General Nelson Miles, who exiles Geronimo and his followers to Florida, promising to allow them to return to Arizona in two years. The promise is broken and the Apache are held prisoner until 1913, when they are transplanted to Oklahoma. By 1886, with the Apache neutralized, Arizona's Indians have become more of a social problem than a military one.

Prompted by confusion with Hayden's Ferry, which has since become Tempe, the Mesa post office changes its name from "Hayden" To "Zenos," taking its name from a prophet in the *Book of Mormon.* During this year there is also a significant event in Tempe: the opening of Tempe Normal School, which in the course of 100 years will become Arizona State University.

1887: Mesa's first archaeological expedition, led by Frank Cushing, provides the first analysis of the Mesa Grande ruins. His group spends 16 months in the Mesa area, studying Mesa Grande to a small degree, but spends more time at a remote site called Los Muertos, west of present-day Chandler. Former Mesa city engineer Omar Turney writes: "Cushing preferred to concentrate work on the ruin now known as Mesa Grande, believing it would yield the best results of any in the valley, but on account of the annoyance of curio seekers, he selected a ruin thought to be farthest from town."

1888: Yet another unusual industry develops in Mesa: ostrich farming. Women's fashion dictates that no stylish bonnet is complete without an ostrich plume. Since the climate of Mesa and the valley is very similar to that of northern Africa, the birds flourish, and ostrich farming becomes a major valley industry. This continues until World War I, when ladies' fashions turn toward more modest headgear. On December 6, 1914, roasted ostrich is added to the menu of the Palace Cafeteria in Phoenix.

Mesa's population reaches 300. To open up more irrigatable land for colonization and farming, the Highland Canal in north Mesa is constructed. This canal is longer than the Mesa Canal, completed 10 years earlier, and construction is considerably more difficult in that the new canal does not follow in the path of the prehistoric Hohokam canal system. Surprisingly, it is used little until the Great Drought of 1901.

1889: The community's post office finally changes its official name to Mesa, with George Passey as postmaster. The name "Mesa" is derived from the Spanish word for "table," descriptive of the broad "tableland" that the original square mile of the community is built upon.

1890: A chapter of Mesa's formative history is ended when orders are received to abandon Fort McDowell. Troops withdraw, and for four years the structures of the fort remain undisturbed. Later, however, the site becomes a popular health resort, before ultimately being designated as the Fort McDowell Indian Reservation, which it remains today.

A large building near the Silver King Mine is dismantled and moved to Mesa. It is rebuilt in the center of town, as Mesa's first downtown hotel, the 21-room

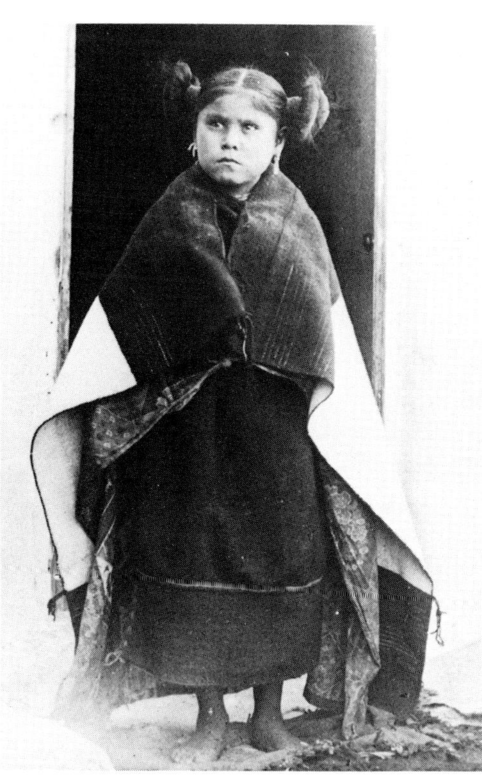

A young Hopi maiden wears traditional tribal dress for this 1904 photo taken by a valley resident who traveled around the state documenting Southwest culture at the turn of the century. Courtesy, Douglas R. Brown Collection

Hakes House.

1891: Gold! The closest strike ever made to Mesa, a few miles away in the northwestern foothills of the Superstitions, is discovered by four Mesans. The boomtown of Goldfield springs up around the Mammoth Mine, which will yield more than one million dollars' worth of gold over a six-year period. The Mormon influence of its owners results in its becoming known as "the only Prohibition mining camp in the territory."

The discovery touches off an "Arizona gold rush." Prospectors flock to the east valley, providing a shot in the arm for Mesa's growing economy. This activity stimulates the publication of Mesa's first newspaper, the *Mesa Free Press,* which in 1893 reports mining activity to be at its peak: "There literally seems to be gold everywhere!"

A major flooding of the Salt River plays havoc with valley settlers during the month of February. Most of Lehi and much of Phoenix are under water, and the flood destroys the one railroad bridge in Tempe, effectively isolating Phoenix from Mesa for several months. Despite the river flowing at 300,000 cubic feet per second, Mesa suffers no casualties.

1892: Adolph Bandolier excavates the Casa Grande ruins near Coolidge, but only notes Mesa Grande in passing: "The plain between the Salt and Gila Rivers south of Tempe also contains numerous ruins . . . I traversed it rapidly, catching a glimpse of the huge mounds at Mesa City."

1893: Mesa continues its growth as a community, witnessed by an editorial in the *Free Press,* which states: "Now is an opportune time for our growing city to take the initiatory steps toward providing a city park." Meanwhile, the Zenos Co-op advertises itself as the agent for "celebrated Myers Pumps . . . the famous Featherbone Buggy Whips . . . and the unexcelled Canton Clipper Plows." The Mesa public schools serve more than 200 students.

1894: The Pioneer Hotel is built, one block south of Main Street. More than 90 years later it will still be in operation as the Alhambra, Mesa's longest-operating place of lodging.

1895: A further economic boost occurs when Mesa is connected to the rest of the valley, and the state, by the railroad. The Maricopa, Phoenix, and Salt River Railroad connects Mesa to Tempe and Phoenix, and Santa Fe opens a line connecting Phoenix with northern Arizona. Among other things, this makes the shipping of lumber from the northlands much more feasible for Mesa settlers.

Electricity for the community is not far away, as Dr. A.J. Chandler, veterinarian, canal magnate, and successful farmer (for whom the neighboring community of Chandler will be named in 1912), begins construction of a powerhouse on his crosscut canal. Upon the powerhouse's completion three years later, Mesa will enter the electric age.

1896: E.M. Reavis, a Superstition Mountain hermit known as the "Keeper of the Lost Dutchman Mine," is found dead not far from his home high in the mountains. He lived there as a hermit for almost

The automobile first appeared on the Apache Trail in 1908. The long, steep Fish Creek Hill offered quite a challenge even to this modern contraption. One account of a group of Mesa men who made the trip stated that one man had "to push the car up one hill." His additional comments were not suitable for publication. Courtesy, Norman Mead Collection

This Mesa statehood rally held near the intersection of Main and Macdonald in late 1911 gathered support from all factions. The statehood efforts were successful; Arizona became a state on February 14, 1912. Courtesy, Mesa Southwest Museum Collections

60 years, making his living from 15 acres of vegetables that he cultivated and sold to Mesa hotels. He had developed a near-legendary reputation among Indians and townspeople alike, and although his ties to Jacob Waltz and the "Dutchman's Mine" are speculated upon, they were never confirmed.

Another death in Mesa typifies the spirit of the pioneer women that have helped to tame this western territory. Sophronia Standage, wife of Henry Standage, one of the founders of Stringtown, dies at the age of 75, when, gathering hens' eggs from atop a ten-foot stack of hay in her barnyard, she falls from a ladder and breaks her neck.

1897: Arizona's harsh elements, only six years after the greatest flood the territory has known, produce the longest period of time the Mesa region has ever experienced without significant precipitation. This "Great Drought" will last until 1905, causing massive crop failure and resulting in the arrests of dozens of farmers on water-theft charges. During the latter stages of the drought, the reduced water flow in the rivers even impacts the availability of electricity, just as Mesa residents are beginning to stock up on electric fans.

1898: Mesa experiences its first major fire. The Cosby Grocery Store and Passey & Mets Furniture Store, on the south side of Main Street in the center of town, burn to the ground. Only a 17-inch-thick brick wall in the Johnson Brothers store next door prevents the entire block from going up in smoke.

A volunteer fire department is formed as a result of the blaze, and fire-prevention guidelines are set. But lack of organization coupled with the drought make fire the predominant hazard for downtown Mesa merchants for the next several years.

1899: Mesa stages a mammoth May Day celebration, which attracts more than 1,500 visitors from neighboring communities—more than twice Mesa's population at that time. The celebration doubles as a victory party in observance of Commodore George Dewey's capture of the Spanish fleet in the Philippines. The Mesa City Council, obviously in a festive mood, states in its minutes, "Owing to it being May Day, and some of the members desiring to get away

early, not much business was transacted."

1900-1902: Mesa's population reaches 722 as the century turns. Agriculture in the east valley continues its evolution, as the cantaloupe industry begins to develop. In 1904 Mesa cantaloupes will take first prize at the St. Louis World's Fair.

In 1902 a development that will more significantly stimulate Mesa's growth occurs: the establishment of the U.S. Bureau of Reclamation, an agency that will soon take steps to regulate Arizona's flood-or-drought water availability.

1903-1905: Mesa's growth includes the arrival of new ethnic groups to the community, as the first Japanese and the first black families move into town. These and other members of the community celebrate the opening of the new Vance Opera House. Many traveling stock shows are booked into this auditorium instead of Phoenix, due to its sizable stage. The floor of the hall is frequently converted to a roller skating rink, with musical entertainment provided by the Vance Sisters.

The Apache Trail, originally called Roosevelt Road, is constructed in 1904. This 60-mile stretch of road leads from Mesa to the site of the Reclamation Bureau's first major project: the construction of a dam just below the confluence of the Salt River and Tonto Creek. The narrow, winding road is the scene of many accidents and near-tragedies, complicated by the introduction of the automobile to the Mesa area at about this time.

1906-1910: More progress is made in the effort to control the flooding of the Salt River. The construction of the Granite Reef diversion dam just north of Mesa is authorized, and the dam is dedicated in 1908. Work continues on Roosevelt Dam, further north, which will reach completion in March of 1911. The *Arizona Gazette* describes much public rejoicing over these projects, and on completion of Granite Reef Dam reports: ". . . Mere words fail to express the appreciation felt, not only by the farmers, but by every merchant, businessman, and everyone else . . . [this is] one of the greatest days in the history of the Valley."

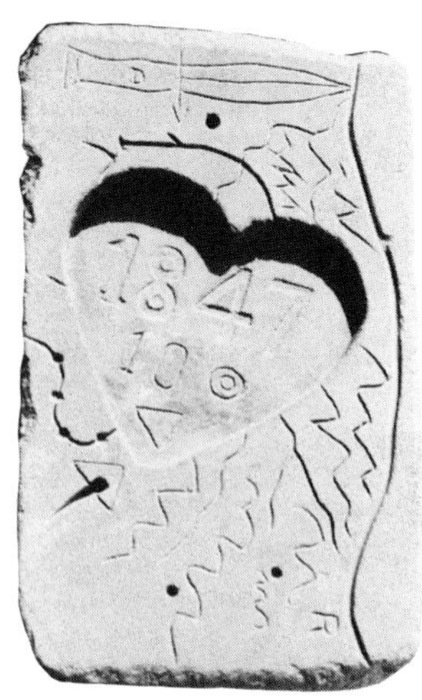

The four Peralta stones, on display at the Mesa Southwest Museum, were made famous by a 1956 *Life* magazine article. The stones are purported to have been carved in the mid-1800s and rediscovered in 1949 just southeast of the Superstition Mountains by a tourist traveling through the Mesa area. Courtesy, Mesa Southwest Museum Collections

Arizona and Mesa begin to show signs of becoming popular vacation spots, and a variety of celebrities pass through. Zane Grey first visits Arizona during this time, and will later incorporate actual Mesa citizens and settings into his popular Western novels—under assumed names, of course. And President Taft himself passes through Mesa en route to a speaking engagement in Tempe. Mesa's population has reached 1,692, but disease once again counters the community's growth, as scarlet fever and diphtheria epidemics close Mesa public schools in 1910.

1911-1915: On the eve of ratification of the first Arizona State Constitution in 1911, constitutional convention Chaplain Seaborn Crutchfield prays: "Lord, we hope that President Taft will not turn down the Constitution . . . don't let him be so narrow and partisan as to refuse us self-government." His prayers are answered on February 14, 1912, when Taft signs a proclamation admitting Arizona to the Union as the 48th state. George W.P. Hunt is elected as the first governor, and Carl Hayden is the first to represent the state in the U.S. House of Representatives.

Despite statehood, the Old West still lives in Mesa, albeit with some concessions to progress. This is best exemplified when, in November of 1913, Mesa Marshal Hyrum Peterson is gunned down in the street by a pair of *bicycle* thieves, Atha Leonard and John Tomlin. The ensuing manhunt involves lawmen statewide, and the two men are captured and sentenced to death on the gallows in 1914. But their sentences are commuted to life in prison, and both are eventually released on parole.

Mesa's development continues, with the first Chinese restaurant opening in the community, established by Wing Wong; an experimental farm is established in Mesa by the University of Arizona's College of Agriculture; and the Maricopa County Fair is held in Mesa for the first time. The U.S. battleship *Arizona* is christened on June 19, 1915, with water from the Salt River.

1916-1920: The last lynching to take place in the state of Arizona occurs in Mesa, when an accused murderer named Starr Daley, while being transported to Florence by sheriff's deputies, is chased by a convoy of more than 50 automobiles through town. They catch up to the deputies near the actual scene of the crime, which was within the current city limits of Mesa, and hang him. One year later, Arizonans reinstitute the death penalty.

The municipality of Mesa purchases its own gas and electric company, the existing Southside Gas & Electric, which will serve as such a prime source of revenue that no city property tax will ever need to be instituted. However, no public transportation system for Mesa is in the offing, and the Mesa-to-Phoenix stage raises its round-trip fare to $1.25.

At the peak of World War I, Mesa contributes many of its young men to the armed forces, and patriotic sentiments run so high in the community that it becomes the first Arizona city to sell its quota of Liberty Bonds. But that same loyalty is not necessarily held toward Maricopa County, as a group of Mesa citizens organizes to secede from the county, along with Chandler, Gilbert, Tempe, and Egypt, today known as Goodyear. The secession never comes to pass, however.

1921-1925: Rollin P. Jones, principal of Mesa's Lehi School, is the victim of one of the most overt acts by Arizona's Ku Klux Klan. He is dragged and beaten with a leather quirt, and branded on his face with acid, allegedly for his reprimand of a female student (the accused whipper in the attack is found to be the girl's father). His attacker is tried and found innocent, and this triggers an increase in Klan activity in Arizona during the 1920s.

The Nile Theatre is opened on Main Street in 1924. Mesa's most ornate movie theatre—in the words of the *Mesa Tribune,* "Arizona's most beautiful show house"—opens with a screening of *The Sea Hawk,* starring Milton Sills and Wallace Beery, and also features some "novel vaudeville acts." A $25 reward is offered to anyone reporting front-row patrons throwing objects at the brand-new screen.

1926-1930: Mesa's growth continues, with an eye on tourism. Mesa's population is reported at 3,711, and a community hotel, El Portal, opens in the center of town. The new hotel is financed by the sale of stock to Mesa residents, and it is hoped that this facility will be able to compete with Chandler's famous San Marcos Hotel. But soon after the hotel's opening in 1928, the Depression severely impacts the lodging habits of the nation, and El Portal soon flounders with financial difficulties.

A longer-lasting Mesa landmark is dedicated when the Arizona Mormon Temple opens its doors, 50 years after the arrival of the first Mormon pioneers at the Lehi settlement. Between 10,000 and 20,000 visitors are expected for the ceremonies, and the *Tribune* reports Mesa's Mormon families hosting an average of "six to six-dozen friends and relatives" in town for the festivities.

1931-1940: The modernization of Mesa continues, as a multipurpose municipal building is completed at the corner of First Street and Macdonald. The building, which includes the police and fire stations as well as a library in the north wing, now exists as the Mesa Southwest Museum. Mesa's first zoning ordinance and building code is adopted, and the Mesa-Tempe highway is enlarged to four lanes. Population increases to 7,224 by 1940.

On January 20, 1937, Mesa experiences its most substantial snow fall ever, as three inches of snow and a low temperature of 21 degrees is recorded. Snowmen abound, schools are closed, and local merchants experience a tremendous run on cameras and film as residents seek to obtain a pictorial record of this unusual occurrence. The snow remains for about one week before Mesa returns to its usual, sun-drenched self.

1941-1950: As World War II rages, Mesa's population more than doubles, to 16,790. Mesa gets its first two radio stations, KARV and KTYL. Not far from the ancient Hohokam ball courts of Mesa Grande, the Mesa Country Club golf course is constructed.

Another major development in the world of sports helps to put Mesa on the map: the Chicago Cubs baseball team formally announces that it will locate its spring training camp in Mesa beginning in 1952.

In 1946 an 82-year-old woman and long-time Mesa resident named Phoebe Jones is arrested and convicted of arson in a devastating fire that destroys the William Deatherage house in south Mesa. Kerosene, oil-soaked rags, and candles are discovered in her home, which was next door to the Deatherage house, and she is implicated in four other blazes. She spends her remaining years in the State Hospital for the mentally ill.

1951-1960: By the end of the 1950s, Mesa's population has once again doubled, to 33,772, and is still on the rise. Now firmly established as a popular vacation spot and winter residence for U.S. citizens from all over the country, tourism is established as Mesa's prime industry, bringing in more than $10 million annually.

Average daily attendance at Mesa public schools tops 10,000. Yet Mesa maintains its small-town feeling; when the 1953 Mesa High School student elections are held, the results are front-page news in the *Mesa Tribune*. Members of the Alma School PTA ac-

tively lobby for increased traffic signals and railroad-crossing signals, and installation by the city is stepped up in these areas.

A poll is taken of civic organizations, asking if the current city policy of banning Negroes from using public swimming pools should be maintained. A compromise is reached, as most favor designating certain days of the week for use by blacks. Later that same year, Veora Johnson, a black school principal, is named "Mesa Citizen of the Year."

In 1959 fire claims the Mesa Civic Center, built in 1948. The city will lack such a facility for years to come, eliminating east valley hosting of the Maricopa County Fairs and other large-scale events.

1961-1986: The upward spiral of growth in Mesa continues unabated into the twenty-first century, with no end in sight. Over this 25-year period, Mesa's population will increase by nearly 10 times, reaching nearly a quarter of a million in 1986. In part this boom is reflective of growth throughout the Southwestern U.S. during this time; however, Mesa's continued steps to facilitate this growth can be directly attributed to its success as a city.

Recent years have seen such developments as the creation of two major shopping centers, Tri-City Mall and Fiesta Mall, providing the east valley with a solid retail base; the construction of the Superstition Freeway, leading from Interstate 10 near the Phoenix-Tempe border across Mesa and east toward Apache Junction; and the opening of several major new manufacturing plants by corporations such as Motorola and McDonnell-Douglas. In fact, the local business climate is so good that it is recognized nationally, when John Naisbitt, in his book *Mega-Trends,* ranks Mesa third in the nation for development of new businesses.

Recognized in its centennial year of 1978 as an "All-American City," Mesa continues to be referred to as a family-oriented city, largely due to its Mormon beginnings; by 1980, however, only 16 percent of the population is Mormon. The median age of Mesa residents at this time is 29 years; the average household income is $17,840.

1987: The city of Mesa has grown to a geographic area of 100 square miles, 100 times larger than the town's "original square mile." But it is that square mile that is the subject of concern in the mid- to late 1980s. In an effort to rejuvenate this historic section of town and fight decay, the Mesa Town Center Redevelopment Corporation is formed. New storefronts are built, new business and office space is developed, new restaurants open, and, finally, Mesa comes full circle when restoration is completed on the Sirrine House, built in 1895 by Mesa pioneer Joel Sirrine and his father George. The house is open to the public as a living history museum, to preserve Mesa's heritage for the decades to come.

The moody Superstitions are now a favorite recreation area for backpackers. A multitude of well-maintained trails and year-round springs make this a delightful wilderness experience for the adventurous. Courtesy, Norman Mead Collection

CHAPTER I

THOSE WHO HAVE VANISHED

The citadel of ancient power still stands 40 feet tall. Built only a few centuries after the birth of Christ, it has silently witnessed more than 1,000 years of Arizona's turbulent history. The citadel was large to begin with, and was expanded almost constantly, growing in scope and size as the empire of its creators spread—the empire of the magnificent Hohokam Indians. The mysterious Hohokam, a culture advanced in the ways of science, of trade, and of social organization, was a civilization that had suddenly and completely disappeared by the time Columbus landed on the American shores.

The citadel, which remains undisturbed to this day in northwest Mesa, was christened as "Mesa Grande" by the early Anglo settlers in the region; in Spanish, it means "large table." Mesa Grande was the largest temple structure ever built by the Hohokam culture, which had its beginnings about 300 B.C., along Arizona's Salt and Gila rivers. The Hohokam, most archaeologists believe, descended from the early Paleo-Indians, or "Stone Age" Indians that lived and hunted along these same rivers for thousands of years.

The Paleo-Indians hunted giant bison and the great mammoth. These early Stone-Age tribesmen would drive and entrap the large, lumbering animals into the bogs and marshes that existed at the time, in what was a much wetter, more humid, prehistoric Arizona. As recently as 1984 Mesa Southwest Museum archaeologists unearthed mammoth remains along with those of other prehistoric mammals just a few miles from the Mesa Grande site.

Did these ancient Paleo-Indians adapt from a hunting life-style to an agricultural one, as the large game animals migrated or were killed off? Did these early farmers evolve into a people responsible for a sophisticated system of irrigation canals spanning hundreds of miles—canals that utilized highly advanced scientific survey

This is an excellent example of the ancient Hohokam ruins; the largest of all the Hohokam ruins still standing are in Mesa—the Mesa Grande Ruins. The walls in the foreground date back as far as A.D. 1000. Courtesy, Norman Mead Collection

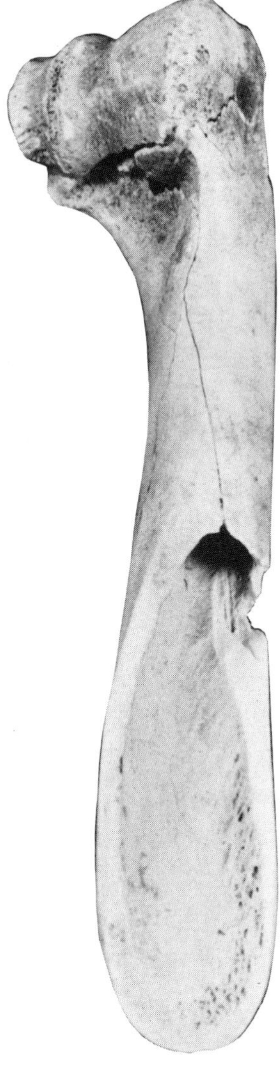

This type of flesher was widely used in the Southwest from prehistoric times until the turn of the century. Prehistoric peoples, such as the Hohokam, used bone tools they crafted from animal bone to flesh out slain animals. The flesher was wedged between the skin and flesh of animals to separate the pelt, for later use. Courtesy, Mesa Southwest Museum Collections

techniques? Did they evolve into the highly developed culture that traded for rare tropical bird capesand copper bells with the peoples of central Mexico, and shell and coral with the peoples of Baja?

This is indeed what the archaeological evidence suggests. Not only did they become successful farmers and industrious tradesmen, but they were also our nation's first true scientists. Archaeology has proven that the Hohokam developed the scientific practice of "acid etching" 300 years before Europeans discovered the same technology. This is a complicated process in which intricate designs are carved on a surface coated with a substance that will not react to acid. The carved surface is then immersed in the acid, which cuts or etches a design into the desired surface.

The Hohokam made intricate etched shell jewelry as well as finely inlaid jewelry of turquoise and coral. In fact, Hohokam bachelors may actually have been the first in history to invite local maidens to come and "look at their etchings." This jewelry may well have been used as money or for barter during their prolific trading. They exchanged goods within an expansive region nearly as large as the continent of Europe. Like Europe during this same period, the great Southwest consisted of a variety of kingdoms and cultures, of which the Hohokam was one of the greatest and most advanced.

The Hohokam "kingdom" was roughly the size of England, with its major population centers along the Salt and Gila rivers, the site of the civilization's inception nearly 2,300 years ago. The earliest phase of the Hohokam culture, called the Pioneer Period by archaeologists, lasted roughly eight centuries, until A.D. 500. This is the period of Hohokam civilization that, more than any other, is shrouded in the mystery of the past. Just how did the caveman-mammoth hunter metamorphose into the advanced Hohokam farmer?

The leading theory suggests that the high cultures of central Mexico, which were more advanced at the time, influenced the change. Archaeologists are still debating whether the Paleo-Indians absorbed elements of these cultures through their own expanding trade, or whether these neighboring cultures to the south sent colonizing missions to the north.

Regardless of the means, the Hohokam of the Pioneer Period had well-established farming communities by the year 300 B.C. They grew a multitude of crops, including corn, squash, beans, and peppers. They also cultivated cotton, which they wove into cloth. Its softness and durability has historically made cotton the preferred material for all desert dwellers, from Arizona to Egypt. Remnants of cloth obtained from Hohokam cave sites indicate that they were master weavers, with difficult and intricate designs common in their work.

The ability to fashion and fire clay into ceramic vessels is one of the major traits archaeologists use in differentiating the so-called "cavemen" from the early Hohokam. Very early in their culture, the Hohokam developed a distinct form of pottery that changed little throughout 1,500 years. The clay was fired to a buff-colored background, with a red hemetic base paint baked onto the surface.

The Pioneer Period was followed by an active period of growth known as the Colonial Period. This period of the Hohokam, which lasted from A.D. 500 to 900, saw the population boom. As a result, their civilization expanded into all the major river valleys in central and southern Arizona. It was during this period that the Hohokam of prehistoric Mesa built the temple now called

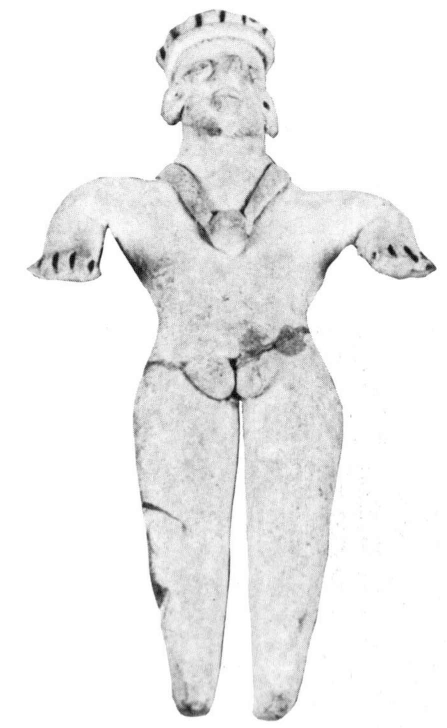

Above: One of the hallmarks of the Hohokam culture was the crafting of stone palettes, which range from simple flat stones to sculptured works of art. These stone artifacts are associated with the death ritual, possibly used for the burning of incense. Courtesy, Mesa Southwest Museum Collections

Right: This Hohokam stylized frog pendant made with pectin shell with mosaic overlay of turquoise and argillite dates from A.D. 1150-1450. Courtesy, Mesa Southwest Museum Collections

Mesa Grande. It consisted of a large central platform mound or pyramid, on which a temple structure was built, surrounded by thick, adobe walls. These mounds provide the most direct archaeological link to the high cultures of Mexico, who built the same type of ceremonial structures. And like the pyramids of Mexico, Mesa Grande is also surrounded by large plazas beyond its compound wall.

Archaeologists speculate that the plazas had two main uses: as regional trade centers, a sort of prehistoric combination of a swap meet or farmers market; and as staging areas for ceremonial rituals. Excavations conducted by the Southwest Archaeological Team in 1986 uncovered a series of massive "ornos," communal cooking ovens, within a plaza adjoining Mesa Grande on the north side; this strongly confirms the theory of communal use and gathering.

Recreation also played a major role in the life-style of the ancient Hohokam, much as it does for Mesa's current-day residents. The community would gather for sporting events held in sunken

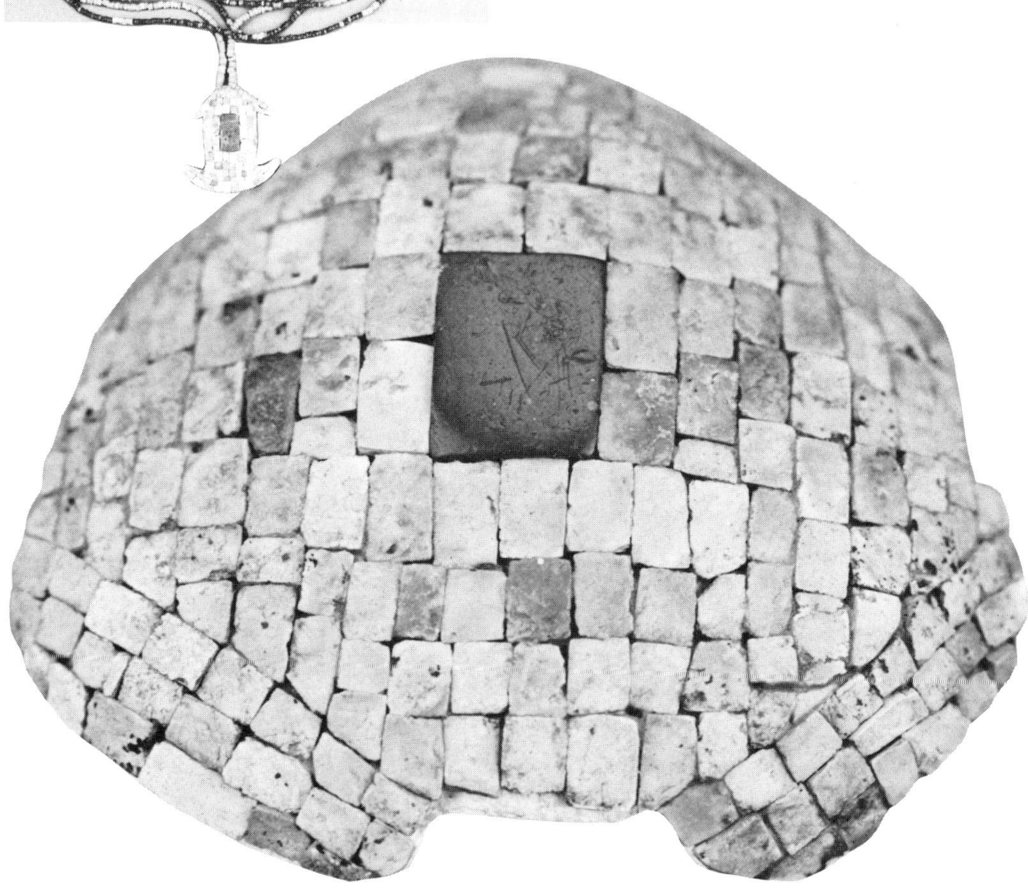

Left: This Colima ceramic figurine dates from 300-100 B.C. Courtesy, Mesa Southwest Museum Collections

ball courts, the size of which approached today's football fields. From evidence obtained on-site, and from ethnographical comparison with a similar game played in Mexico, archaeologists have been able to piece together what the game must have been like.

It was apparently a mixture of basketball, football, and soccer. Like basketball, there was a round hoop at each end of the court, extending out from a side wall. The object of the game was for the team to put a ball through that hoop. While it sounds simple, the ball, which was about the size of a modern-day baseball, could barely squeeze through the hoop; and as in soccer, players were not allowed to touch the ball with their hands. Each team wore mock or stylized armor of wood and leather, not unlike current football players' padding; this was definitely a contact sport.

Early Spanish explorers who witnessed the version played in Mexico between competing villages likened the game to open warfare. It seemed that the best winning strategy was to beat your opponents into unconsciousness and then, using your elbows, pick up the ball and push it through the hoop. Upon a victory, the crowd would go wild, for two good reasons: first, the winning villagers would jubilantly claim their prizes; and second, since those prizes generally consisted of the jewelry worn by the losing villagers, the losers would be scrambling for cover! Not surprisingly, the abilities of one's team dictated how nicely attired and bejeweled the villagers would appear at the game. Villagers not finely attired showed disrespect and lack of confidence.

The Colonial Period, a time of massive colonization, ended around A.D. 900. The era from that point on until approximately 1100 is known as the Sedentary Period. As the name might suggest, this was not a time of great change.

During this period, as with previous periods, the Hohokam family typically lived in a house that was partially submerged in the earth. With this so-called "house in a pit," the Hohokam had actually discovered the solar-heating properties of the sun and thermal temperature transfer of the earth some 1,000 years prior to its recent popularity. These homes utilized two important principles that current home designs are just now beginning to develop:

1. The adobe walls of the house gathered heat during the day, which was given off at night. These cooler walls kept temperatures down during the day, as they gathered more heat for the evening. As a result, they maintained a consistent, comfortable climate. Many desert-dwelling cultures still utilize adobe structures in this manner.

2. If the house is partially underground, it can utilize the winter-summer heating cycle of the earth. The earth lags from four to six months behind the surface temperature, effectively serving to cool an underground home in the summer and warm it in the winter.

The Hohokam, with their partially submerged pit houses, merged these two principles of daily and seasonal temperature swings into a structure ideally suited to the harsh desert environment, one in which a swing of 60 degrees during a 24-hour period was not uncommon. The Hohokam learned to adjust to these shifts in reasonable comfort through their advanced desert engineering.

The Hohokam's greatest engineering feat, however, was the elaborate and monumental canal system, one that has not yet been surpassed by any pre-industrial culture in the world. This desert civilization put thousands of acres of land under cultivation by using canal irrigation. They built literally hundreds of miles of canals, some as far as 20 miles from their water source. Most of the canals in the system were built during the Colonial Period, and enlarged during the Sedentary Period. As a result of the canal system, by the end of the Sedentary Period the great power citadel, Mesa Grande, was surrounded by villages and towns with a combined population in the thousands. There had been a generally steady increase in prosperity during this time, despite relatively short periods of drought, flood, and famine.

A middle class of tradesmen and craftsmen was developing during this time, supported by the larger population base. There were artisans, carving stone and sculpting clay figurines; jewelry makers at the height of their craft; and potters making intricately decorated and painted ceramics. The tradesmen and merchants were in turn developing ever-expanding markets for the export of Hohokam goods in exchange for the exotic wares of other cultures to the north and south.

Burials of this period show wide diversity of

the grave objects that were buried with the individuals, indicative of the existence of significant differences in status and wealth. A relatively complex social order was obviously in place within the Hohokam culture.

The final period of the Hohokam lasted from 1100 to 1450. This period is referred to as the Classic Period. Although archaeologists have studied this period of the Hohokam more than any of the others, there is substantial disagreement on what was truly happening to the Hohokam civilization at this time.

For more than 1,000 years, the Hohokam had a strong, consistently growing empire, but all of this changed during the Classic Period. Large, continuously occupied settlements such as Snaketown, just a few miles southwest of present-day Mesa, were suddenly abandoned; whole canal systems throughout that region were simultaneously abandoned. The traditional single-family dwellings gave way to above-ground, fort-like structures, known as "compounds."

Something very significant was happening to the Hohokam during this time, and there are many different theories as to exactly what it was.

Some have likened it to another civilization that, like the Hohokam, lasted more than 1,000 years and then fell—the Roman Empire.

By 1500 the Hohokam empire had, in effect, vanished. In the case of Rome, it was the internal political and religious structures that had deteriorated, leaving the Romans susceptible to barbarians from the north. History tells us that it was a slow fall. Different sections of the Roman Empire pulled away from the whole, and individually fortified themselves. Some made their own separate peace with the northern Germanic tribes, either by being absorbed by them or paying tribute to them.

During the Hohokam's Classic Period, there were forces at work that must have caused similar internal destruction, or, at least, a decided reorientation of their society. They may also have had their own version of barbarians descending from the north. This might explain the abandoning of smaller dwellings in favor of multifamily, fort-like structures. The fear of raiding barbarians might also explain the abandonment of peripheral, high-maintenance, easily vandalized canals, and the abandonment of settlements not

constructed for defense. External pressure from outside tribes could explain much, although not all, of what happened to the Hohokam.

It is known that the Apache were pressing to the south during this time span. Could they have been the force that caused such tremendous change within the Hohokam culture? Archaeologists first argued this theory in the 1930s and 1940s, but today most believe it too simplistic an explanation for the disruption and demise of the Hohokam. It is not unreasonable to believe, however, that pressure from an outside group such as the Apache could have been a contributing factor.

Like the Romans, Greeks, and Egyptians before them, the Hohokam built their greatest structure near the end of their civilization. Casa Grande, the most well-preserved of all the great Hohokam structures, was built during the Classic Period. The Casa Grande Ruins have been preserved as a National Monument, located just outside of Coolidge, 35 miles southeast of Mesa. Besides serving as a religious center, Casa Grande also housed an astrological observatory. Scientists have documented that special sight holes and marks in the massive two- and three-foot adobe walls could be used to determine the summer and winter solstice, as well as other astrological events. Were the powerful Hohokam astrologers using the stars to chart the destiny of their people?

It is believed that future excavations in Mesa will prove the Mesa Grande Ruins to also have contained an observatory. It was during this Classic Period that the Mesa Grande structures were enlarged again, and became the largest of all Hohokam structures ever known to have been built. But shortly thereafter, between 1450 and 1500, the Hohokam completely vanished.

What caused their disappearance? Was it drought, or floods? Was it crop failure? Was it warfare from either external tribes or internal strife? Or was it a great religious calling that told them to leave the Salt River Valley? Hopefully archaeologists will one day unlock the final secrets of the Hohokam. And it is very likely that these secrets may be contained in the last and greatest of all the Hohokam citadels, Mesa Grande. Until that time, the Pima translation of their name will have to serve as their epitaph: "those who have vanished."

FROM CORONADO
TO KIT CARSON

Who was the first white man to gaze upon Mesa and the Salt River Valley? Like the reason for the disappearance of the Hohokam, this has also been a much debated issue for the past hundred years. Early historians believed it was Cabeza de Vaca, a Spanish explorer whose name translates as "Cow's Head," who shipwrecked on an expedition intended for Florida. According to their reports, he and his black slave, Esteban de Dorantes, wandered for eight years across the vast reaches of what is now the Southern and Southwestern United States. Upon reaching Arizona, he turned south into New Spain (Mexico), where he regaled his fellow Spaniards with tales of great golden cities that he had seen. But in reality, he based his legendary tales of the "Seven Cities of Gold" on stories that were told to *him* by natives he encountered on his wanderings.

He was originally believed to have come down the Salt and Gila rivers, which led into the Colorado River and on into New Spain. Although the issue is not settled, most historians now believe that de Vaca followed the San Pedro, and not the Salt; in this case, he would have just missed being the first explorer to travel through the Salt River Valley. In either case, he is still important as he was the first European to set foot in Arizona, or, for that matter, the continental United States.

If not Cabeza de Vaca, then who was the first European to cast his eyes on the Valley of the Sun and its winding Salt River? Three strong contenders for the honor are de Vaca's black slave, Esteban; Fray Marcos de Niza, a Spanish priest; and the early Jesuit missionary, Padre Eusebio Francisco Kino.

Esteban was certainly the first black man to set foot in the United States. Esteban's accounts of travel with Cabeza de Vaca in the South and Southwest were colorful and detailed. In fact, it

Francisco Vasquez de Coronado led an expedition of Spanish soldiers, Indians, and padres from Mexico City into Arizona in 1540. Western artist Frederick Remington recreated this historic exploration party. Courtesy, Arizona Historical Society

Weapons from all over Europe, such as this hand-crafted steel dagger with incised geometric designs on the hilt and ornamented cross-piece, were imported into the American Southwest both during and following the Spanish Colonial period. The dagger's triangular concave iron blade would have been an effective tool for close encounters. Courtesy, Mesa Southwest Museum Collections

was Esteban's supposed first-hand knowledge of the infamous Seven Cities of Gold that led to his purchase by Don Antonio de Mendoza, viceroy and governor of all of New Spain.

Fray Marcos de Niza, with Esteban as his guide, was sent on an advanced mission into Arizona, to further search for the Seven Cities. The following excerpts are taken from de Niza's own words, from his journal *The Story of the Discovery of the Seven Cities by Fray Marcos de Niza,* as translated by Father Bonaventura Oblasser in 1938:

In obedience to the instructions of the most illustrious Sir Don Antonio de Mendoza, I, Fray Marcos de Niza, member of the order of Saint Francis, set out upon this journey . . . I left the town of San Miguel in the Province of Cuiliacan on Friday, March 7, 1539. My party consisted of: Padre Onorato, my companion; Esteban de Dorantes, a negro; some Indians, whom the viceroy had purchased and then set at liberty and whom the Governor of New Galicia Francisco Vasquez de Coronado had entrusted me.

The actual route taken by Marcos de Niza is subject to much controversy, for his account contained many geographical errors and seeming impossibilities. It can be deduced, however, from the routes described, that his journey took him along the west coast of Mexico, from which he entered Arizona in the San Pedro Valley, and proceeded north to the Gila and Salt rivers. Father Oblasser's translation put Fray Marcos de Niza in the Salt River Valley from April 30 through May 3, 1539. De Niza wrote:

I spent three days in visiting the various places in this valley, and the natives went the limit to feast and entertain me. I saw more than two thousand buffalo hides in this valley. They were tanned perfectly. And I saw more turquoise and necklaces made of them in this valley than in all the others that I had passed. They tell me that all this is brought from the city of Cibola . . . A great number of people live there. They are of a pleasant disposition. The valley itself is so well stocked with provisions that more than three hundred horsemen could subsist there. It is all under irrigation and presents the appearance of one immense garden.

Father Oblasser's translation puts de Niza in Mesa on May 2, 1539. Oblasser has de Niza visiting Mesa Grande, and seems to indicate from notes on his prepared route map that it was his belief that the Apache were responsible for the fall of the early Hohokam cities in the Salt River Valley. His notation refers to the ruins as having been "Pima villages, prior to the Apache invasion . . ."

According to this translation of de Niza's account, it was at this time, while in the Mesa area, that de Niza actually encountered a man from Cibola. De Niza states: "At the place where I am now I have come across a native of Cibola. He was forced to leave that place by the one whom the overlord had placed in charge."

It was while de Niza was in the Mesa region that he received word from Esteban that he was nearing Cibola. Esteban, with Indian guides and runners, had been sent ahead to scout the route, and his correspondence was indeed encouraging. De Niza said:

At this place, some messengers brought word from Esteban that he was about to leave for the last uninhabited region. He was very glad he had waited until now, for he had been able to acquire greater certainty concerning the grand things of the country.

As a formality, just before leaving the Salt River Valley area, de Niza claimed the land for God and Country; in his own words, "What I had been doing right along, in other villages, I repeated in the valley. I erected crosses, made the inscriptions and performed the rites prescribed for taking formal possession of a place." And with that, the land that would become Mesa fell under Spanish rule.

If de Niza's 1539 expedition and Father Oblasser's 1938 translation are correct, de Niza's claim of the Mesa and Salt River Valley area for Spain would have occurred 81 years prior to the Pilgrims setting foot on Plymouth Rock.

Understandably, when de Niza relayed the account of his journeys after returning to New Spain, he launched a near "gold-rush" level frenzy, culminating in a great expedition into the Southwest.

Viceroy Mendoza commissioned Francisco Vasquez de Coronado as leader of the expedition, on January 6, 1540. Two hundred and ninety-two fighting men, plus priests and Indians, comprised the expedition.

Coronado's was the first military expedition to enter what is now the continental United States, and again Arizona had the distinction of being "the first of the first." It is clear from the more accurate records of Coronado's expedition that he and his men did not enter the lower Salt River Valley. They passed just to the south and east of the Mesa region. However, his men did cross the Salt River higher in the mountains by raft, bestowing upon the river the name "River of the Rafts," or, in Spanish, "Rio de las Balsas." Even today, more than 400 years later, nearby mountains continually yield evidence of the early Spanish explorers.

Charles Winecoop, a resident of Mesa in the 1930s, found a cache of Spanish armor in the Sierra Estrellas, to the south of Mesa. It was typical of the type of armor tossed aside by the Spanish conquistadors of Coronado's expedition while experiencing the hot Arizona desert. Other mountains surrounding the Salt River Valley, especially the Superstition Mountains east of Mesa, have produced a number of Spanish artifacts from the time of Coronado.

If neither de Vaca, Esteban, de Niza, or Coronado ever saw the east valley, the first Spaniard that is *known* to have gazed upon Mesa was the Spanish priest Eusebio Francisco Kino. The story of Father Kino's discovery of the valley was related by Mesa's foremost historian, the late Earl Merrill, in a 1973 newspaper column.

On March 2, Kino and his party reached the Sierra Estrella, coming upon them from a different direction than they had planned to on their previous journey. Indian guides accompanied them to the top of one of the peaks.

"We could plainly see the Verde River," wrote Captain Manje, one of the group, "which takes its rise in the land of the Apaches . . . with a grove of trees along its banks. It is joined by another salty river, running from east to west, and the two, merging together, flow into this Rio Grande [Gila] River, the junction of which we were able to see . . ."

Aside from Father Kino's adventures, the latter 1600s and early 1700s were times of little activity for the Anglos in the Salt River Valley. Primarily as a result of an increased threat of an Apache attack in central and southern Arizona, coupled with a decisive defeat suffered at the hands of the Yuma Indians in 1781 at Yuma, the Spaniards had essentially abandoned

Ceremonial armor such as this circa 1575-1599 gilt brass Renaissance parade armor breastplate was crafted in France, Italy, and Germany for export to armies throughout Western Europe, but primarily to Spain, which had become the dominant world power at that time. Although not sufficiently protective for combat, this breastplate is of the style that would have been available to the Conquistadors. Courtesy, Mesa Southwest Museum Collections

Trapper, hunter, mountain man, guide, and legendary hero Christopher (Kit) Carson piloted General Stephen Kearny across Arizona in 1848. He later settled in New Mexico and led a troop of Union volunteers from that state in the Civil War. In 1863 Carson commanded an expedition against the Navajos in their Canyon de Chelly stronghold. Courtesy, Arizona Historical Society, Tucson

central Arizona to the Indians and their wars by the end of the eighteenth century. The valley became a war zone, a sort of no-man's-land, between two great Indian peoples: the Apache and the Pima.

These two tribes could not have been more different. The Pima were agriculturally based, using advanced irrigation technology. They claim that the Hohokam, meaning "those who have vanished" or "the ancient ones," were their direct ancestors, and much archaeological evidence supports this supposition. The Pima would, therefore, have continually lived along the Salt and Gila river basins for more than 2,000 years, starting their civilization 300 years before the birth of Christ. The lifetime of their civilization rivals that of the great Roman Empire. And just as the Roman Empire had the marauding Vandals from the north, the Pima had the Apache.

The Apache, whose society was based primarily on raiding, and was only supplemented by small-scale agriculture, had quickly adapted to (and benefited from) the Spaniards' introduction of the horse. This revolutionary new mode of transportation allowed the Apache to become one of the most effective raiding societies the world

has ever known.

Many of these Southwest Indian wars were documented by Philip St. George Cooke, who commanded the Mormon Batallion through Arizona in 1847. He described in particular detail the situation in which the Pima allied with the neighboring Maricopa against the raiding Apache to the north and east, and the hostile Yumas to the southwest.

Among the first of these intrepid Americans were a breed of itinerant explorers and trappers known as "mountain men." The mountain men began their exploration of the Salt River in the 1820s, providing the earliest, although sketchy, accounts of the Salt River Valley region, as well as their frequent run-ins with the Apache.

Our country's most well-known frontier explorer, Christopher "Kit" Carson, was no stranger to the Mesa region. Carson was born in 1809 in Madison County, Kentucky. His family moved to Missouri when he was still an infant. At the age of 15 he was apprenticed to a saddler, but, hating the trade, ran away and joined a party headed for Santa Fe in 1826. From Santa Fe he left for Taos and became the cook for another legendary mountain man, Ewing Young, thus beginning a lifetime of adventure in the Southwest.

The following is an account from Kit Carson's autobiography, concerning his first expedition, one in which he fought Apache at the fork of the Salt River and the San Francisco (now known as the Verde) River. It seems amazing that what is now one of Mesa's favorite picnicking and recreational areas, just beyond the present-day city limits, was the site of a running battle between Carson and the Apache. He recounts:

. . . we continued our march, trapping down Salt River to the mouth of the San Francisco River, and up to the head of the latter stream. We were nightly harassed by the Indians, who would frequently crawl into our camp, steal a tarp or two, kill a mule or horse, and do whatever damage they could.

Although Ewing Young's party with Kit Carson was one of the early expeditions down the Salt, an earlier expedition led by James Pattie was related by Earl Merrill in one of his weekly historical columns in the *Mesa Tribune.*

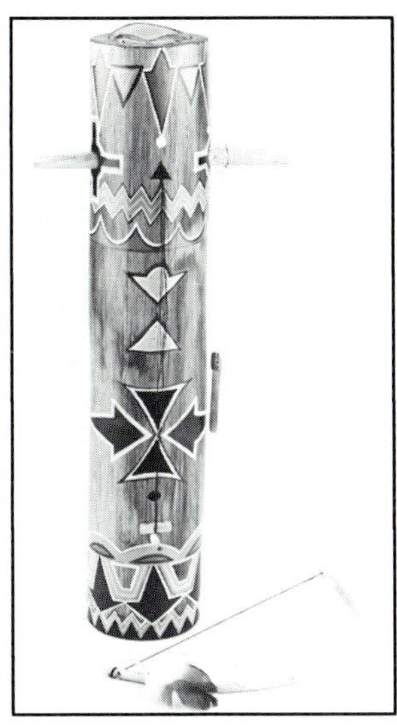

Above: This Apache fiddle was crafted on the San Carlos Reservation by Salton A. Reed in 1981 in the traditional manner, utilizing the hollowed flower stock of a dried agave with horsehair strings to produce sound. The bow, ornamented with a feather, is made from a bent twig flattened on the interior side and horsehair strings. Courtesy, Mesa Southwest Museum Collections

Right: Pima basketry skill is apparent even in strictly utilitarian baskets, such as this grain basket. It was used to store grain both for food and for the next season's planting. Following the introduction of wheat by the Spanish, the traditionally agricultural Pimas became noted wheat producers. Baskets of this style were often large enough for a man to hide in, or large enough to store 50 bushels of wheat. Courtesy, Mesa Southwest Museum Collections

On the morning of February 1, if Pattie was remembering correctly, the party, now mostly Anglo-Americans, began the ascent of a river that he called the Black, but which several scholars agree could "hardly be anything but the Salt."

"We found it to abound with beavers," Pattie related. "It is a most beautiful stream, bounded on each side with high and rich bottoms." They traveled upstream to where the river forked "in the mountains,. through Mesa to the Verde River." Charles D. Poston, called the "Father of Arizona," made his first expedition into Arizona in 1854:

. . . We could not explore the country north of the Gila River, because of the Apaches, who then numbered fully twenty thousand. For three hundred years they have killed the Spaniards, Mexicans, and Americans, which makes about the longest continuous war on record.

The Apache Indians, who had at least one of their home bases in the Superstition Mountains overlooking Mesa, terrified other Indians as well as Anglo settlers of Arizona. Poston makes a strong case why early Anglos teamed up with the Pima against the common enemy, the Apache:

The Apaches have robbed [the Pima] time immemorial, and they in turn make frequent campaigns against the Apaches. When they return from such a campaign, if they have shed blood, they paint their faces black, and seclude themselves from the women. If they have not shed blood they paint their faces white, and enter the joys of matrimony.

The brutality of the Apache was matched by many of the early frontiersmen. James Kirker, instead of trapping for beaver, collected another marketable commodity: human scalps. Hunting the populated river valleys of the Southwest, Kirker and his band of cutthroats killed and collected an estimated 10,000 Indian scalps. The government of Mexico, in a last-ditch effort to control the Apache in their northern empire, offerred $50 for each Apache scalp turned in. In 1837, Kirker's most profitable year, he is purported to have

Above: Viola Taylor and her mother, Cecelia Henry, San Carlos Apaches, are producing various sizes of burden baskets. The craftswomen use only traditional materials: willow for lighter-colored portions and cat claw for the darker designs. Courtesy, Norman Mead Collection

Above right: Edith Johnson, a San Carlos Apache, weaves willow between pliable twigs to form a burden basket. These baskets range from extremely crude, with minimal decoration, to those more finely woven with elaborate decoration. Courtesy, Norman Mead Collection

Right: Apache Gan or Mountain Spirit Dancer masks of this style were used in ceremonies to cure the ill. Most of Apache ritual deals with the diagnosing or curing of illness and is presided over by a shaman. In Apache culture both males and females could function as shamen. Courtesy, Mesa Southwest Museum Collections

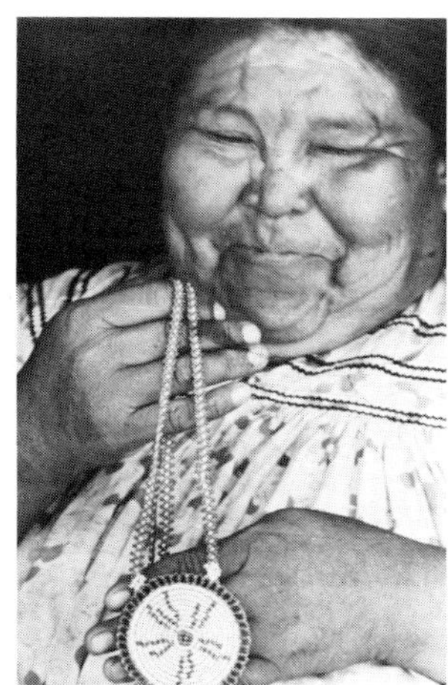

Above: A San Carlos Apache woman wearing traditional camp dress displays a fine example of tribal beadwork. Throughout their history, the Apaches have done some of the finest beadwork in the West. However, their warring in defense of their lands often overshadowed their artistic and cultural achievements. Courtesy, Norman Mead Collection

Right: Chief Chil Chuana stands in front of a traditional Apache wickiup. Although his nickname was "Chin," the Apache word for "devil," with his encouragement many of his people later became churchgoing Lutherans. Photo by Walter J. Lubken, courtesy, Norman Mead Collection

Left: This tuts-ah, or Apache burden basket, is decorated with buckskin fringe and tinklers. Originally burden baskets were utilitarian, and worn by Apache women to carry gathered nuts and berries as well as wood and other supplies. The small metal cones or tinklers produce a rhythmic sound when striking each other. Courtesy, Mesa Southwest Museum Collections

made more than $100,000.

The Kirker party was only one of a number of scalping companies that operated in the Southwest. Yet it took many years of immigration and progeny by the Anglos of the territory to equal the population that Kirker's group annihilated.

Apart from the Apache and their raidings from strongholds near Mesa, there were at this time several other significant events that influenced the future development of Mesa and the Arizona Territory.

In 1821 Mexico won its independence from Spain, placing Arizona under Mexican rule. In 1846 President James K. Polk declared war on Mexico. The Mormon Battalion, led by Lieutenant Colonel Philip Cooke, played a central role in the capture of Arizona, and many members of the battalion later were some of the earliest settlers of Mesa. In 1848 the Mexican War officially ended with the signing of the Treaty of Guadalupe-Hidalgo.

United States possession of Arizona did not end the Apache menace. In 1861 U.S. Cavalry Second Lieutenant George Bascom betrayed a white flag of truce and treacherously attempted to capture the Apache chief Cochise. Cochise narrowly escaped and launched a new round of Apache wars throughout Arizona. It was during this round of wars that the Apache warrior Geronimo rose to prominence and left his legendary

This 1847 photo by Ed Irwin is one of the few surviving photos of the famous Apache chief Medicine Man. As a younger man he regularly scouted for the white men and became very knowledgeable in their ways. When he led his people in raids against Arizona settlers he was extremely successful and became the most feared of all Apaches, thereby creating a legend that lives today. Courtesy, Norman Mead Collection

mark on history.

In 1862, as the Apache threat continued, Arizona was claimed as a territory of the Confederacy. In sheepish response the next year, the U.S. Congress belatedly passed a bill making Arizona a separate territory of the Union, apart from New Mexico. But despite its popularity with both the North and the South, Arizona did not play a significant role in the Civil War. During this entire period, the Apache raids were heating up, continuing to make the Salt River Valley a battleground not fit for settlement. It was not until 1865, when the Civil War ended, that the U.S. turned its attentions to the Apache Indians.

As part of this renewed effort, Fort McDowell was established, near the present site of Mesa,

MARYVILLE
Mesa's First Incarnation

▼ ▼ ▼

It should not be assumed that the Lehi party of 1877 formed the first attempt at settlement in the vicinity of present-day Mesa. In fact, it may have been the remains of Maryville, located just across the Salt River from the Mc-Dowell Crossing, that enticed the Utah group to establish the community that would become Mesa.

Maryville grew from a station on the Salt established by William Rowe in 1868. Rowe's Station, which catered to travelers to and from Fort McDowell, soon generated enough traffic to warrant the opening of a general store, owned by Charles Whitlow. The troops stationed at nearby Fort McDowell were among the most frequent customers. The name "Maryville" was chosen for the community by Whitlow in honor of his daughter, Mary Elizabeth. As owner of the town's prime source of goods, his selection met with little resistance.

The village that sprung up around the store was short-lived; the Maryville post office opened April 25, 1873, and closed a mere eight months later. Frequent Indian attacks were not a small factor in its downfall; raids on livestock were common, and left many of the families that had attempted to settle there destitute.

But the major reason for Maryville's demise was the 1871 establishment of Hayden's Ferry, several miles to the west, which proved to be a much safer and more convenient crossing of the Salt. With activity at Fort McDowell on the decline, Whitlow left the area in 1874 and moved to Florence. Although William Rowe continued to do business until 1875, the downfall of Maryville was swift, and by the time the Lehi party arrived less than two years later, Maryville was nothing but a ghost town. Much of the lumber from the abandoned buildings was salvaged and used in the first dwellings of the first Mesa settlers. Such was the legacy of Maryville.

▼ ▼ ▼

Some people speculated that Jack Swilling, a promoter and gambler, was a man running from the law. He is known as the founder of Pumpkinville, a farming community that supplied food and fodder to the Army at Fort McDowell. Pumpkinville is now known by another name, Phoenix, state capital of Arizona. Courtesy, Norman Mead Collection

representing the first real U.S. military presence in the Salt River Valley. This presence soon grew, and the last major campaign in the region against the Apache was about to be waged. A bloody battle known as the "Battle Of the Caves" was fought about 40 miles upriver from the present site of Mesa, by General Crook's cavalry unit, with help from members of the local Pima tribe.

As day began to dawn, a party of Apaches emerged from the cave, feeling secure in the belief that no enemy knew of this secret passage to their den. At the word a volley was poured into them and six Apaches fell; the survivors were called upon to unconditionally surrender, but their only reply was a yell of defiance and the chanting of war songs. Two hours of brisk skirmishes followed. The Indians seemed confident that by their superior numbers they could conquer, but this cost them dearly, for they made charge after charge in which they were mowed down with slight loss to the troops, and to the last they fought desperately and well. As the silent winter's day was closing, the impatient troops were ordered to charge and with a tempest

of cheers the command moved forward and gallantly closed the work.

The number of Indians killed is not known, but about 60 bodies were found, and 30 women and children were made captives. Considerable property was taken, much of which had been issued by Indian agents, and passes and tickets for rations were found, obtained from the same source.

Two small communities quickly popped up to supply fodder and food for the fort, setting the stage for the permanent settlement of Mesa. In 1867 Jack Swilling, a rogue of dubious background, started the farming community of Pumpkinville, and just east, directly across the river from present-day Mesa, the village of Maryville was founded. Maryville, located at the river ford called McDowell Crossing, prospered for about 10 years, until Hayden's Ferry was built at the site now known as Tempe. The more-convenient Hayden's Ferry put the town of Maryville out of business. And what happened to the town of Pumpkinville? It changed its name and continued to flourish. It is now known as Phoenix.

Chief Talkalai was an Apache chief who once controlled the territory northeast of Mesa. Courtesy, Norman Mead Collection

THE JOURNEY TO MESA

We were much surprised on entering Salt River Valley. We had traveled through deserts and mountains for a long ways. Now there opened before us a sight truly lovely. A fertile looking soil, and miles of level plain, in the distance, green cottonwood trees.

So wrote explorer, missionary, soldier, interpreter, and pioneer Daniel W. Jones of the first Mormon expedition into central and southern Arizona in November 1875. The "sight truly lovely" he described? A broad tableland overlooking the smooth-flowing Salt River, the future site of a settlement that would in turn bear the names of Utahville, Jonesville, Lehi, Hayden, Zenos, and, ultimately, Mesa, Arizona.

"But," he might have added, "there's no point in settling here, when an even more beautiful site lays ahead . . . in Sonora, Mexico!" For settling the Salt River Valley was not the plan of the first Mormon expeditions that ventured south from their Salt Lake City base.

The road to Mesa's settlement, however, began with the accounts given by Daniel W. Jones. A rugged, single-minded veteran of the Mexican War, Jones was sent on his expedition by Brigham Young, president of the Mormon Church, who dreamt of colonizing the vastly unpopulated lands to the south of Salt Lake City.

Scouting parties of the church were not uncommon in Arizona during the middle 1800s. In fact, much of northern and central Arizona was included in the Mormon "State of Deseret," a large intermountain geographic domain laid out by the Mormon Church soon after its relocation in Utah. Church missionaries were exploring the northwest portion of the state as early as 1857.

Young, however, was interested in continual expansion to the south. Following the Mexican War's end in 1848, Mexico, and specifically the northern state of Sonora, was a logical site for

Arizona artist Gertrude Rust depicted the Mormon pioneers arriving at the site that would later become Mesa, Arizona. Courtesy, Norman Mead Collection

a colony. Sonora was the destination of the Jones scouting party that departed from Nephi, Utah, in 1875.

Traveling on horseback, the seven-man party, including Jones and his son Wiley, crossed the Colorado River at Lee's Ferry, just a few miles south of the Utah-Arizona border, and passed through the lands of the peaceful Hopi Indians in northern Arizona, doggedly pursuing their final destination. Along the way they heard what surely must have been one of the first sales pitches for "the Valley of the Sun." Two gentlemen in Pine Springs named Wharton and McNulty enthusias-tically told them tales of the Salt River Valley, and of its inviting climate and appeal for settlers. This came as news to the group, since, as Jones himself wrote, "strange as it may seem, at the time we started, the valley of the Salt River was not known even to Brigham Young."

Despite this sales job, the party pressed on, passing through Tucson, meeting with Territorial Governor Anson Safford. He welcomed them to Arizona with open arms, and was enthusiastic about future Mormon settlement in the territory. They proceeded south, toward Sonora, but soon encountered one aspect of Mexico that Young had not foreseen: its propensity for political turmoil. They found it to be in the midst of a revolution, and wisely chose to move on to El Paso, where they entered Mexico through "Paso del Norte." They enjoyed a pleasant four-month stay south of the border before returning to Utah to present their positive findings to Young and the church elders.

Brigham Young was enthusiastic about the party's findings. With the church in the midst of a substantial growth phase, he appointed Jones to lead a settlement party to these new lands.

Young's goal was for the group to eventually settle in Mexico, but he also allowed for the "spirit of inspiration" to guide them toward a suitable point for settlement, should they fall short of the Mexican border. At least, thought Young, there

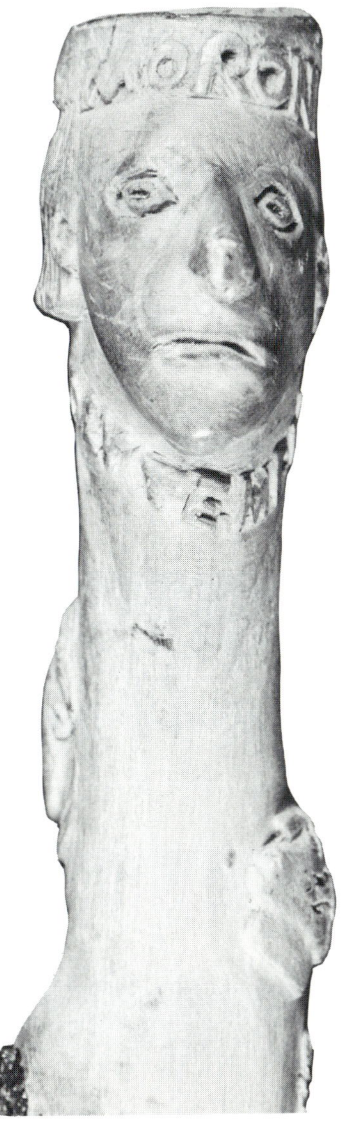

Above: According to the Mormon faith, the angel Moroni, depicted in folk sculpture, revealed the location of the Golden Plates hidden in Palmyria, New York, to Joseph Smith, founder of the Church of Jesus Christ of Latter-day Saints. Mormons believe that Joseph Smith's transcriptions of the plates, which became the Book of Mormon, are the history of the ancient tribes of the Americas. Courtesy, Mesa Southwest Museum Collections

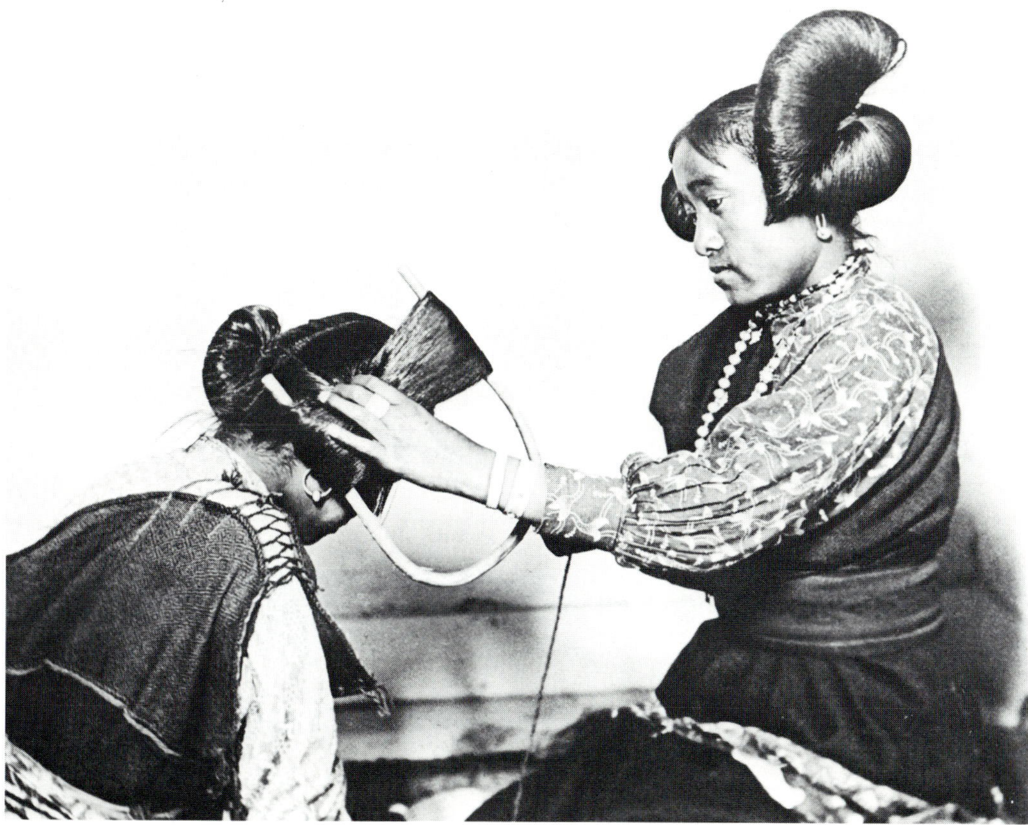

should be one more outpost on the way to the golden hills of Sonora. And, almost certainly, those first glimpses of the Salt River Valley flashed through the mind of Daniel W. Jones.

Leaders of the church put out the call for those willing to form a settlement in the "far south," maintaining the vagaries of destination. They were instructed to gather in St. George, Utah, a small town about 10 miles north of the Arizona border on the Virgin River. Jones soon set about organizing a party of working-class pioneers with the grit and determination to carve a community out of untouched desert country. It was not a mission for the weak of heart or the faint of constitution. The cast of characters was a diverse, yet inspired, lot. The party included Jones, his wife Harriet, and their 10 children, ranging in age from 20-year-old Daniel P. Jones to one-year-old Almina; his first counselor, Philemon C. Merrill, a farmer, and his wife and seven children; Henry C. Rogers, his second counselor, a wagon maker, along with his wife and nine children; and Thomas Biggs, company clerk and engineer, with his wife and four children.

It was Rogers who formed an image of the group's final destination, one he frequently described to the others in the party. As he remembered Brigham Young's reference to the "spirit of inspiration," he drew a picture in his mind's eye of a distinct but less than idyllic setting: a clear stream, a row of large cottonwood trees, a small adobe building with a flat roof, and a man and a horse. It can be assumed that his "vision" met with polite (but largely unconvinced) response. At *that* time.

Other members of the company were of great help owing to their practiced trades: Joseph McRae and Isaac Turley were blacksmiths; Ross Rogers, Henry's brother, was a surveyor; and George Steele was a nurseryman. The group totaled 84 men, women, and children.

Bundling up their life's possessions, with a moderate supply of livestock, the pioneers departed from St. George on January 17, 1877, after receiving a few final words of instruction from church leaders. The 21 wagons were jam-packed with their personal effects; in fact, many of them were overstocked. Unaware of the rigors to come,

DANIEL W. JONES
In Search of "A Sight Truly Lovely"

▼ ▼ ▼

Daniel W. Jones' early background rendered him a highly unlikely candidate to lead a Mormon expedition toward settlement in an unpopulated desert. And even though the sturdy character and strong-willed personality of Daniel W. Jones, chief scout and leader of the initial settlement party, clearly proved him to be the man destined for the job, it took a strange twist of fate to lead him to that destiny.

Born in Howard County, Missouri, on August 26, 1830, Jones lost both parents prior to his 12th birthday, and soon found himself an apprentice in the leather-working trade. He succumbed to wanderlust as a teenager and headed for Mexico in 1847, volunteering his services for the Mexican War. Following the war he found himself in no hurry to return to the states, and remained in Mexico until 1850, developing a fluency in the Spanish language that would prove extremely beneficial in his later pursuits.

After leaving Mexico he worked at odd jobs, and in time found himself on an expedition driving 8,000 sheep from New Mexico to California. It was in Utah that a most significant accident occurred: a severe gunshot wound caused Jones to drop out of the expedition in order to recuperate.

Jones' pistol accidentally discharged one day while he was mounting his horse, and wounded him in the groin. The injury was so severe that Jones considered taking his own life: upon examining the seriousness of the wound, he "took out the other pistol from the holster with the intention of 'finishing the job' . . . almost everyone in the company expressed the belief that I would die."

The citizens of a small Mormon settlement in Provo County, however, did not agree, and took him into their community, nursing him back to health. Taken with their kindness and the openness of the townspeople, Jones became intrigued with the Mormon way of life. Soon after, he abandoned his California journey and dedicated himself to teaching the Indians of the West his newly adopted beliefs.

His travels as a soldier and scout worked to his advantage in his dealings with the Indians, and his success soon came to the attention of church president Brigham Young. Young approached him first to gain his assistance in the printing of a Spanish-language version of the Book of Mormon, and later to form a scouting party to explore lands to the south of the State of Deseret. It was on one such expedition that he passed through Phoenix, to be told that "the most likely ditch site on the Salt River" had not yet been claimed.

Through conducting scouting trips and his eventual command of the first Lehi settlement party in 1877, Jones developed a reputation as a strong-willed, stubborn leader. He was used to working with Indians, and often placed himself in a position of sympathizing with most of their causes, resulting in friction with other settlers. To compound matters, his single-mindedness and unilateral decision making often drove fellow settlers off into other directions. In one instance several families left the Jonestown settlement in August of 1877.

Jones himself acknowledged that his methods of administration could occasionally stand restraint. He approached this subject in describing the aforementioned incident, which resulted from his persistence in special treatment of Indians:

Some of the Indians expressed a desire to come and settle with us . . . I naturally supposed that all the company felt the same spirit, but I soon found my mistake, for, on making this desire of the Indians known to the company, many objected, some saying that they did not want their families brought into association with these dirty Indians. So little interest was mani-

Jones was understandably very popular with the Indians of the area, and he succeeded in spreading the Mormon faith throughout the local villages. However, these ties continued to lessen his popularity with the Anglo settlers of the region, and eventually he was formally charged by residents of Tempe and Phoenix with protection of Indians who had trespassed upon crops. Conflict and controversy became more common as time went on, with Jones becoming more headstrong in his advancing years. Eventually, the constant struggles and a disenchantment with the politics of the church resulted in his moving his family north of the valley, to the Tonto Basin.

Tragedy would soon follow. Soon after their arrival, his wife and child were killed when a snow-covered shed collapsed on them. Jones, distraught, left the area almost immediately. He proceeded to travel the West, roaming Arizona, Utah, and Mexico, where a son-in-law who had accompanied him was accidentally killed, before returning to the Salt River Valley. Soon after his return, however, two more sons died, and he set off once again, this time heading north to Salt Lake City.

For the remainder of his life, he turned his attentions to writing, compiling his memoirs, *Forty Years Among The Indians,* and inventing, developing such items as adjustable saddles and a road-grading machine. He finally returned to Mesa in 1914, to live with his son, Daniel P. Jones. Even at the age of 84, he continued work on his road grader. It was while purchasing parts for the machinery in a local hardware store that Jones suffered severe injuries when he fell through a trap door. He died soon after on April 20, 1915, and was laid to rest in the Mesa Cemetery. Ironically his grave remained unmarked for many years before his final epitaph was written, identifying him as "Daniel W. Jones, Father of Lehi."

The famed Salt River winds through the picturesque desert landscape. The river that once saw Kit Carson fight off Apaches now supplies wild water raft trips for thrill-seekers. Photo by Norman Mead

many families had packed their favorite sewing machines, kitchen tools, and clothing, leaving little if anything behind. Determined to bring "civilization" to the wild desert as quickly as possible, their best of intentions soon went awry.

The fully loaded wagon train proceeded exactly as far as Santa Clara, seven miles south, in that condition. With the teams puffing and the wagons inching their way along the haphazard trails, the group realized that this journey would be unconducive to the portage of needless material goods.

Reluctantly, and no doubt tearfully in many instances, the members of the party began to liquidate whatever could not be construed as a "necessity." The townspeople of Santa Clara, on the other hand, who were fairly removed from the mainstream of American merchandising, excitedly leapt at the opportunity to acquire such fine new possessions at bargain prices. The party was soon stripped to the bare essentials.

These transactions, heartbreaking as they might have been, did serve to greatly enhance the financial standing of most of the members of the party, a development that would serve them well in the very near future. Jones had initially suggested recruiting citizens of small means for the journey so that they would lack the resources to turn back in the event of rough going. Although he had foreseen the need to "reduce the load" prior to leaving St. George, no one seemed to believe that it would be a problem. He turned to Brigham Young for advice, who recommended that the party take off fully loaded, knowing that Santa Clara was a scant distance away. This turn of events did much to solidify the group's overall financial picture, which would soon be further taxed by a need to overcome two major obstacles: a raging Colorado River and a profiteering ferryman.

Stone's Ferry was the crossing site utilized by the party, and the toll was steep: $10 per wagon, which soon added up to a bill in excess of $200. Even following the profitable excursion through Santa Clara, most of the families in the party could ill afford this sort of expenditure. It was Joseph McRae who was largely responsible for making the crossing possible: in an unselfish transaction, he traded one of his wagons, several of his horses, and some additional cash in exchange for complete ferriage for the group.

The journey continued, and the Utah party

Ross R. Rogers used this spirit level in 1877 to determine the exact point at which to locate the canal head for the Utah Ditch in Lehi, Mesa's original settlement. Courtesy, Mesa Southwest Museum Collections

steadily made its way through a typical northern Arizona winter, enduring freezing nights and the occasional snowstorm. Spirits in the group, however, remained high. Daniel W. Jones wrote of the journey in his autobiography:

The trip was made without losing an animal or suffering in any way worth mentioning; in fact, to this day many of the company speak of the trip as one of pleasure rather than suffering. Everything was under strict discipline. No one can travel safely through a wild, dangerous country and be neglectful, no matter what those may say who are too lazy to stand guard without grumbling.

It is not unlikely that the leader's memories of the trip may be a bit more pleasant than those of some of the participants; however, discounting normal hardships, there was apparently no loss of limb, life, or animal, making it a remarkable trip for that time period.

The descent from the mountains into the desert was difficult, but, as Jones mentioned, was completed successfully, without loss of stock. The end of February saw travel progressing rapidly, as the party approached the Salt River Valley, and the ground between Wickenberg and Phoenix was covered quickly. According to Daniel P. Jones, the leader's eldest son, "the whole town of Phoenix," in fact, was purported to have come out to see the party passing through, a spectacle of "22 wagons, with lots of children sticking their heads out from under the wagon covers." The party spent little time there, however, continuing east, looking closely at land along the Salt River. The rugged band was definitely weary, but still awaited the "right place" to settle.

That place was soon in appearing. It was the morning of March 6, 1877, one day out of Phoenix, that Henry C. Rogers' vision, duly noted some three months prior, manifested itself upon the rugged countryside. Daniel P. Jones described it as follows:

There was a high bank on the other side of the river, with a row of large cottonwood trees growing on it. They looked like they had been planted there. They were very large and must have been at least 30 years old. At the upper end was an adobe house that had been used as a post for soldiers to guard people through the pass that led to Fort McDowell.

The well-worn group was only too willing to accept this as the ending milepost. By nearly unanimous consent—one hardy pioneer recommended continuing —the travelers agreed to end the journey.

The journey ended at a canal head on the Salt River, directly across the river from the abandoned settlement of Maryville, the remains of which matched the description of Rogers' vision. Their stopping point was 10 miles from Fort McDowell, eight miles east of Hayden's Ferry, and 15 miles east of Phoenix. Upon the site of what was to be their new home, the haggard, well-worn pioneers took a respite . . . for about an hour. Maybe two hours. But regardless, construction of the first canal from the Salt River was under way *by that afternoon.*

It was a matter of course that canal construction would be vital to the development of any settlement in the hot Arizona climate. And the industrious Jones was not one to sit back and bask in the glory of a simple accomplishment such as traveling more than 300 miles in 49 days by wagon train.

Henry Rogers and his brother Ross took charge of the project, armed only with a spirit level and a straight edge—a far cry from today's engineering tools, but miles ahead of those employed by the Hohokam Indians of 1,000 years prior. The party's 18 men and boys worked the canal head until they were exhausted, day after day, week after week, making slow but steady progress on their mammoth undertaking. Work was finally completed, May 15, 1877, and the first stream of water flowed to the settlement referred to as "Fort Utah."

The "fort" was an adobe-walled structure that measured approximately 50 by 75 feet. Originally designed for protection from the nearby Apache who were still actively raiding from nearby settlements, the fort was utilized as lodging for several of the families prior to more permanent single-family dwellings. A well was dug inside, and the interior was divided into separate rooms for the individual families.

The comforts of civilization were taking root in the small settlement. The thorny charms of desert life were beginning to entice even the most skeptical of the group. However, back in Salt Lake City, the leaders of the church, while mildly pleased with the group's accomplishments thus far, were still expecting the party to reach Mexico. Brigham Young gently prodded the group in a letter written that summer, expressing his praise for their settlement on the Salt, but inquiring, ever so politely, as to the itinerary of the next leg of their journey:

We should like to know what your intentions are with regard to settling the region for which you originally started. We do not deem it prudent for you to break up your present location, but, possibly next fall, you will find it consistent to continue your journey with a portion of those who are now with you . . . we do not, however, wish you to get the idea from the above remarks that we desire to hurry you away from where you are now.

Despite Young's queries, the St. George party showed little inclination toward further exploration. This little encampment was quickly becoming "home," and friendships were now established with the residents of the nearby communities of Phoenix and Hayden's Ferry, as well as an uneasy alliance with the neighboring Indian tribes, most notably the Pima.

Originally centered around the Gila River to the south, several families of Pima were brought north to the Salt by settlers in Hayden's Ferry, to form a "buffer zone" between them and the Apache. They were still located on the river when the Jones party arrived, and Jones saw the value in developing relations from three angles: for the help they could provide on canal construction; for the possibility for additional converts to the Mormon faith; and indeed, as insurance against Apache attacks.

His efforts in conversion, while largely successful, resulted in one amusing incident. A common ceremony employed by many missionaries in the Western U.S. was to present Indians with a gift, often an article of clothing, immediately following their baptism, to welcome them into the "civilized" world. Shortly after his arrival, Daniel Jones had found himself beseiged by Pima Indians requesting that they be baptized. This unsolicited zeal baffled Jones, until he learned that his overly enthusiastic Indian translator was promising a new shirt to every Indian male to be brought into the faith!

In the beginning, the cohesive spirit of the community at Fort Utah was pervasive. In fact, some scribes went as far as to describe the Mormon life-style as a successful form of "communism," which, although eyebrow-raising in the present day, may have been an apt description. This was especially true in the case of the canal construction, in which, as the *Prescott Miner* reported, "all share equally in the returns, regardless of capital invested." It was a form of the "United Order" plan of living, which, although not officially connected with the Mormon Church, was an outgrowth of Mormon settlements in the West. In this communal plan, crops and the results of all industry were gathered together at a common center, for common use by the members of the community, and it served this first settlement well, at least in the beginning.

Another communal effort involved the selection of an official name for the community. There would prove to be little correlation between "official" names and those popularized by general

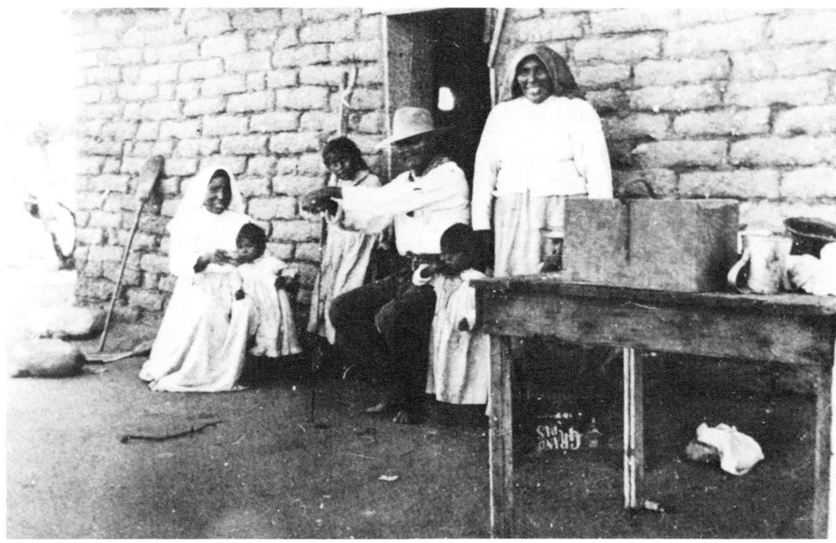

A Pima Indian family posed for this portrait around the turn of the century. The Pimas' homes were adobe, well suited to the Arizona climate. Courtesy, Douglas R. Brown Collection

public usage. A vote taken of the residents a few months after their arrival resulted in "Utahville" as a nearly unanimous choice for their new community. However, as Daniel Jones' influence continued to swell, and knowledge of his exploits grew in the neighboring communities, the settlement began to be referred to just as frequently as "Jones' camp," or "Jones' settlement," and, inevitably, "Jonesville." Some of those in the camp *not* named Jones were less than ecstatic about this development, but often found themselves referring to the settlement by this name anyway, in deference to public usage.

As the names changed, it became apparent that the newly found settlement was not without conflict, much of it rooted in a growing resentment toward the increasingly authoritarian style of leadership adopted by Jones. While this method of management was instrumental in the success of the party in the journey from St. George to the valley, it did not wear well once the party had reached its destination.

However, elsewhere all was positive. Word of the Jones party's success and final destination soon spread like wildfire throughout the State of Deseret, and it was not long before a second party was prepared to strike out for the much-heralded Salt River Valley. This time the party was made up of individuals and families from all over the West; but the bulk of them were from Bear Lake County, Idaho, and Salt Lake County, Utah. They set out with 79 men, women, and children and 25 wagons on Sep-

tember 14, 1877, and headed south.

Leading this second party was a quartet of family patriarchs, common only in their desire to relocate in a new land of opportunity: Charles Crismon, a cattleman and miller, interested in setting up business in a moderate climate after suffering heavy livestock losses from the cold winter; Francis Pomeroy, a multifaceted businessman looking for relief from chronic rheumatism; Charles Robson, lawman and former warden of the Utah Territorial Penitentiary, and Pomeroy's son-in-law; and George Sirrine, a successful merchant and rancher, and Crismon's son-in-law.

The journey was cold as the winter of 1877 proved a harsh one. Nevertheless the party made good time, considering that they had a substantially larger amount of livestock to drive—some 340 head of horses and cattle. Crossing the Colorado at Lee's Ferry was not an easy task with so much stock; with a capacity of two wagons per trip, crossing after crossing had to be attempted on the rickety barge across the rapid river, and at least three men were needed to row on each trip.

The stock was herded into the river to swim across, but proved reluctant to brave the waters. To transport them by ferry would be even more time consuming, but Francis Pomeroy came up with a clever solution. Spotting a young calf in the herd, he carried the calf onto the barge, and proceeded across. The calf's mother became understandably worried, and took off after her runaway offspring. Soon the entire herd began to follow her lead, and within minutes the entire herd of livestock had forded the mighty Colorado.

After the crossing at Lee's Ferry, things did not get much easier. The party ran into continued inclement weather on the northern plateau, and opted to rest in the Verde Valley soon after Christmas. The four leaders, Robson, Pomeroy, Crismon, and Sirrine, formed a scouting party with hopes of reaching the Jones settlement by the first of the year. In the case of George Sirrine, he had little time to get acquainted with the baby daughter that his wife Esther had delivered just days before.

It took the scouting party a mere four days to cover the 125 miles between their temporary camp and Jonesville, and they did indeed spend New Year's Eve with Jones and his settlers. Jones, eager for new residents in a community growing divisive, recommended a site for settlement in close proximity to Jonesville. However, it was decided that, to avoid crowding, the second party would locate on higher ground, about five miles to the south. They scouted the land upon a large mesa, running 10 miles across the east valley, and found it more than appropriate for settlement. Robson, Sirrine, and Pomeroy returned to the main party while Crismon remained behind to supervise construction of a canal to the proposed new site. The rest of the group arrived on February 14, 1878, including six-week-old Florence Sirrine and two other baby girls who were born during the journey.

To construct a canal of the magnitude envisioned by the leaders of the second party would have been nearly impossible, considering their limited man power, equipment, and the unyielding lay of the land—the water would need to flow *uphill.* Many scoffed at their plans, and waited for them to relocate nearer to the free-flowing Salt.

This well may have happened, had it not been for one striking coincidence: the Hohokam Indians had had the same idea, in the same spot, more than a thousand years earlier, and the remains of their handiwork still lay upon the newly reclaimed land.

This prehistoric canal followed nearly the exact gradient mapped by Sirrine and Pomeroy. After discovering the ancient ditch, it took eight months before water reached the townsite. Canal construction understandably had become the community's first major industry, out of necessity. Canal builders received an average daily wage of $1.50; but many agreed to receive their pay in shares of the Canal Company. Those not working the canals were readying building construction, poised to begin as soon as the first drop of water from the Salt reached the mesa. When this event occurred in October 1878, Mesa was born.

In the meantime the Jonesville settlement had fallen into disarray. Disagreements over the treatment of the local Pima, coupled with a general dissatisfaction with Daniel Jones' leadership, sparked the departure of the majority of the company until only four families remained. This greatly diminished the resources of the company, and most went to work at Charles Hayden's flour mill a few miles down the river. A plan to divide the settlement among the four remaining families failed dismally. For the next few years, Jonesville, soon to become known as Lehi, would continue to struggle. The early settlement in the eastern Salt River Valley was rapidly fading into the growing shadow of its new neighbor on the hill.

Families from the second party began their move onto the mesa from their temporary settlement a short distance above the McDowell Crossing. Many utilized lumber and materials found at the abandoned village of Maryville. While there is disagreement about which of the pioneers constructed the first dwelling on the mesa, it is generally attributed to the William Newell family.

His wife Rena described it in extremely modest terms: "We have the most comical little house, six posts with forks set in them. The wood out of a species of cactus set up around the sides and plastered with mud . . . the roof is a flat dirt roof. Newell built it for haste . . ." The first wood floor in Mesa belonged to Jesse Hobson, as did the first newborn child.

Francis Pomeroy's dwelling came soon after, and was adopted, more or less, as the settlement's official "community center." It was a brush shed some 30 feet square, with a dirt floor and a roof covered with arrow weed, grass, and dirt. Though rough-hewn, it was truly palatial when compared to the surrounding dwellings, and many families took shelter there until their homes could be completed. In addition, it was the site for frequent community get-togethers, such as dances and religious services. It also served as a makeshift school, with Zula Pomeroy, the teenage daughter of Francis, as teacher.

And so it began. The community on the mesa began to thrive, with canals spreading across the parched land, bringing life where there was previously only dust. Houses, shacks, and hovels sprang up with each new arrival as neighbors, friends, and strangers pitched in to slowly build a town. After months on the road, the adobe huts and brush-walled lean-tos were considered quite homey by the settlers. Word quickly spread of their success, and wagon trains from the north were soon beating a path to the modest settlement in the east end of the "newly discovered" Valley of the Sun.

Yes, the journey was over for the original settlers of Mesa. But the hard times were just beginning.

THE HARD YEARS

I t didn't take long for the achievements of the first two groups of settlers in Mesa to reach church officials in Salt Lake City. Soon a third and fourth party were under way, and, after them, groups arrived regularly.

The third party arrived January 17, 1879, bringing with it the Mesa pioneer families of Hibbert, Phelps, Dana, LeSueur, Davis, and Warner. The fourth party contained the families of Standage, Rogers, and Pew. All of these names are familiar even to modern-day residents who know nothing of the community's history: virtually all of the major streets in Mesa's center district bear the names of these first settlers.

The latter party, arriving in January 1880, opted to settle about one mile west along the mesa in a settlement that became known as Stringtown. It is still debated whether this community took its name from the string and ropes used to support the early tent town, or from the fact that the dwellings were "strung out" along a dirt trail. Today that road still exists as Alma School Road in Mesa. The corner of Alma School and Southern Avenue has become Mesa's most heavily traveled intersection. Land in this as-of-yet uninhabited section of the valley was quite easy to come by. In fact, upon his arrival in 1883, a settler named Conrad Kleinman was able to obtain his 80-acre tract in a swap for one able-bodied work horse.

The majority of the newcomers, however, continued to set up housing in the little settlement on the mesa, and by 1881, its population had grown to more than 300. But Jonesville had remained essentially stagnant. Following the departure of many of the original families, the riverside settlement housed only a handful of residents. As of 1884 their ranks no longer included one Daniel W. Jones.

Lehi remained a quiet farming community for a time after Jones' departure, but soon fell victim to the unpredictable flood-or-drought cycle of the Salt River. Several major floods, including one in 1891 that submerged nearly all of the little

A typical harvest wagon makes its way to town. As the harvest got larger, more sideboards were added to the wagon to accommodate the load. Courtesy, Norman Mead Collection

The MITCHELL

Members of a prominent pioneer family in the Mesa area, the Rogers brothers—Walker, Otis, and Oscar—display in the 1890s how dapper young men were generally attired. Courtesy, Mesa Southwest Museum Collections

settlement, discouraged new arrivals from taking up residence below the mesa; however, some hard-core Lehi townsfolk tenaciously held their land despite the ravages of nature. Lehi has grown little since then, and was officially annexed to Mesa in 1970.

During the flood of 1891, the river carried in excess of 300,000 cubic feet of water per second. Many of the adobe structures were reduced to large piles of mud. No settlers were killed by the torrential waters, but five Indians lost their lives. This may be because the Maricopa and Pima Indians, often unable to feed and clothe their elderly tribe members, had tried to take advantage of floodwaters to dispose of them, in a crude form of euthanasia. Several aged Indians were placed in the path of the floodwaters, with bedding, clothing, and food, and left to die.

While Lehi was losing its footing, the town of Mesa was experiencing the tribulations that accompany the birth of a community. House and road construction was a slow process and materials for homes consisted of adobe and salvage. The Francis Pomeroy house, in fact, was constructed partially from the structural remains of now-vanished Maryville. The nearest source of lumber was Prescott, more than 100 miles away and not yet accessible by train.

Attempts were made to transport lumber by floating logs down the Salt River. Charles T. Hayden devised a plan to build a sawmill in the nearby Sierra Ancha and float the lumber to the valley. But the box canyons along the river played havoc with the floats, destroying most of the lumber, and the plan was abandoned.

Land was divided among the members of the original Mesa Company soon after the move, and was distributed based on each individual's contribution to the construction of the Mesa Canal. Townsite lots were valued at $50 each, and canal shares were $200 each. Some lots were held by trustees for more than a decade, still selling for $50 as late as 1890.

Gradually the community began to take shape. The town was laid out as Brigham Young proposed: in a one-mile square, with streets wide enough to allow for a complete U-turn by a full team of livestock pulling a wagon. Despite some initial reservations about the maintenance of such wide streets, the plan was followed. Years

Above: The Mesa Dairy & Ice Company, founded in 1895, gave regular ice service via horse-drawn wagon to the homes and businesses of Mesa. Prior to this, ice was freighted in from Phoenix at great expense. Courtesy, Mesa Southwest Museum Collections

Above right: A Mesa family picnics in the desert. Joel Sirrine stands on the left with a friend in the tall saguaro cactus. The 1895 Sirrine House is the first historic structure in Mesa to be preserved by the city, and has been restored to the year 1904, when the Sirrine family left the house. Courtesy, Mesa Southwest Museum Collections

later, Mesa residents would proudly point to the 100-foot-wide thoroughfares as the most progressive and practical in the valley.

The controlled growth dictated by Young's plan was beneficial to the community in many ways, and paved the way for its incorporation in 1883. On July 5 of that year, a petition was presented to the Maricopa County Board of Supervisors requesting incorporation. By August 6 the newly "official" village, at that time called Mesa City, was holding its first election.

Alexander F. Macdonald was elected the town's first mayor. Macdonald was a feisty Scottish immigrant who had come to America in 1854 at the age of 29, four years after embracing the Mormon religion.

Macdonald and his wife traveled west to Salt Lake City upon their arrival in America. Eventually they moved on to Springerville, where he served as mayor, and later Provo, where he spent 10 years as postmaster. After returning from a two-year missionary stint in his native Scotland, he was recruited by the church to head the brand-new Maricopa stake in Mesa. He became heavily involved in the local political scene there, and was instrumental in the drive for incorporation.

Familiar names made up the remainder of the first town council and village officers: Elijah Pomeroy, George W. Sirrine, Alvin Stewart, and William Passey served on the council; Charles I. Robson was elected city recorder; and Hyrum Phelps served as pound keeper. Agenda items for the early council included the building of some

small footbridges across the town's growing canal system, the construction of a city hall, the regulation of saloons, and the purchase of an iron jail cage for $150.75.

But there were more than these minor problems on the horizon. The lack of water, the lifeblood of the desert, continued to cause trouble. So serious were the disputes involving the precious commodity that, at one point, armed guards stood watch over the canals to prevent diversion into neighboring communities and lands.

One story reported by the *Mesa Free Press* stated that:

Lehi has had quite a good deal of trouble during the past week over the water question. A scrap occurred Wednesday evening in which guns, revolvers, and other weapons figured conspicuously . . . if it continues to get much worse, it has been suggested that the sheriff call out the National Guard.

Incidents of tampering with the canal headgates and locks were commonplace, and water theft was high among the list of common crimes in Mesa. Even disputes that made their way to the high courts of the territory weren't always settled peacefully. One courtroom battle in Prescott about water rights ended with the two attorneys engaged in a fist fight, and the defendant stabbing two of the litigants before being fatally wounded himself!

The close-knit nature of the Mesa and Lehi

settlements did not in itself serve to alienate the remainder of the valley; but when issues such as water rights arose, it did tend to make the community as a whole an easy target. One incident involved a party of 15 armed men from Tempe who demanded of George Sirrine that the community cease and desist *all* use of waters derived from the Salt River!

Sirrine defused the situation by gesturing to a small trickle of water in a small ditch, explaining that the amount they were using was paltry indeed. He made a deal with the group: he proposed that Mesa close its canal gates for one day.

If the small stream was not substantial enough to reach Tempe in that time, then surely it could not be considered a major diversion of precious waters. The Tempe delegation agreed, and relented when the diverted water fell more than a mile short of its destination.

Attacks of a different sort began to take place upon the predominantly Mormon settlements in the 1880s, as public sentiment resulted in the passage of federal legislation outlawing polygamy, which at that time was intrinsic to Mormon doctrine.

Beginning with the Edmunds Act of 1882, and the subsequent Edmunds-Tucker Act of 1887, those practicing polygamy or cohabitation were barred from voting or holding office, and were subject to fines of $300 and as much as six months in jail. Federal officers began a vigorous pursuit of "polygs," filling the territorial prisons and penitentiaries with an almost exclusively Mormon clientele. The media of the day played out the drama for all it was worth, and then some. One Western newspaper warned of "the Mormon Monster," citing that "at least 1,000 Mormons reality, about 150–have been colonized in Maricopa County" to wrest control of the Arizona Territory.

George W. Sirrine prevented Charles Crismon from falling victim to the authorities on one Mesa raid. A number of male residents had been subpoenaed, but Sirrine had arranged for Crismon, who was 78 at the time, to hide out at a

The self-proclaimed Baron of Arizona, James Reavis, right, and his wife, left, lived the life of royalty for more than a decade. He purported to hold the title to the Peralta Land Claim, which included Mesa and most of central Arizona. Many paid his demands of tribute before the courts, and after a lengthy battle, declared his claims to be forgeries. Courtesy, Norman Mead Collection

nearby home. A bench warrant was then issued for Crismon's arrest.

Sirrine, however, chose not to pass this information on to Crismon; instead, he arranged for a doctor to accompany him, along with the federal officers, to pick up Crismon, and told him only that he would soon be arriving with the doctor for a quick check-up. Sirrine instructed the old man to cut his gums in several places as soon as he saw them arrive, so that he would be able to produce a blood sample for the doctor. "Spit the blood into a spittoon and cough," ordered Sirrine.

When Sirrine accompanied the officers to the house, Crismon did as he had been instructed, coughing so hard he was unable to answer the door. When the men entered, the doctor, who was in on the ruse, exclaimed, "My God! He's having a hemorrhage!"

The officers, having the decency not to arrest this sickly old soul on death's door, returned to the court empty-handed, and Crismon's name was stricken from the judicial calendar. He lived in good health to the age of 83, a good five years after his "hemorrhage."

Through that subterfuge, Crismon avoided spending time in the Yuma Territorial Prison, a fate that awaited hundreds of Mormon men who were charged and convicted of polygamy during this time. Many more, however, fled south of the border until the furor died down.

Many Mesa residents fled not out of fear, but to aid their friends and relatives. In fact, none of the original Lehi settlers actually had more than one wife, even though Daniel W. Jones, always the idealist, frequently lectured on

"Polygamy as Understood by the Mormons—And Why It Cannot be Abandoned." A.F. Macdonald, after serving his term as mayor, was among the many called south by church leaders to help establish settlements in Mexico for the fugitive Mormons.

After several years of persecution and legal battles, during which the Edmunds-Tucker Act was confirmed as constitutional, a manifesto was composed by church president Wilford Woodruff. In it, he declared his intention to "submit to antipolygamy laws, and to use my influence with the members of the church over which I preside to have them do likewise." While it took many years for these practices to dissipate, enforcement of the laws slowed greatly upon Woodruff's pronouncement, and most of the expatriate Mormons returned to the country.

If being forced into hiding wasn't bad enough, Mesans were doubly surprised when a claim filed with the surveyor general's office in Tucson designated their newly settled community, and indeed, the majority of the Salt River Valley, as the property of one James Reavis, the self-proclaimed "Baron of Arizona." This news arrived a mere four years after President Hayes had summarily awarded their lands to the Indians!

Reavis had produced a varied and impressive assortment of documents identifying himself as heir to the land, which had originally been granted to rancher Miguel Peralta by the king of Spain in 1748. Taking advantage of the clause in the Treaty of Guadalupe-Hidalgo pledging to honor all existing Spanish land grants, Reavis lay claim to most of central Arizona, and collected monies for quit-claim deeds from hundreds of farmers and ranchers who were currently doing business on "his" lands.

He decked himself and his family out in the finest of fashions, carried himself royally about his holdings, and, although his claims were never quite taken seriously by residents of Mesa or Lehi, collected enough fees and payments from others to support his kingly life-style for more than a decade. Ultimately, however, his documents were proven to be forgeries, and in 1895 his claims were declared fraudulent. He was convicted and sentenced to a long prison term.

Mesa soon found itself confronted with others attempting to procure a living through less-than-honorable, and considerably more violent,

During the 1890s mining was an important industry in the mountains surrounding Mesa. Silver and gold were mined in the beginning; later, copper became the mainstay for the state. Courtesy, Norman Mead Collection

means. In 1883 an attempted robbery of a Chinese peddler brought about the community's first criminal manhunt. When it was determined that the felons included the well-known villains "Curley Bill" Brocuis and "Three-Fingered Jack" Williams, a posse of 75 men was quickly assembled.

Mesa historian Frank Pomeroy recounted the events that followed the attempted capture of these desperados:

Scouts were sent out to cut the trail surrounding Mesa, and discover the direction taken the outlaws . . . John Blackburn, Ben Blackburn, Martin Pomeroy, and James Thurman cut the trail north and west of Mesa. They found two fresh horse tracks which they followed toward the Salt River . . . Emerging from the river bottom, they saw at a distance several horsemen winding their way casually through the mesquite and chapparal northward. On seeing the pursuers, the group halted and awaited the arrival of the boys. When the boys were about 100 feet distant, they were told to stop, but one of them was invited to come on and "spill" what was wanted . . . John Blackburn rode on up to the group and told them he had come to arrest them for attempting to rob a Chinaman. He was asked if he had a warrant for their arrest. When he informed them he had no warrant, the leader said he would not go with them without a warrant . . . John Blackburn

started to draw his gun, when Curley Bill rode up to him and shoved a gun in his ribs, and said with an oath, "Drop that gun, or I'll put daylight through you!" John Blackburn did not pull his gun, and Ben Blackburn, with a bead on Curley Bill, did not pull the trigger. Curley Bill lowered his pistol and advised John and the boys to go back home and get their warrant . . . The boys saw the light and returned.

The posse headed north again within the hour, this time with an arrest warrant and additional firearms. But by that time the outlaws had too good a jump on them, and escaped to the north.

Man-made hardships did sometimes slow the development of Mesa; however, these paled in comparison to the natural obstacles that continually impeded the growth of the valley community. Apart from the regular flooding of the Salt River that threatened to wash away the settlement of Lehi completely, there was severe heat, disease, drought, fire, and even an earthquake to deal with. The hot scorching summers were the most continual problem, and the bane of all valley residents. It is suggested that the Mesa of today would not exist had the original settlement parties arrived in July or August, as opposed to January and March. How did the earliest residents beat the sweltering dry heat of the desert? One method involved bedsheets and watering cans. During the evening, after the harsh sun had descended, sheets were hung from the porch roofs and trees, and thoroughly watered down. The wind then blew through the damp sheets in a primitive form of evaporative cooling, lowering the temperature of the porch, upon which the families would sleep. Watering cans, or simply jars of water with holes cut into the lids, were also used by early Arizonans to sprinkle water upon themselves during the days and evenings.

Even the "miracle" of electricity was not always a final solution to the heat. During extremely dry periods, the Salt River's flow was so diminished that not enough energy could be generated to serve the needs of the community and its newly invented motorized fans.

Severe heat caused its share of health problems, but other common diseases of the day were also responsible for inhibiting Mesa's early growth. The most dreaded of these, smallpox, took a heavy toll on the early community. The most devastating outbreak of smallpox came just days after Mesa's official incorporation.

Forty-four townspeople died during the summer of 1883, depleting the ranks of the community by nearly 15 percent. An equivalent loss of life today would result in more than 40,000 deaths. Mayor Macdonald's 11-year-old son John was the first victim. Initially diagnosed as a heat rash by a doctor who didn't want to create a panic in the community, the young Macdonald's case worsened until it became obvious that an outbreak was at hand.

The flames were fanned by the fact that Macdonald's wife was at that time operating a store and post office out of the family home in downtown Mesa. Dozens of community residents passed through their doors daily, and many were contaminated with the disease before a quarantine could be established. By the end of August more than three dozen people had died.

Long-time resident Clarence Dana recounted his memories of the plague to the *Mesa Tribune*:

People were dying every day . . . We lived near the pest house quarantine center, also on the road to the cemetery. It seemed that they were almost continuously passing with bodies. At the time of death they were in such terrible condition that their flesh would almost drop from their bones. They had to be rolled in sheets before being placed in their coffins.

Prior to the epidemic, most Mesans were buried in the Tempe cemetery, but the increasing frequency of the burials soon brought about the need for a graveyard in Mesa. Two small lots just outside the townsite were designated for this purpose, but were soon outgrown. In 1891 land was purchased for a new city cemetery one and a half miles north of the city. The fact that a few dozen unmarked graves were known to exist at the original site has fueled speculation throughout the years that perhaps not all of the graves were moved; however, recent trenching for gas and water lines at that original site, now at the corner of Center Street and University Drive, turned up no evidence of this . . . or at least none so far.

The havoc wreaked by Mesa's severest earthquake was no match for the rage of smallpox, yet did serve to raise a few eyebrows when it struck on May 3, 1887. Centered in northern Sonora, Mexico, the quake jostled southern Arizona communities. In Mesa its impact was limited to rocking the waters of the irrigation canals and rattling dishes in cupboards. At nearby Fort McDowell, a side of a small mountain was dislodged, and the shock was reported to be "very severe." The quake of 1887 ranked as one of the most severe ever recorded in the Rocky Mountain region.

Drought was another natural phenomenon, one especially harsh in an area with so little water to begin with. Brief periods of no precipitation were common, but in 1897 a drought began that would continue for an amazing eight years.

During the Great Drought, as it became known, the population of all valley communities, Mesa included, decreased. Many thousands of acres of farmland simply dried up and became useless. Skirmishes involving water rights flared

Wide prehistoric Hohokam canals, later enlarged by pioneers, brought life-giving water to the valley. The beautiful reflections in the water connote a peaceful serenity of days gone by. Courtesy, Mesa Southwest Museum Collections

once again during this era, and tempers were short. At times it seemed that the fates wanted the fledgling Arizona settlements to dry up and blow away. One report cited rains "in California within three hundred miles of us on the west, and within a couple of hundred miles on the east, but we got not a drop." It took strong encouragement from Mormon church officials in Salt Lake City to keep many Mesa residents from packing up and moving elsewhere as they watched their crops wither year after year.

By the time the rains finally resumed their regular schedule in 1905, the point had been hammered home: some sort of reservoir and water-control system was desperately needed if life in the Salt River Valley was to continue.

With drought came fire hazard. "The small boy with firecrackers will be rigorously suppressed," wrote the *Tribune* on one dry Fourth of July. And the following edict was issued from the office of the mayor in July of 1898:

To the Citizens of Mesa City: In view of the possible loss of life and property to fire during our coming 4th of July festivities, it is desirable that all parents and guardians should caution those under their watch and care concerning the danger arising from careless use of matches, firecrackers, and all kinds of fireworks. The fact of our city being practically without water should admonish every citizen to be on the alert, prepared to work in harmony with the city officials for our mutual protection. Please, fellow citizens, be on your guard.

The townspeople, well aware of the potential of fire hazards, were careful, but despite this it was only a matter of months before the town's first major fire erupted. On October 21, 1898, the blaze broke out in Cosby's Grocery Store. The ensuing story was eloquently reported by the *Mesa Free Press*, which had just been ready to go to press for its weekly edition when the alarms sounded:

Mesa had its first fire this morning. The alarm of fire rang out upon the air, and in almost a twinkling, the street was full of people rushing to the scene of the fire, which was in Cosby's grocery store, adjoining the Passey and Mets furniture store. Everybody worked with a will in trying to

extinguish the fire and in carrying goods out of Cosby's and the adjoining stores. The two buildings . . . were of wood and corrugated iron, and it was soon apparent that they could not be saved. All efforts were then directed to saving the Johnson block containing the Johnson Brothers' store and the post office, and Abell and Wilbur Company's hardware store. The fire fiend licked up the two wooden buildings quickly, but the gallant work of the boys, the gentle east wind, and the solid seventeen inch brick wall of the Johnson block stayed the flame. The losses, outside of damage to the goods removed, are: Cosby, about $500, no insurance; Passey & Mets, building and contents, $1,500, insurance, $1,500; George Passey, building, $650, insurance, $400.

Fire protection became a hot issue, both in the papers and on the city council agenda. Prohibition of the construction of wooden buildings in the town center area was an immediate result, and several proposed firefighting plans were generated. Water supply was still a major problem, however; during the fire, the only sources had been a handful of nearby wells, which were quickly depleted, and a small canal about 50 yards away. Mesa's first volunteer fire department was organized as a result of the fire, although the *Mesa Free Press* would later criticize it as being "in an unorganized condition."

There was one act of nature that *was* within the power of Mesa's early residents to control, and that was the rapid proliferation of the area's cottonwood trees. The rich groves that sprouted along the banks of the Salt, and had provided Daniel W. Jones with a "sight truly lovely," were starting to be deemed a nuisance by the townsfolk.

Although they provided much-needed shade, they were criticized for using too much water, spewing brittle branches on homes and residents during windstorms, and filling the air with small fluffy seeds. New trees that were easier to maintain were being planted around the community, and their cleanliness and appearance generated public support for the efforts to eradicate the cottonwoods. As the 25th anniversary of the founding of Lehi and Mesa settlements neared, that first stand of trees along the Salt, which contributed to settler Henry Rogers' vision and prompted settlement, were chopped down, because they were "unsightly."

GOLDFIELD
Mesa's Own "Sutter's Mill"

▼ ▼ ▼

There may be legends galore about Jacob Waltz and his legendary mine, but there was little mystery surrounding the second most noteworthy chapter in the history of Mesa-area mining: the Mammoth mine and the short-lived town of Goldfield, just five miles northeast of Mesa in the Superstition foothills. And although it may pale in mystery and romance in comparison to Waltz' mine, it was eminently more worthwhile from a practical standpoint, making rich men of the four lucky Mesans who happened to stumble onto it and providing a great shot in the arm for the area's economy.

It was discovered in the fall of 1891 by the Merrill brothers, Orrin and Orlando, along with C.R. Hakes and J.R. Morse. The party literally "stumbled onto a gold mine." While wandering not far from an existing mining camp, they uncovered a rich outcropping of gold ore, and upon digging further, they found ample evidence of what was to become one of the richest strikes in Arizona's history.

In description of the mine's great quantity of riches, it was called the "Mammoth," and the four operated it until selling out to a Colorado firm two years later. The mine continued to prosper, even more so with the new capital investments facilitated by its new owners, and it is believed to have produced in excess of one million dollars in gold. The accompanying boomtown of Goldfield prospered as well, providing goods and services to the miners and employing many out-of-work Mesans in its stores and saloons.

Like any mine of the era, the Mammoth was not without its tragic accidents. One incident in 1897 brought the residents of Goldfield and Mesa together in a vigilant show of support that saved the life of a miner nearly given up for dead.

The accident occurred at 10 P.M., July 3, just as the night shift was coming on. James Stevens was working 50 feet down into the

This photograph is believed to document prospectors from Arizona's "gold rush" at the Goldfield area. The photo of these two rough-looking characters seems to bring out the "gambler" in them as they boldly display their cards. Courtesy, Mesa Southwest Collections

mine when the company's carpentry shop sank through the front portion of the shaft, sealing him off from the outside world. "Stevens had two gallons of water and several candles with him," reported the *Free Press;* "he can hold out for sometime, unless he dies for want of fresh air. If he gets hungry before he is rescued, the candles in his possession will be sufficient to sustain life for some time."

The *Free Press* revised its story in the next edition, stating that "parrafin candles . . . have no nutritional qualities whatever."

Efforts to dig through the debris were slow and painstaking. After five days of sifting through the collapsed mine, there was still no sign of Stevens. The *Phoenix Gazette* wrote his epitaph in its July 9 edition: "NO HOPE FOR STEVENS . . . THE WORK OF ATTEMPTING HIS RESCUE HAS BEEN ABANDONED."

Yet the following day there was a remarkable occurrence, as reported by the *Gazette:* "One of the employees of the mine reached a wooden airshaft from the surface and tapped it several times. Much to his surprise and delight he heard distinctly three taps in answer, which was followed by several taps in rapid succession."

From this point on, the company spared no pains in working to extract the trapped miner. Stevens' tapping became lighter as the days dragged on, yet his presence was still confirmed a remarkable 11 days later, on July 14. Each day brought optimistic headlines —"Hope For Stevens," "Entombed Miner To Be Released Today"—but to no avail.

Finally on July 16 the crews came to within 12 feet of the miner, at which point his voice could be heard. Several hours later, the *Gazette* reported the breakthrough:

The picks broke the sheet and a cloud of dust and rocks fell through, and a head and shoulders were shoved through the aperture. The two miners in the shaft eagerly grasped the arms and were about to haul the man through . . . in a second the wasted form of James Stevens was lying in the shaft.

Despite losing more than 60 pounds and living for 13 days with no sustenance, Stevens survived the cave-in. "He gave not the slightest indication that his mind had become unhinged from mental torture," reported the paper; "cool temperament and steady nerves saved his life." After the incident, James Stevens became a sort of folk hero, and his fame outlived the mining operation.

Goldfield's end was soon in coming. A mere four months after the mine collapse, the owners suddenly closed the mine. The town folded up soon after, and this colorful chapter— providing a sample of the boom years that were ahead for Mesa—was over.

THE BOOM YEARS

The turn of the century signaled a new beginning for Mesa. It was the beginning of a boom period that would continue virtually uninterrupted for the next 30 years. The West had been tamed; the Apache were no longer a threat. The Age of Steam was in progress, with man convinced that he and his machines were ready to conquer and civilize the world. Queen Victoria had sat on the English throne for more than 60 years, and even in Mesa, Victorian culture, fashion, and architecture were all the rage.

The feeling among Mesa residents was one of optimism. The *Mesa Free Press* reported the following account of a Fourth of July celebration in 1898, reflecting the mood of the time and a patriotic fervor inflamed by the Spanish-American War:

From midnight until daylight, the town was ablaze with rockets, Roman candles, and other pyrotechnic contrivances. At sunrise, a salute of 13 guns was fired, and Company E, drawn up in line in front of the armory, fired 13 volleys.

At about 7:00, the throngs of people, buggies, carriages, and other vehicles began to crowd the streets. By 8:00, the time set for the grand parade, the streets were packed, but for some reason, it was after 10:00 before the procession formed.

After this long wait, the procession formed with the Mesa City Band in the lead, followed by the magnificently decorated float of the charming Goddess of Liberty with Company E, as a guard of honor, fair Columbia and Uncle Sam, next a handsomely decorated float, then followed 200 little tots, school children from four to ten years old.

The float of the Y.M. and Y.L.M.I.A. was beautifully artistic, and its attractiveness was largely enhanced by the charming young ladies who rested beneath the artistic canopies of flags and bunting. The floats of the I.O.O.F. and Rebeccahs, the Woodmen and Woodmen Circle, B.M. Johnson and Bros., the Farmers' Exchange, the Mesa Hay and Grain Co., and the Mesa Lumber Co., followed

In addition to the large block stones, more decorative, smaller stonework can be seen in the towers on top of the Roosevelt Dam. The Italian stonemasons created a work of art, blending Old World and New World architecture. Courtesy, Norman Mead Collection

in order, and they were handsomely decorated.

Captain Saba's Rough Riders followed next, about 80 strong, and they made a fine appearance. The buggies and carriages completed the procession, which was the largest ever seen in Mesa.

The fireworks in the evening called together an immense throng of people on the streets and the dance at night in Co-op Hall was well attended.

Later editions of the *Mesa Free Press* indicated that the parade generated such a rich array of floats that it actually took the judges several days to declare a first-prize winner!

The community, bound in spirit, continued to welcome new arrivals from all parts of the nation, and could no longer be construed as simply a Mormon settlement. The new century brought with it the establishment of the first Catholic church in Mesa, foreshadowing the dramatic changes that would soon occur in this sleepy farming community. Even so, the strong Mormon domination of Mesa politics would last another 50 years.

In 1901 a new building was constructed to house the Arizona capitol, which had moved from Prescott to Phoenix in 1889. The gradual gravitation of the territorial government center to the Salt River Valley propelled Mesa to the geographic center of Arizona politics, which were beginning to heat up about the Southwest's most precious and sought-after commodity: water.

Throughout the late 1800s every community along the Salt River had been plagued by floods and droughts. Numerous independent irrigation canal companies had formed along the Salt, and developed loose agreements on how much water each company could have.

These agreements caused few difficulties when water was in good supply. But with increased demand and major droughts, the companies went to war, both in the courts and in the trenches.

Mesa, the community located farthest upstream and still looked upon as a close-knit Mormon community, was especially targeted during these "water wars." Stories have been told about irrigation locks and hand gates being broken and smashed in raids against the Mesa community.

A number of the early non-Mormon settlers were encouraged to settle in Mesa to beef up the town's defenses. One of these early residents was Ramon Mendoza, a native of Sonora, Mexico. Mendoza was the town's first *zanjero,* a Spanish word roughly translated as "water guard." Mendoza, a tough no-nonsense individual, later moved from his job as armed water guard to armed police officer. Years later, his son Ramon, Jr., would serve as police chief for the City of Mesa.

With the water wars escalating, the time had come to act. In 1901 the territorial legislature raised $30,000 through a special tax, which was supplemented by the federal government, for preliminary surveys of a dam to control the Salt River. On January 21, 1902, when the kingpins of water finally incorporated as the Salt River Valley Water Users Association, it was the culmination of a tortuous process. But it was this unification that paved the way for the next major step, one that would prove to have far-reaching effects on Mesa, the entire Salt River Valley, and the future state of Arizona.

On June 17, 1903, President Theodore Roosevelt signed the Reclamation Act, and four months later the Department of the Interior and Bureau of Reclamation, in cooperation with the Salt River Valley Water Users Association, authorized the construction of Roosevelt Dam. Roosevelt Dam was the first project to be approved under the act, and the first one to repay the government in full. At the time the dam was known as the

Irrigation was vital to the development of the Salt River Valley. This 1910 pumping plant helped Mesa get water to its residents. Courtesy, Special Collections, University of Arizona Library

Tonto Dam of the Salt River Project, and would not receive its current name until its dedication nearly a decade later. But regardless of its name, the decision to build this dam and its effects proved to be the single most important event in the history of Mesa, Arizona.

At the time, Mesa was a quiet, dignified, small yet progressive community. Many other economic milestones were being reached when plans for the dam were announced. Electricity had come to the town five years earlier, and virtually every home had now become "electrified." This was accomplished largely through the efforts of one of the town's most influential and prominent citizens, Dr. A.J. Chandler.

Along with his brother Harry, Chandler found that he could take the Mesa Canal water diverted from the Salt miles upstream and utilize it on the mesa to generate power. Just east of Crismon Road, now called Country Club Drive, at the edge of the mesa itself, the Chandlers built their generating plant, the first in the state. Elec-

tricity was soon to be followed by that marvel of modern communications, the telephone. It was in 1902 that a completely operator-assisted telephone system was implemented in Mesa.

Another boon to the area's economy resulted from a market for a commodity in good supply throughout the Southwest: horses. Mesa had them, and the British wanted them. The Boer Wars of South Africa were raging to their conclusion and the British armies were still utilizing horse and mule power as their prime means of transport. This need provided a boost to Mesa-area ranchers.

Many believed that it was the strain of the Boer Wars that led to the death of Queen Victoria, ending her 63-year reign of what was then the world's most powerful country. That mantle, however, was beginning to slip to the United States. The Industrial Revolution, coupled with the belief that "Yankee ingenuity" could accomplish anything, were generally responsible for the shift in power.

Above: This view was taken from the top of a grain load just starting into the mountain area that is the present site of Canyon Lake, just a few miles north of Mesa. Courtesy, Norman Mead Collection

Right: The name of this early entrepreneur is barely visible on the small side boat—*The Cartcaters.* The ferry had limited room: one wagon and a few additional horses per trip. Horses, people, wagons, and supplies had to be ferried across Roosevelt Lake, as the lake was rising and had already covered the town of Roosevelt at the bottom. Courtesy, Norman Mead Collection

That "ingenuity" was grandly realized in the construction of Roosevelt Dam. The project was much more than a construction job and it required much more than ordinary construction workers. From Mesa's vantage point, the work force that the project generated was like an invading and occupying army!

In addition to a sizable contingent of construction personnel, there were multitudes of others associated with the project. Engineers and architects were responsible for the dam's design. Cooks fed the hordes of workmen. Blacksmiths kept the army of mules and horses shod. Lumbermen operated a sawmill built especially for the dam construction site.

Mule skinners and horse freighters moved 30,000 pounds of material daily. Explosives experts blew away mountains to prepare the bedrock dam site, and exploded other mountains to obtain granite for the stone dam. Italian stonemasons were imported to carve the granite into large stone blocks.

Merchants quickly moved in and built a temporary town of tar paper and wood, in what would soon become the bottom of Roosevelt Lake. And, in addition to everyone else, there were the omnipresent Washington bureaucrats who were on hand to supervise—or, as the workers would eloquently put it, who were "gummin' up the works."

Mesa was the railhead for the project, so everything shipped to the project went either to

Right: Cottonwood, sycamore, and oak supplied many of the main timber braces in the construction of Roosevelt Dam. Notice how the large beams almost dwarf the draft horses used to pull the load. Courtesy, Norman Mead Collection

Right: The construction of the Roosevelt Dam involved a mixture of power: steam power and back power. The large equipment depicted had to be disassembled and hauled by wagon more than 50 miles, from Mesa up the Apache Trail. Courtesy, Norman Mead Collection

Below: Freight wagons from Mesa wait to board the ferry that would take them across the rising Roosevelt Lake. Courtesy, Norman Mead Collection

or through Mesa. From Mesa north to the dam site was some of Arizona's most rugged country. There were no roads; the main thoroughfares were little more than old Apache trails that wound along the twisting and treacherous Salt River.

Because of this, the first order of business was to get a road built from Mesa to the construction site. Phoenix and Mesa each sold bonds totaling $71,000 to fund this highway construction, which took place during 1903 and 1904. The first stage of the project, consisting of expanding and extending the road across the flat desert to the base of the Superstition Mountains, went quickly. But the second phase of the plan, road building through those rugged Mazatzal Mountains, was a slow and arduous task. It was also low-paying, backbreaking work.

It was during the construction of what became known as the "Apache Trail" that the first real wave of emigrants came to Mesa, supplying a labor force for the road construction. The first Oriental family arrived in Mesa in 1903, and the first blacks came soon after, in 1905.

Surprisingly, however, it was the dreaded Apache, coaxed off the reservation by the promise of 50 cents for a day's work, that supplied most of the labor for the construction of the roads, dams, and canals associated with this major reclamation project.

Dr. Ralph Palmer, a Mesa physician who played a major role in the dam's development,

Above: Roosevelt Dam was photographed as it appeared in the middle stage of its construction in about 1907. Roughly hewn stones can be seen in the center area; finely squared stones were used for the exterior. Courtesy, Norman Mead Collection

Above right: Most of the buildings in the town of Roosevelt were left at the bottom of the lake bed where the original town was formed. However, official institutions such as the Roosevelt Post Office were moved to higher ground. Courtesy, Norman Mead Collection

Right: As in many of the other boom towns of the West, tar paper shacks and board and batten buildings quickly sprang up in Roosevelt to fill the needs of the miners. Here a wood vendor has a load of firewood to sell to local merchants. Courtesy, Norman Mead Collection

recounted the first days of the project:

My first job was to assist the acting superintendent Charles Olberg in laying out the camp at the dam site, and we started on this immediately. On a low bluff on the south side of the Salt, our survey gang staked out a location for a large corral, an engineers' mess tent on a higher level, a field hos-pital tent, sleeping tents for engineers and guests, and numerous tent sites for working men, a black-smith shop, carpenter shop, etc. As the work pro-gressed, we laid out a town site adjoining on the east, the lots to be leased to individuals on permit for business purposes at no rental but under re-striction as to conduct, especially in regard to li-quor, which was prohibited with a three-mile limit of the entire project. We also located an excellent spring and brought water in by gravity to a large storage tank supplying the entire camp to be established on a high bluff across the river on the Tonto side. Of the early tents set up were two in a cottonwood grove across the Salt and on the Tonto where Mr. Olberg had them placed—one for himself and one for us.

During the next five years of Mesa's history, new arrivals from all corners of the earth would arrive and find a niche in the town's rapidly swelling economy—an economy built around supplying the needs of both the men who worked on the project as well as the project itself.

There was a wide variety of needs to fill, social and otherwise. In 1904 John T. Vance built the largest auditorium in all of Arizona in down-

town Mesa. Many a heart was set a flutter, and many a heart was broken within the walls of the Vance Opera House. The 1908 *Directory of Phoenix and the Salt River Valley* stated: "There are two theatres in Mesa—the Mesa Opera House and the Vance Opera House. The last named is the largest structure of its kind in the southwest, with all modern improvements . . . and the best dance floor in the territory."

Both opera houses attracted their share of entertainment to Mesa—everything from opera to traveling theater groups and vaudeville, which provided local residents with a wide array of musicians, magic acts, and assorted one-nighters. Even noted speakers such as William Jennings Bryan, the silver-tongued orator and three-time nominee for president, visited the Vance Opera House.

Also a constant source of entertainment to Mesa and the Arizona Territory during these years was the Mesa Brass Band. The "band boys," as they were called, organized in 1898, and enthusiasm intially ran high. As reported by the *Mesa Free Press* on August 10, 1900: "Last Saturday night the Mesa Brass Band gave another concert. These concerts are getting to be quite a feature in Mesa . . . The streets were filled with vehicles, and the sidewalks were lined with people who came out to enjoy the fine program of music dispensed by the band boys. The city fathers, it is understood, will be requested to buy a band stand." Subsequent reports, however, would indicate that the band found itself in a continuing series of reorganizations and attempts to "revive interest"; but today, the Mesa City Band is still in existence, ranking among the premier community bands in the state.

Not all of Mesa's entertainment was so innocent. At the height of the dam construction, Mesa boasted nine drinking establishments along Main Street, along with a number of pool halls. Prostitution was well documented in the early Mesa jail records, as was a high incidence of fights and drunk and disorderly conduct.

This is not hard to explain. Since alcohol was not allowed on the construction site, or at the lower Granite Reef division just outside Mesa, Mesa became the workers' watering hole. Workmen came into town to drink, play cards, shoot pool, and carouse. Many of the businessmen of early Mesa made a good living making sure that their needs were met.

The battle to enforce the dam site prohibition laws forced the hiring of a grizzled Texas Ranger named Jim Holmes to keep things "dry." Dr. Ralph Palmer recalled this "enforcer" and one of the many alcohol-related incidents that were commonplace during this turbulent time:

Before Roosevelt Dam could be started, a road had to be built from Mesa to the dam site. Today the Apache Trail winds through some of the most rugged sections of Arizona. Courtesy, Norman Mead Collection

Today, skateboards and 10-speed bikes are popular modes of transportation for the young. Here the members of a family proudly show off their means of getting around in 1900: a goat cart. Courtesy, Mesa Southwest Museum Collections

The Le Sueur family and friends show off their new automobile, with Red Mountain in the background. The Le Sueurs' auto was said to be the first owned by a Mesa family. Courtesy, Mesa Southwest Museum Collections

Jim was a small, wiry, blue-eyed Dane who had seen rough days on the Texas-Mexico border, and was entirely adequate to handle the job. He was the typical two-gun man of western fiction . . . Many mornings I would ride over a flat across the river and throw cans up in the air for him. An ordinary tomato can he would keep in the air shooting alternately from right and left hips until there was nothing left of the can or both guns were empty. When trouble was brewing, Jim always shot first and got his man so that his reputation was quickly established and no one seemed anxious to tangle with him. One of Jim's early shootings in connection with liquor occurred late one evening when word came to him that a Mexican bootlegger had come into Cottonwood Canyon on Tonto Creek with a pack outfit and two barrels of whiskey. Holmes deputized a man named Bagsley, and they walked across the suspension bridge and up Tonto. To reach the cottonwoods they had to go 100 yards or so through a dense growth of tules higher than their heads and with a trail just wide enough to walk single file. It was just getting dark when they came to the bootlegger's camp. Several customers beat it into the brush, but one Mexican stood his ground with his hands in the air. Holmes took a gun from him and told him to come along. When they entered the tules Holmes was ahead, Bagsley next, and the Mexican following. All at once the Mexican shot Bagsley, but before he could get in a second shot Holmes had drawn and got in his regulation five holes in the Mexican—one in the forehead, one in the neck, one in the chest, and two in the abdomen.

The subject of alcohol was one of the more controversial aspects of Mesa's economic development. At one point, the city's mayor led a heated debate over the day's most burning issue: should or shouldn't the City of Mesa permit the sale of liquor on Sunday?

The mayor argued that it *should*. At the time, it was not allowed; and as a result, the dam workers would head for Tempe and Phoenix for their Sunday drinking and extracurricular activities. It was pointed out that the city was sending thou-

Top: These trade tokens, used by Soapy Smith's Saloon of Mesa, were issued by the Los Angeles Rubber Stamp Company. Courtesy, Mesa Southwest Museum Collections

Bottom left: This trade token, used by the Cooley & Dykes company of Mesa, was good for 12.5 cents in trade. Courtesy, Mesa Southwest Museum Collections

Bottom right: This trade token was good for one-half gallon at Davis Dairy in Mesa, Arizona. Courtesy, Mesa Southwest Museum Collections

Above: At the height of the construction of Roosevelt Dam, Mesa had nine drinking establishments and numerous pool halls. It was a ripsnorting Western boom town where even shoot-outs in the streets were not unheard of. Courtesy, Mesa Public Library

sands of dollars to these neighboring communities needlessly, money that should have stayed in Mesa. The town leaders, however, were not sympathetic to his liberal views, and the mayor eventually resigned over the matter.

Indeed the whiskey, tobacco, billiard parlors, and ladies of the night were of grave concern to parents raising their children in what had previously been an idyllic, closely-knit community. This resulted in a city ordinance passed in 1917 that read as follows:

Any minor, except when in pursuit of necessary business, who shall visit, hang around, or loiter in or about any bawdy house, billiard, or drinking saloon, bar, or other place where intoxicating liquors are kept and sold, or who shall loiter about any street, street corner, alley, or other public highway, or who shall prowl about or enter any public building or private building without permission of the owners thereof, on Sundays, or other days not legal or local holidays, or who shall loiter or hang around when occupied, shall be guilty of a misdemeanor.

It is not certain if this ordinance resulted in a decrease in "hanging around," but a 9 p.m. curfew instituted soon thereafter helped matters substantially.

Three special men left perhaps the most lasting impressions on Mesa during this time of excitement and progress. They were Walter J. Lubken, official photographer for the project; the project's chief engineer, Louis Hill; and the aforementioned Dr. Ralph Palmer, the official surgeon and physician for the project.

Walter Lubken was designated photographer

for the Roosevelt Dam project in 1904. Lubken documented construction progress by taking thousands of photographs of the dam, the men, and the machinery involved in this enormous undertaking.

His photographs of the dam and other Western scenes have been published in hundreds of books, journals, and magazines, but the vast majority of his work was not credited. In 1977 the Mesa Southwest Museum was the site of the first comprehensive exhibit of his work. Following that show, Lubken's photographs were exhibited at the Smithsonian Institution. Today he is regarded as the most important historic photographer in Arizona and the Southwest.

Lubken was always fascinated by the Indians of the Southwest, and frequently selected them for his photographic subject matter. He thoroughly documented the participation of the Apache in the construction of the dam.

Although the use of these local dwellers as laborers would today seem a sensible move from a business standpoint, their hiring caused a commotion that nearly lost Chief Engineer Louis Hill his job and brought the entire project into question. This was due, of course, to the still predominant anti-Indian sentiments and bigotry that had even permeated the federal government.

Hill defended the abilities of these Apache workers, and often sent them out on the job in unsupervised squads. This policy did not set well with the bureaucrats, and soon Congress held hearings regarding Hill's use of Indian labor. Hill was called "an impractical dreamer, a shady engineer who was building an unnecessarily large power plant for the fun of it, or for purely speculative purposes." Hill answered his critics in his customary straightforward manner, and succeeded in convincing the governing body that "all he had done was what he believed was best for the majority."

Two years following Roosevelt Dam's groundbreaking, Dr. Ralph Palmer had opened Everybody's Drug Store in downtown Mesa. Everybody's continues in operation today in its same location, and has become a historic landmark in downtown Mesa.

While at Roosevelt, Palmer kept a journal that was later used as the basis for a book titled *Doctor On Horseback*. From his writings, one can obtain a glimpse of what life was like during the

WALTER J. LUBKEN
A Master of the Camera
▼ ▼ ▼

Shortly after the turn of the century a young photographer, Walter J. Lubken, left New York City and came to Arizona to seek adventure and perhaps fortune.

Through the eye of his camera lens we see the intricate designs of early Indian baskets—baskets that were made before these items became trade goods and were redesigned to suit the traders. We can see how native Arizona Indians used nets to fish the natural streams. We see what the early steamboats of the Colorado River really looked like as they prepared to make their journeys from Yuma upriver. There are pictures of early Phoenix when trolley cars were used for transportation and pictures of the Superstition Mountains when they could be reached only by foot, horse, or wagon trails.

From Lubken's camera came the only known pictures of Camp Verde and Tonto Apache with their proud chiefs such as Chilchuana and Taklia. On glass plates he recorded the life-style of these Apache people before they became lost in the culture of the Anglos. He had a natural rapport with the Apache as they patiently waited and posed for long periods while he set up and manipulated his early and cumbersome cameras. He rewarded his subjects with highly prized sticks of peppermint candy.

It is uncertain where Walter Lubken acquired his expertise in photography or why he selected Mesa as his headquarters. It seems fairly safe to say that he settled on Mesa as it was the closest town to the United States' first reclamation project. Lubken was the official reclamation photographer for more than 45 years—from the beginning of the Roosevelt Dam project through part of the Hoover Dam and Lake Mead undertaking. Between 1901 and 1911 the headquarters for the developing of this "photo history" was the Lubken Company Commercial Photographers in Mesa, just east of what is now the Mezona Motel on Main Street.

▼ ▼ ▼

Above: Walter J. Lubken is pictured in his rig stopped at the town of Goldfield, at the foot of the Superstition Mountains, in about 1905. A raging flood from the Superstitions washed Goldfield away and buried the site under several feet of dirt and rock. Courtesy, Norman Mead Collection

Right: The proud Apache had a difficult time making the transition from tribal life to the white man's society. Working for a dollar a day, Apache men could earn enough to buy white man's clothing and shoes for themselves and their families. Photo by Walter J. Lubken, courtesy, Norman Mead Collection

development and building of Roosevelt Dam.

Work was hard and dangerous. A desert river can be one of the most unpredictable forces that nature can muster. The citizens of Mesa had lived with this unpredictability for nearly 20 years, but the angry moods of the Salt River were new to many of the dam workers.

Palmer told of one incident that illustrated to those workers the potential force of the raging Salt, as he observed the raging river with one of the project engineers:

About the time the contractors had their first coffer dam in and a lot of heavy equipment down in the canyon, the rivers put up a rather considerable flood, with water in the canyon reaching the bottom of the suspension bridge, which meant about fifteen feet of water. The heavy equipment was buried in the sand and everything movable, including the coffer dam, went down the river.

Mesa residents would see the dam wash away twice more before the project could withstand the mighty force of the river. Palmer himself nearly fell victim to the raging waters when a medical emergency required that he cross the river during a flooded stage. He related his failed attempt to cross the rushing river on horseback:

About halfway across the river, the horse stumbled and went down over the riffles into deep water. As I went down, I grabbed his mane and floated downstream with him. However, he had gotten one foot through the tied reins and instead of swimming, he was floating on his side. Someone on the bank had seen me and let out a yell. Several cowboys got out their ropes and tried to throw one out to me. They couldn't make it for the distance even though they had tied rocks in the end loop. Finally, one of them . . . waded out on the crossing and went down over the riffle. When he came to me hanging onto the root, I was about exhausted and don't remember any more except that he grabbed me as he went by and together we went underwater in the channel. When I came to an hour or so later, I was in the hospital with the water pumped out of my stomach and getting warm in hot blankets with sips of whiskey.

The first stone of the dam had been laid in September 1906, and the last one was put into place in February 1911, four and a half years later. It was on March 8, 1911, that the formal dedication of the dam took place. Former President Theodore Roosevelt presided over the ceremony.

Roosevelt was well acquainted with Mesa. His son Archie was at that time attending school at the Evans, later Mesa, Ranch School, an exclusive boarding school south of town that specialized in incorporating the basics of Western

Right: In the 1920s the Cohen brothers opened what was called a cigar shop. In addition to selling a "little bit of everything," the store served as a pawn shop. During the Great Depression the Cohens also acted as a mortgage company; when foreclosures were numerous, the brothers had a store in which the owners could sell their belongings. Courtesy, Norman Mead Collection

Above: Sam L. Williams' Mix-up Shop and Second-Hand Readin' Store was located in downtown Mesa. As bicycles were rapidly replacing horses as a means of transportation in the early twentieth century, they were a major commodity of this particular business. Courtesy, Mesa Southwest Museum Collections

by the United States, and for 50 years it remained the highest stone dam in the entire world. At the time there was nothing to compare with it, and it was considered one of the man-made wonders of the world, on a par with the Great Wall of China and the pyramids of Egypt. It is still considered one of the major engineering feats of man.

Mesa was never to be the same again. Just as Dodge City became a great boomtown upon news of the Comstock Silver Strike, Mesa became a full-fledged boomtown as news of the nation's first reclamation project spread. But this time it was employment, not precious minerals, that drew the new arrivals.

Despite not being allowed to sell whiskey on Sunday, Mesa did continue to grow and prosper in other areas. And one of the earliest successful businesses, appropriate to a city striving to retain its clean image, was the broom factory, owned by Elton "Curley" Weller.

The factory, primarily a family-owned and operated concern, constructed brooms from the rawest of materials: the company grew its own broom corn plants on land leased from Mesa farmers, and processed the plant materials—cutting, sorting, grading, and fastening the brooms together—by machine as well as by hand. Workers would then trim, label, and inspect the final product.

All types of businesses were flourishing during the first two decades of the twentieth century, including several successful general mercantile operations, such as the Mesa Co-op and the O.S. Stapley Store. One of the most versatile was the Johnson Pearce Company, which during the course of 75 years dealt in produce, feed and

ranch life with regular scholastic curriculum— "readin', writin', and ropin'," as one wag put it. Roosevelt and his wife Edith stayed at the school as guests of Professor Harry Evans during the dedication trip.

In his speech he expressed his satisfaction with the project and Reclamation Bureau in general, and his appreciation to those who had named the dam in his honor. He then flipped an electric switch that opened the sluice gates, unleashing a torrent of water to the riverbed below.

Upon its completion in 1911, the dam stood as the largest reclamation project ever attempted

seed, coal and wood, beer and wine, and even homemade ant poison, exemplifying the pioneer spirit and showing an ability to adapt to Mesa's changing consumer demands. Founded by future mayor Zebulon Pearce and L.B. Johnson in 1911, it continues in business today, just a few doors down from its original location.

Many early businesses were directly related to the construction money brought in by the dam projects, but not all. The merchandising of desert wildlife was one example. Rattlesnakes were selling for 40 cents a pound, and gila monsters would go for as much as $10 a dozen. However, perhaps the strangest industry to enjoy a prosperous but brief heyday was ostrich farming.

Ostrich plumes had become the rage for ladies' high-fashion hats, and enjoyed a worldwide demand. These large feathers commanded as much as $300 a pound, making them a very lucrative venture.

The Salt River Valley, as luck would have it, turned out to be an ideal climate for ostrich raising. It is described in detail in *A Short History of Mesa,* a 1907 Chamber of Commerce promotional booklet:

These local Mesa bathing beauties were believed to have been photographed in Walter J. Lubken's studio in 1910. Although Lubken had a commercial studio, his major interests were in documenting Arizona Indians and historic events such as the Roosevelt Dam construction. Courtesy, Mesa Southwest Museum Collections

For climate, fertility, and natural products the Salt River Valley had been compared to northern Africa. In no case is this likeness more apparent than in the ease with which the ostrich has been domesticated here. Already the Salt River birds number three-fourths of all the ostriches in the United States. One valley farmer has a flock of a thousand birds. Ostriches are pastured in the same way as cattle, and like cattle, they do without shelter. The eggs are hatched by an incubator, the young bird maturing about as rapidly as a cow. The birds sell at from $150 to $500. Their wealth, of course, is in their plumage. At plucking, which occurs once in eight months, a bird yields from $30 to $50.

This fact introduced another novel new crime into the books of the Mesa city courts: plume theft! As reported by the *Mesa Free Press* on March 14, 1908:

The case of Al Edwards was disposed of about 5 o'clock last evening. Two fine ostrich plumes were found in the possession of Edwards and he confessed to cutting them from Dr. Chandler's ostriches. He said the ostrich came to the fence and he cut them off, thinking to keep them as souvenirs, and not realizing the value of the plumes.

According to Earl Merrill, Mesa's most prosperous ostrich farmer was indeed A.J. Chandler, whose ranch was now well within the city limits. He also raised alfalfa, a favorite food of the ostrich, as well as hogs.

The ostrich industry, unfortunately, was an early casualty of World War I. Priorities shifted from frivolities such as hats with ostrich plumes to more basic pursuits, and the great ostrich ranches no longer had a market. New ostrich-marketing strategies, however, were attempted, as evidenced by a report in the *Phoenix Gazette* from 1914: "The first ostrich that has ever been baked in a public eating house in Arizona will be on the bill of fare today at the Palace Cafeteria."

During the late 1910s and early 1920s, the healthy Mesa economy afforded town residents an unprecedented amount of leisure time. One of the main pastimes for the community was following the exploits of the town baseball team, the Jewels. Mesa had become known in the valley as the Gem City, a nickname which would surface in many businesses and organizations. Many old-timers say the nickname was derived from elusive mineral riches in the nearby Superstitions, while others relate it to the precious stones uncovered in the nearby Four Peaks region. One of the largest amethysts ever discovered came from this area, ultimately finding its way into the Crown Jewels of England.

Managed by First National Bank teller H.G. Dixon, the Mesa team traveled the state, and, after winning several games, saw fit in 1919 to declare themselves state champions. While this claim was immediately challenged by teams in Superior, Bisbee, and several other Arizona cities, the Jewels usually made good on their boasts. In fact, a *Mesa Free Press* reporter nonchalantly recounted a Mesa victory over Phoenix with the following summary: "This writer was there with scorebook and all, but quit counting early in the game. Somebody said afterward that the score was 21-6. Let's let it go at that."

Increased ties with neighboring communities stepped up the need for improved roadways. Construction of the Mesa-Tempe Highway, now known as Main Street in Mesa and Apache Boulevard in Tempe, was begun in the early 1920s. Paving of neighborhood streets and sidewalks was a top priority; the town's dirt streets simply produced too much dust during the dry months, and became rivers of mud during the rainy seasons.

The rains played such havoc with the unpaved thoroughfares that wooden planks stretching across the mud-filled streets and running up and down the sidewalks were commonplace in downtown Mesa during the winter months. Mesa's enterprising merchants, however, once again made the best of a bad situation, as told by the May 3, 1915, *Mesa Tribune:* "The Mesa merchants did a remarkably lively business in rubber shoes today. The cold rain and attendant mud made pedestrian stunts uncomfortable, even with rubbers."

During dry seasons, the Mesa town "sprinkler," a modified truck carrying a large tank of river water, was used to keep the dust to a minimum. This, however, created other problems, as evidenced by a brief note in the December 16, 1918, *Tribune:* "Several people who have been sprinkled when passing along the

sidewalks or crossings in the paved section have suggested to the *Tribune* that it would be a very much appreciated favor if the flushing could be completed before the time for the morning up town traffic." In the meantime, paving of the city's streets and sidewalks would continue, and within 20 years the city's sprinkler truck was retired for good.

New arrivals to the area continued to gravitate to the east valley, and home building continued as a major industry. But on September 24, 1919, came the decision to build what has become perhaps Mesa's best known and most elegant structure: the Mormon Temple.

Despite a steady influx of non-Mormon residents to the community, Mesa was still largely populated by the offspring of those first missionary groups from Utah. Their enthusiasm for their new-found valley oasis had held the interest of church officials for more than 40 years, and local church officials began formally promoting Mesa as a temple site as early as 1912. Church leaders from Salt Lake City eventually arrived to inspect several proposed sites, but declined, prompting a California faction to propose construction of the next temple in Los Angeles. With the outbreak of World War I, however, a decision was delayed.

In the meantime, more than $200,000 was raised in and around Mesa for construction of the temple. Church officials returned and agreed upon a 20-acre site, at what is now the corner of Main and Hobson streets just outside the orig-

The Mesa Coliseum was an outdoor amphitheater where plays, political oratories, and traveling theater troupes were often seen. Courtesy, Norman Mead Collection

inal square-mile town center.

News of the decision reached the valley rapidly, and within days a special "Temple Fund" had been established through the *Mesa Free Press* to solicit donations toward the construction of what was to be a truly massive structure. Small donations had been adding up for some years, the first coming in 1887 from a poor Graham County widow who, just prior to her death, designated five dollars to be put toward the construction of an Arizona temple. This money did indeed find its way to the Mesa Temple Fund some 30 years later. Today thousands of visitors, both Mormon and non-Mormon, visit the temple each year.

While Mesa was becoming a fairly sophisticated Western city, it still had more than a trace of the Old West in its citizenry. One colorful incident reported by the *Mesa Free Press* dated July 31, 1919, described an unfortunate incident that befell a town magistrate: "Judge J.W. Pruitt woke up this morning with his clothes all gone, and worse than that, he had slept in the yard and didn't wake up until the sun had lifted the curtains of darkness." A thief, who had been an apparent acquaintance the night before, had made off with the judge's trousers, which had contained his watch and chain and $1,000 worth of Comanche County oil stocks.

Obviously, along with economic boom came unsavory strangers. More pressure than ever before was placed on the shoulders of Mesa's law enforcement forces. Providing a grisly rite of passage for the sleepy village in its growth into a major city was the unprecedented murder of the town marshal, Hyrum Peterson, on November 12, 1913.

The *Arizona Gazette* reported the incident as follows:

No crime in the history of Mesa has so worked upon the population as the brutal murder of Marshall Hyrum Peterson last evening. Business is practically suspended and almost every ablebodied male citizen in town has joined in the search for the murderers.

Mesa's sandlot, semipro, self-proclaimed state baseball champions for Arizona traveled throughout the state around 1903 defending their championship status successfully. Courtesy, Mesa Southwest Museum Collections

The spacious El Portal Hotel was built by the Mesa community just prior to the great Wall Street crash. It suffered some hard years, closed, and eventually reopened as the Maricopa Hotel. Courtesy, Mesa Southwest Museum Collections

Despite some imaginative early speculation that the killer was none other than Butch Cassidy, whom some biographers purport survived his South American adventures and retired to the Globe area, the murderers were eventually found to be a pair of youthful bicycle thieves, Atha Leonard and John Tomlin. Following them to the edge of town, himself on a bicycle, Peterson finally overtook the pair, ordering them to dismount and surrender. They complied, but then opened fire with automatic revolvers and "shot him to pieces."

A posse was immediately formed, and the duo was captured some 30 miles west of Prescott the following day. The pair had stopped to fry some bacon for their supper, which was quickly consumed by the hungry members of the posse.

Leonard and Tomlin were found guilty, but their death sentences were commuted to life imprisonment. Both were eventually pardoned and released, Tomlin after serving 19 years, Leonard after serving only seven. This turn of events was violently opposed by the townspeople. Leonard and Tomlin were never heard from again.

One of the most unique civic projects ever undertaken in the state of Arizona was also one that met with an untimely end. That project was "El Portal," Mesa's first community-owned hotel and resort.

In 1927 Mesa was beginning to taste the fruits of tourism. Improved transportation and communication with the rest of the country began to establish the east valley as a "not unreasonable" place to go for a Western vacation, and the hotel industry was flourishing. City leaders seized this moment to propose a "not unreasonable" idea: that of a community-sponsored hotel, built from funds collected through sale of public stock.

Optimism was rampant—these *were* the Roaring Twenties—and enough money was raised to complete construction the following year. Built at the corner of what is now Main Street and Center Street in downtown Mesa, the structure cost a whopping $190,000 to build. Completely steam-heated and air-cooled, El Portal was a state-of-the-art resort for the valley.

El Portal was a grand display of modern engineering and community involvement. Its name, the Spanish word for "entrance way," was derived from Mesa's latest nickname, the "Gateway City," as it served as the gateway to the valley for visitors from the east.

On January 19, 1928, El Portal opened its doors, and was proclaimed by the *Mesa Tribune* as marking "a new era for Mesa." That new era, unfortunately, lasted precisely 21 months. The Great Depression of 1929 made a shambles of the thriving hotel industry, and El Portal soon found itself in severe financial difficulties. The facility was foreclosed June 29, 1931, a mere three and a half years after its grand opening.

During the hard years immediately following the crash of 1929, the *Tribune*'s presses continued rolling, and at their offices on South Macdonald Street passersby could gaze through the front window and watch the gas-powered flat-bed presses printing the news. When the banks closed, the presses worked overtime, printing not only the newspaper, but also a special scrip that would be accepted by local merchants in place of hard currency until things stabilized and the banks could reopen. This inspired solution was the brainchild of publisher Charles Mitten, which helped to keep Mesa's economy intact during those lean and hungry years.

Zane Grey relaxes near his Tonto Rim camp in about 1920. His customary style while writing was always on a lapboard. Many of his famous books, including *To the Last Man*, were written here. Courtesy, Norman Mead Collection

CHAPTER 6

FROM COWBOYS
TO CADILLACS

By the early 1930s Arizona was coming of age as a tourism destination, and Mesa, situated in the center of the state and adjacent to the towering Superstition Mountains, was in a position to take prime advantage of this development. From 1930 right up to the present day, Mesa has struggled to cope with this tourism demand and the tremendous growth that it triggered.

In the 1930s Mesa's number-one business was still agriculture and its related industries. However, tourism and the convention business were beginning to emerge as contenders for the top spot. The front-page headline of the *Mesa Tribune* on January 15, 1931, exclaimed, "CITRUS FAIR OPENS TODAY," with the subhead announcing "Exhibits From All Parts of State Crowd Mesa at First Arizona Exposition." Admission to this fair was 25 cents for adults and 10 cents for children. It was clearly the first major show of its kind to be held in Mesa.

The $600 in prize money offered was truly a princely sum in 1931, and did indeed attract exhibitors in great numbers from all parts of the state. Local bands marched in the streets, and a performance by popular local songstress Betty Verrue won acclaim. This enormously successful event was coordinated by entertainment chairman William Menhennet, who would go on to become a major force in the Mesa Chamber of Commerce, continuing to push Mesa into the epicenter of Arizona's convention and tourism industry.

Another development instrumental in bringing people to Mesa took place that same year, when the new Mesa train station was dedicated. The $60,000 structure was hailed as one of the finest along the entire Arizona rail system. Prior to this, Mesa had little more than a spur line that came from Tempe down Transmission Road, now known as University Drive. The new depot provided direct access to the rail-riding tourists and

Tortilla Flat, situated on the Apache Trail north of Mesa, is now being restored after it was destroyed by fire, and was a collecting point for prospectors, cattlemen, and a variety of characters. Courtesy, Norman Mead Collection

CURIOS
PICNIC SUPPLIES
BEST HAIRCUTS LOWEST
TORTILLA FLAT
BIGGEST LITTLE
TOWN IN ARIZONA
SERVING ARIZONA'S LARGEST

The Phoenix-Miami-Globe stage line was one of the privately owned lines that provided transportation through Mesa for tourists seeking the scenic Apache Trail as well as businessmen headed for Globe and Miami. Courtesy, Norman Mead Collection

traveling businessmen, and also opened up travel for Mesa residents.

The very day the depot was dedicated, the *Tribune* announced the imminent arrival of more than 200 women from throughout the state for the annual convention of Arizona Women's Clubs. Better transportation through rail service, coupled with regular convention business, was setting the groundwork for a rapid spurt of growth for Mesa.

Wild West tradition contributed much to Mesa during this time. "RODEO STARTS TOMORROW" shouted the banner headline of the *Journal-Tribune* on July 4, 1936. Governor B.B. Moeur was guest of honor at this large community rodeo and parade. Sponsored by the American Legion, this rodeo drew top performers from across the country, and some legendary animal performers as well.

The paper talked about some of the beasts

Arizona's Cotton Parade, a major annual event, was held in Mesa, home of the state's Cotton Festival. Even the cars got into the act. Courtesy, Mesa Southwest Museum Collections

that would be going up against the fearless cowboys. "The famous bull 'Rocking Chair,' ridden only twice in 102 attempts, from Joe Clark's ranch, will be on hand to find a rider, and 'Mae West,' one of the worst outlaw horses of the old DX string, once owned by Dan Kleinman, will be seen both tomorrow and Sunday."

All sorts of wild animals, trick horses, and other special entertainments were promised for the spectators, for whom the total package, including an all-you-can-eat barbecue dinner, cost a whopping 50 cents.

Community spirit ran high during this period, and much of it centered around Rendezvous Park, near the center of town at the corner of Second and Center streets. The site for the big

helped to facilitate an unprecedented growth in the construction of civic buildings and other community projects, again with assistance from the Works Projects Administration. These projects included expansion of the Southside District Hospital, the construction of a new city hall, library, and jail facility, which currently houses the Mesa Southwest Museum, major irrigation pipe and gas line installations, and increased construction of curbs, gutters, and sidewalks.

Mesa in the 1930s was a charming blend of the Wild West and a young community striving to become a major city. Representing the more romantic Old West were the rodeos, the Indians who sold crafts from horse-drawn wagons, old bearded prospectors with their heavily laden pack

This Hopi kiva was located at Billingsley's Hopi House Trading Post of Mesa. M.W. Billingsley, seated, center, was one of the few white men adopted into the Hopi tribe. A kiva is a subterranean ceremonial room used for performing sacred Hopi rituals. Billingsley's trading post was a regular and colorful stop for the Hopis leaving the reservation and coming to Mesa and the valley. Courtesy, Mesa Southwest Museum Collections

rodeo, the park hosted virtually every community function, and was the site for a new, state-of-the-art community swimming pool in 1937.

Arizonans by this time had learned to take their swimming pools quite seriously, and the Rendezvous Pool, funded by the Works Projects Administration to the tune of $35,000, featured a high dive, a large pool more than 130 feet long, and two small pools for younger children. Rendezvous Park would become a source of community pride for the next 20 years, featuring, in addition to the pool, softball diamonds, a large indoor skating rink, a children's playground, and a baseball field, which became the eventual spring-training site for several major league baseball clubs.

During this same time, Mayor L.B. Werner

mules plodding along Mesa's Main Street, and a fellow by the name of Johnny Hale.

John Hale was the world's leading expert on branding irons, and had amassed the world's largest collection from working ranches around the world. A Mesa educator, Hale received his first branding iron from a friend as a joke, but soon fell in love with the legends and lore that the brands carried. He referred to them as "scepters of power for the kings of cattle." Many ranches in the Southwest were indeed larger than some European kingdoms, and their irons served as coats-of-arms that marked their owners' wealth and cattle.

One front-page *Tribune* story, announcing the upcoming publication of Hale's first book on

Above: Ranching has been a major industry and trade center for many years in Mesa and in the nearby desert riverine environment along the Verde River System. Courtesy, Norman Mead Collection

the subject, featured a photo of Hale leaning back in an old mesquite rocking chair, while wearing a ten-gallon hat and holding a huge branding iron: the image of "old Arizona" personified. The caption read:

The most famous of all Arizona cattle brands, the old Hashknife iron, is being shown here by John Hale, nationally known for his collection of branding irons. Hale's collection includes hundreds of irons from all over the southwest and a number from foreign countries, including one of the Duke of Windsor's Canadian ranch. He is co-author of a book, Hot Irons, *the romantic story of the west's cattle industry . . . Hale did the research for the volume. One of Mesa's best known residents, Hale has been one of the community's most active civic leaders.*

The Hashknife brand belonged to one of the largest of the Arizona ranches, the C-O Bar, controlled by one of the state's most powerful pioneer families. This family, still well known to Arizona residents, received nationwide attention when one of its descendants entered the 1988 race for the democratic nomination for president. After serving two terms as Arizona's governor, Bruce Babbitt left the "hashknife" and family ranch behind to pursue his bid for the presidency.

In the 1930s and 1940s, cattle remained one of the state's key revenue producers, and the Babbitts' ranch was a major supplier. Arizona's most important economic factors could generally be summed up by the "Five C's:" copper, cattle, cotton, citrus, and climate. Climate was still making the smallest contribution, but this was beginning to change rapidly. The unexpected arrival of one particular industry in Mesa confirmed the area's potential to rise to heights equal to the paradise called California: show biz!

The same front page that featured the John Hale story in 1940 carried the banner headline: "STUDIO PREPARES TO MAKE FILM HERE." The paper provided the details of what would be the first major feature film to be shot almost entirely on location in Mesa, Arizona. An earlier film, *To the Last Man,* featured some footage shot in the

Above: The stage stop at the bottom of Fish Creek Hill saw many a Conestoga wagon from 1904 to 1911 as passengers traveled from Mesa to the Roosevelt Dam site. This stage stop was also the locale of many early Western films. Buster Crabbe was one of many old-time Western stars who made movies here. Courtesy, Norman Mead Collection

Mesa area, but *The Texas Rangers Ride Again* was Mesa's first real brush with Hollywood. The *Tribune* reported:

Business agents of Paramount studios, here from Hollywood, completed arrangements for filming a full length feature here Wednesday, and if tentative plans are approved, moving picture cameras will be touring here within a week . . . Arrangements have been made for filming part of the picture in Florence, part of it on the Tex Barkley ranch near Superstition mountains, and much of it in Mesa. Most of the arrangements have been made for the studio by the local chamber of commerce . . .

[Richard A. Blayden, business manager] has completed arrangements for use of Hotel El Portal as headquarters for the film company. Not more than 12 or 14 of the group of nearly a hundred will be actors, he said. Extras will be recruited locally. The movie company will buy materials for its sets and other supplies here.

The film was a lively Western of the "B" variety, starring John Miljan and John Howard. Written by a Texas journalist, the film portrayed then-modern rustling methods on a large cattle ranch, and how Old West justice dealt with the problem. Containing such classic lines as "Stick 'em up! We're rangers! You're under arrest!" it featured many locals in bit parts as well as some in featured roles, including Mesa businessmen Lester Farnsworth and Gail Millett, who played a couple of itinerant cowhands.

An old adobe building on North Sirrine Street was transformed into a general store, which was a predominant set used in the film. As the film crews worked, the local reporters expressed fascination with the inner workings of a real Hollywood motion picture:

Camera work drew large crowds of spectators, most of whom were amazed at the hours of tedious work that go into a few feet of film. Rehearsed again and again, with painstaking arrangements of lights and position, a little dab of action might take less than a minute of actual camera work.

The report went on to describe how the street in Mesa took on the look of the fictitious town of White Sage:

The old adobe building, once quite an imposing structure but now pretty well ruined, had its hitching rack and authentic fading old "Billings General Merchandise-Groceries, Supplies" and "Post Office" signs. One or two other "White Sage" city signs were about, and a Sheriff's Office. The store was well-stocked with merchandise and looked particularly authentic when John Miljan was parked in the doorway, a few tough-looking cowhands wearing guns around him, and a couple of Texas rangers. When John Howard, star, rode up, shooting began.

Whether this was the shooting of film or the shooting of blank pistols, the news report did not clarify.

Mesa, with more than 350 days of sunshine a year, was an attractive alternative film site for movie producers, and both movie executives and Mesa business leaders were predicting that Mesa was on the verge of becoming the Hollywood of Arizona. This optimism was reflected in a May 3, 1940, article in the *Tribune:*

New business and new possibilities have been brought to Mesa by Paramount Pictures, which this week completed the filming of the The Texas Rangers Ride Again *here. The picture made in Mesa will be worth more to us, however, as a lever to pry more of the movie industry away from Hollywood to Arizona. Mesa showed Paramount some superb western settings, bright Arizona sunshine even at the time of year when weather conditions are uncertain everywhere, the possibilities of using our nationalities and races as extras at moderate cost, and, not least, real western hospitality.*

Mesa's citizens, like those everywhere else in the 1940s, had been bitten by the movie bug. Many of the younger residents, and more than a few of the older ones, secretly dreamed of becoming stars and working in the movie industry, and sought experience. As a result there was a resurgence of interest in local theater groups and camera clubs. Mesa was a Western town used to creating its own entertainment, and this new motivation brought new levels of professionalism to local theatrical pursuits.

Theater in the pre-TV era was the artistic

Above: The Mesa Camera Club captured a music recital of Mesa residents outside the Lehi school around 1940. There was a resurgence of music, theater, and drama in the Mesa area after Hollywood discovered it as a new and promising setting for motion pictures in the 1940s. Courtesy, Mesa Southwest Museum Collections

heart and soul of many American communities, and Mesa took pride in its productions. Especially popular were crime mysteries like "Among the Stars" by Kathryn Waynes, which played for an extended run at Rendezvous Park in 1940.

Whether it was a local play, a rodeo, or the annual Citrus Fair, Mesans never strayed far from their unique Southwestern roots. The ninth annual Arizona State Citrus Show adopted a Spanish theme, with the local paper anticipating "the bright togs of the gay caballeros and senoritas."

To keep in the civic spirit, the townsfolk were requested to dress in appropriate south-of-the-border garb. The *Tribune* announced, "Saturday is the day for the appearance of everybody in Spanish costume, and nothing less than an appropriate hat, a bright ballero, and a sash will do." The Dress-Up Committee, composed of newspaper publisher Charles Mitten, magistrate Harold Reeb, and Police Chief Joe Maier, was responsible for handing out punishment for those not dressed in costume. Little enforcement was required, though, as most of the enthusiastic citizenry showed up on the specified day in brightly colored regalia.

Such gaiety was curtailed by the no-nonsense era of World War II. Mesa's residents, along with those of the entire nation, were shocked when the battleship USS *Arizona* was sent to the bottom of Pearl Harbor, resulting in a watery grave for nearly 1,200 men. Mesa had already been actively involved in the war effort. Because of its ideal flying weather, the city was selected as the site for two major air force bases.

The July 8, 1941 edition of the *Mesa Tribune* reported:

Within the space of a short two hours Wednesday, the city of Mesa broke ground on two great air bases in the local district. Work started on more than five million dollars worth of defense construction. In a brief, impressive gesture, Mayor George N. Goodman turned over land in which the city invested approximately $50,000 to the agencies which will train war eagles for America and for the United Kingdom.

British Royal Air Force flyers who trained in the area were major contributors to the "Air Battle of Britain," cited by many historians as the turning point in the war. Hundreds of young English pilots were trained at Mesa's Falcon Field, and many fell in love with the Western charm of the area. It was also rumored that the charm of the Britons won the hearts of many of Mesa's eligible young females. After the war many Royal Air Force pilots returned to Mesa and became leading citizens. Mesa's much larger Williams Air Force Base was used to train American forces, who made no less of an impact on the war effort.

Left: Camera clubs had a resurgence of interest after the movie industry started using Mesa as a regular location. Club members would make frequent trips to the desert in attempts to capture unique subject matter such as this large, unusual saguaro. Courtesy, Mesa Southwest Museum Collections

Mayor John Hamblin and the Mesa City Council felt it so important to make both the English and the U.S. "fly boys" feel welcome that they appropriated funding for a special recreation center "to meet the mounting recreation needs of the British airmen . . . and the 2,000 or more men who will soon be training at the Mesa Military Airport Field." A monthly stipend of $125 was approved for maintenance of a drop-in center for the trainees. The council also agreed to furnish power for floodlights at the high school and Rendezvous Park, to be used by the military men.

With the British flyers, U.S. troops from all ethnic backgrounds, and the growing prominence of the Hispanic community, Mesa was fast becoming a miniature melting pot.

The Mesa Citizen of the Year for 1941, Pedro Guerrero, personified the American dream. Born in Solomonville, Arizona, a rough-and-tumble mining town, Guerrero was orphaned at an early age. He battled the still substantial prejudice held by many Arizonans against their Spanish-speaking neighbors and rose to prominence as one of the leading Mesa citizens of the mid-century. The *Tribune* reported:

Primarily because of the intensity of his feeling for what Mesa can do for his fellow Spanish-Americans, Pete Guerrero becomes Mesa's man of the year, chosen by a select committee of Mesa men and women leaders appointed by the Journal-Tribune *to make the selection. He becomes the city's sixth citizen to win this single honor. Harvey L. Taylor was named in 1934; Phil Isley in 1936; L.B. Werner in 1937; John P. Hale in 1939.*

Guerrero went on to achieve great success. He and several partners founded a large Mexican food company that is today one of the Southwest's leading producers in the field. Rosarita Foods, named for Rosaura Guerrero, Pedro Guerrero's wife, was later purchased by Beatrice Foods. The operation expanded and grew to become one of Mesa's larger employers. In addition, he formed, along with Jimmy Lindsey, the Guerrero-Lindsey Sign Company, which celebrated its 50th anniversary in 1985.

The family has continued its prominent role in civic affairs and the advance of the Hispanic culture. Pedro's son Adolfo served as president of the Mesa Little Theater and was a founding board member of the Mesa Southwest Museum. Adolfo's son Zarco has achieved national prominence as an artist who, through his study and lectures in South America and Japan, has become a world ambassador for Mesa and the Hispanic culture.

Another of Pedro Guerrero's sons, Fernando, made equally important contributions to Mesa in the sports realm. Fernando, along with Dwight Patterson and others, was a major force in bringing big-league baseball spring training to the east valley.

The Chicago Cubs came to Mesa in 1948, and continue to sell out every game on the spring schedule today. According to the *Tribune* of the day:

The hotel facilities especially pleased [Clarence Rowland, president of the Los Angeles Angels, a farm club of the Cubs], who said, "50 healthy athletes like plenty of food, a good bed and places to amuse themselves. I'm sure the El Portal can provide all of them. One of the main reasons why the Cubs do not want to train in Los Angeles, now that their Catalina base is being used as a Navy base, is that the city offers too much night life and glamour. He wants the healthful clean fun a smaller city can offer." Rowland gave considerable attention to the Rendezvous park where the players would train, and said that "with a little infield revamping, the field is ideal. The 450 feet from home plate to deep center is just right for young bucks to aim for in early spring." Mesa's spring weather appealed to the coast city baseball magnate because of the warm, sunshiny days and cool, sleep-inviting nights.

An early art exhibit was seen by the Mesa Camera Club in 1935. The exhibit was held at the old Lehi schoolhouse at the corner of Horne and Lehi Road. Courtesy, Mesa Southwest Museum Collections

The Cubs, the movie houses, the local plays, and special events were all distractions that allowed Mesans some respite from the war that raged around the world during the mid-1940s. Every day, more "southsiders," a nickname given to Mesa and Tempe residents, based on their location south of the Salt River, were drafted into the war effort. Almost every issue of the *Journal-Tribune* carried a small article naming the latest draftees, along with the day and time of their induction.

On the home front, civilians joined in the preparation for the very worst that could happen: enemy attack. The *Tribune* outlined the blackout procedure devised by Mesa Civilian Defense Commander Jack Riddle, to be strictly followed by the citizens in the event of an air attack:

1. At 6:30, all members of the council, police, air raid captains, medical and ambulance corps go to their posts.
2. The general air raid alarm will be sounded at 7:55. This consists of intermittent blasts on the air raid siren. This alarm should black out the entire town and the country-side.
3. At the sound of the alarm, all persons are asked to blackout their homes. Get off the streets. All traffic except trains, will come to a halt, and cars should come to a stop at the side of the road and turn off their lights.
4. The alarm will last for ten minutes or until 8:10 when the all-clear sound will be heard for two minutes on the siren.

The war's realities were brought home when a captured Japanese submarine toured the country and Arizona in 1943. Hundreds of Mesans viewed this two-man "suicide sub" during its time on display. The sub, 65 feet long and seven and a half feet wide, was grounded at Pearl Harbor on December 7, 1941. After the war, many former Japanese instruments of war would travel the country on a victory tour, and Mesa was one of the first stops.

A more pleasant diversion continued to be the film industry, which, although disrupted by the war effort, continued to use Mesa as a film locale. The entire front page of the *Journal-Tribune* on May 7, 1943, was filled with a recap of *The House Before the Dawn,* which had finished production just a week before:

All of the outdoor scenes of the movie were filmed here, which included a bombing scene, several domestic farming scenes and a huge haystack fire—part of which make the residents out Lehi way think Orson Welles had brought his men of Mars back for another invasion of our planet. Mesa was chosen for this movie, partly because the terrain north of town supposedly resembles English landscape, but mainly because here, which would hamper filming of the night scenes in the picture. The House Before the Dawn *is the sixth movie to be filmed in this district.* To the Last Man, *a Zane Grey story, started the list. Following that* The Texas Rangers Ride Again, Lady in a Jam, Thunderbird, *and* China *were filmed.*

The story went on to describe how superstar Veronica Lake and the production crew were completing their last day of shooting at the Fitch and Rogers ranches in Mesa. This would prove to be the final film in which Lake's famous long, sexy hair would sweep across her face in her trademark sultry fashion, her tresses having been deemed a safety hazard by Uncle Sam.

War movies and Westerns continued to be the most popular cinematic themes during the 1940s. With Old West landscapes as well as two modern air bases, Mesa could still offer a suitable

Big-name stars of the 1930s and 1940s were popular in such movies as Zane Grey's *Drift Fence,* with Larry "Buster" Crabbe, Katherine DeMille, Tom Keene, Benny Baker, and Glenn Erikson. The Mesa area saw a galaxy of Western stars during this period. Courtesy, Norman Mead Collection

Above: The cast from Zane Grey's *Arizona Mahoney*, including Joe Cook, Robert Cummings, June Marteli, Buster Crabbe, Marjorie Gatson, and John Miljan, among others, are pictured here. This Paramount picture was based on Zane Grey's novel *Stairs of Sand,* and was filmed in the Mesa region. Courtesy, Norman Mead Collection

Right: *To the Last Man,* based on a Zane Grey story, was the first Hollywood motion picture filmed in the Mesa vicinity. However, *The Texas Rangers Ride Again* was the first to be filmed almost exclusively in Mesa. This was the film that launched a decade of movies filmed in the Mesa area. Courtesy, Norman Mead Collection Collection

Above: Western movie star Tom Mix was an associate of Mesa's Mark Barker, also known as "Moxo." Mix frequented the area, often staying at Mesa's Red Mountain Ranch. He was killed in a tragic auto accident on the road between Mesa and Tucson, near Florence, in 1940. Courtesy, Mark Barker Collection

Right: In the movie *Lady in a Jam,* Mesa's Mark Barker was an extra. Starring Ralph Bellamy and Irene Dunne, the movie was filmed in the Mesa area and took advantage of the picturesque scenery including the Superstition Mountains. Onlookers observe Ralph Bellamy autographing Barker's hat the hard way—hat still on. Courtesy, Mesa Southwest Museum

setting for the majority of either of these types of films.

Lady in a Jam, starring Irene Dunne and Ralph Bellamy, was another Mesa favorite. The movie used the El Portal hotel facility, out of business for several years, as a home base. Still making ample use of local extras, *Lady in a Jam* was a true "A" Western, and a step up in quality from Mesa's earlier cinematic works. With a plot centering around a false gold strike that temporarily brought an old ghost town back to life, the film was shot near the base of the Superstition Mountains, utilizing the abandoned Goldfield mining camps as a backdrop.

One of the extras to appear in this picture was local showman Mark Barker. Barker perhaps best personifies what was happening to Mesa from the 1930s through the 1950s. Convinced that Mesa was destined to become more than just another sleepy Arizona desert town, Barker knew that, with its desert surroundings, Mesa's Western mystique could be developed and used to its fullest advantage.

In 1938 Barker was an aspiring young magician with a growing national reputation, and he toured the West frequently, performing regularly at Phoenix's Biltmore and very posh Fox Theater. By happenstance, on one of his tours he spent an overnighter at a small motor lodge just outside of Mesa. When checking out the next morning, he remarked to his wife, "My, what beautiful country. This must be a wonderful place to live. I think I could stay here forever."

The motel keeper's eyebrows raised. "Well, here's your chance," he said. "This place is for sale!" Taken by surprise, Barker and his wife Nena bid a hasty goodbye, and headed for their next performance. But during the next several months of road shows, the innkeeper's words kept echoing in Barker's mind. He finally said to himself, "Why *not* Mesa, Arizona?" picked up the phone, and bought a piece of Mesa's future.

He made a name for himself immediately by tearing down the small motel and converting the

property into Mesa's first trailer park, the first such commercial venture in the state. Called the "Sunset Trailer Ranch," it launched an industry for which Mesa has since become famous. Today there are more than 75 trailer resorts within the Mesa city limits.

Not that Barker knew much about running a trailer resort; his strengths were in promotion and entertainment, and entertain he did. His frequent performances made his trailer park an overnight success. The city hierarchy quickly became aware of Barker's talents for organizing and promotion, and he soon became involved in a host of civic activities.

In 1947 the Mesa Jaycees launched what would prove to become an immensely popular event, their "Rawhide Days" Old West festival. Mark Barker served as event chairman. Helping to make that first event a huge success was an appearance by an old buddy of Barker's, cowboy film star and ventriloquist Max Terhune. For the three-day event, the Jaycees built a complete Old West town, just north of the El Portal on Center Street, using tricks they had learned from visiting Hollywood set builders.

The town was stocked with saloon girls, who were portrayed by local high school girls, and was frequented by outlaw desperadoes like Mesa civic leaders Jim Powers and Dwight Patterson. The

Above: Young Mark Barker, Eastern greenhorn, dreamed of being a cowboy and living the outdoor life in the Southwest. He accomplished his lifelong dream. In the 1930s and 1940s Hollywood filmmakers were predicting that Mesa would become the Hollywood of the Southwest. Courtesy, Mesa Southwest Museum Collections

Right: Yet another side to Mark Barker is the clown. He was an accomplished magician and a ventriloquist as well. Whether playing "Moxo the Magician" or the typical jester, Barker was in much demand as an emcee for many events. Courtesy, Mark Barker Collection

mayor of Rawhide City was Jaycees' President Jimmy Freestone. This event grew annually in prominence and recognition to the point that in 1952 it won the top prize nationally for Outstanding Jaycee Project.

During the five years that "Rawhide Days" rose to prominence, Mesa was seeing a lot of other things happen very quickly. In 1947 the Chamber of Commerce was encouraging the city and the school district to buy a huge gymnasium, built at the now-idle Marana Air Field near Tucson. It had cost the government $250,000 to build, but was available for sale to the city for a mere $56,000. The chamber pushed it as an ideal structure for attracting convention business to Mesa, and the deal was made. The building was purchased, quickly moved to Mesa, and renamed the Mesa Civic Center. It was the largest municipally owned convention center in the state and formalized Mesa's commitment to tourism by regularly attracting a steady stream of major state conventions and meetings.

Another major gathering place, popular for its weekend dances as well as conventions, was the Mezona, earlier known as the Vance Audito-

Right: Mesa's Rawhide Roundup Parade began in 1947 in an exciting "cowboy" era. The Stapley stagecoach was pulled out of mothballs for this special event. The Stapley family later donated the stagecoach to the Mesa Southwest Museum, where it is currently on display. Courtesy, Mesa Southwest Museum Collections

Far right: Mark Barker was instrumental in bringing about Mesa's "Rawhide Roundup." Many storefront sets were built with Mark's know-how, a result of ideas he had learned from show business set builders. Mark is pictured on a trick horse, promoting a Western event. Courtesy, Mark Barker Collection

rium, which was managed for many years by Van Brinton. Its prime selling point was its status as Arizona's first air-conditioned dance hall, using a unique system in which water was pumped over three 100-pound blocks of ice, radiating a cooling effect throughout the building.

In 1948 plans for Mesa's first country club were unveiled by architect William Bell. A membership drive was launched, and construction of the Mesa Country Club and golf course, just north of the prehistoric Mesa Grande Ruins on the edge of the mesa, was completed soon after.

Facilities such as this, coupled with the ever expanding housing developments, used a great deal of water, and once again concerns about the availability of a future water supply began to mount. Many of these fears were quelled with the 1949 signing of the Upper Colorado River Basin Compact. This document guaranteed 50,000 acre-feet of water per year for Arizona use. Despite its signing, however, it took many years and sticky legal battles with the State of California for the terms to be finalized. The U.S. Supreme Court ultimately ruled on the case in Arizona's favor.

That same year Arizona Senator Ernest McFarland tried to get senate approval of his "Central Arizona Bill." A battle ensued that would

Bonanza star Lorne Greene was a special guest on the *Luncheon in Mesa* show in the 1950s. Others pictured are Nena Barker, left, Nona Beaugureau, and Mark Barker, who arranged the event. Courtesy, Mark Barker Collection

be continued by Senator Carl Hayden for many years before he emerged triumphant.

More mundane events were taking place at this time as well, yet they were occurrences that would have significant impact on the community and its growth. Mesa saw the arrival of the first dial telephones in 1949, doing away with the operator-assisted system that had been in place for nearly 50 years. And for those few streets in Mesa that had not been laid out according to the mule-team guidelines, $115,000 in state highway funds were awarded to widen them.

The changes in Mesa's streets continued to be a visible sign of the rapid growth of the city, and a formalized plan was developed by Planning Commission Chairman Bill Passey to replace the previously used "hit-and-miss" method of assigning street names. The new process was explained as follows:

East-west streets north of Main St. would be alternately numbered "streets" and numbered "places," and all existing street names now applied to these streets are to be replaced with numbers. East-west streets south of Main street would be alternately numbered and named "avenues" and the word "avenue" would be reserved to the south half of the city for east-west streets exclusively. All north-south streets would have names followed by the word "street" except in a few cases where "boulevard" or "road" is retained in long-established names.

Mesa's leaders were beginning to plan for the future, as the second half of the twentieth century was fast approaching. Toward this end, the Chamber of Commerce sent a list of civic concerns to its membership for a vote upon the prioritization of these concerns. This list, as published

Top: The Arizona sunset is a gift that never fails to delight Mesa residents and visiting shutterbugs. Photo by Norman Mead

Right: The towering saguaro cacti are familar sights in the desert lands that border Mesa, as are the legendary Superstition Mountains. Photo by Norman Mead

Far right: The mighty Superstition Mountains have been irresistible subjects for a multitude of artists and photographers. Photo by Norman Mead

Opposite top: The desert hillside turns blue with the blossoms of the lupine, and the majestic saguaro cactus in the background. Photo by Norman Mead

Opposite bottom: The fabled Superstition Mountains have lured many a prospector into their depths in search of the Peralta fortune. Photo by Norman Mead

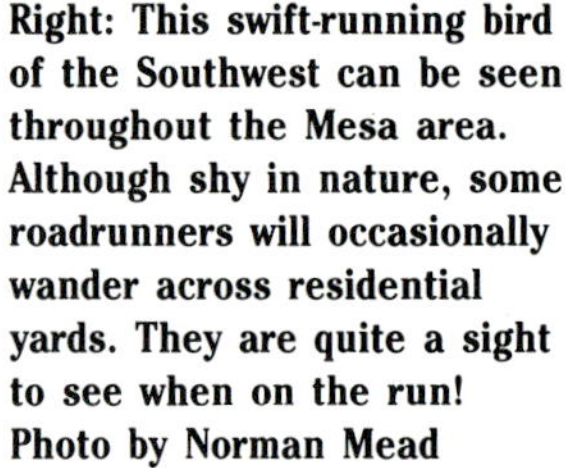

Right: This swift-running bird of the Southwest can be seen throughout the Mesa area. Although shy in nature, some roadrunners will occasionally wander across residential yards. They are quite a sight to see when on the run! Photo by Norman Mead

Above: These Apache Indian women make burden baskets. Photo by Norman Mead

Right: An Apache Indian poses in traditional buckskin along the bank of the Salt River. Most of the Apaches now live on the banks of the Black and White rivers, the two main tributaries of the Salt. Photo by Norman Mead

Right: The Old West spirit still lives within the bounda-ries of Mesa. The annual ro-deo features a special treat— a trick ride in which everyone gets into the act. Photo by Norman Mead

Below: Womens' barrel racing is only one of many popular events at the local rodeo. Photo by Norman Mead

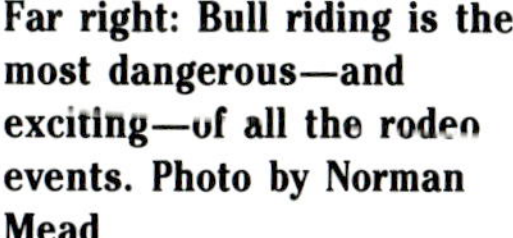

Far right: Bull riding is the most dangerous—and exciting—of all the rodeo events. Photo by Norman Mead

Above: The harsh dry desert turns into a lush oasis when a desert river like the Salt is added. It is little wonder that the early pioneers saw its potential and compared it to the Nile. Photo by Norman Mead

Right: The Mesa Southwest Museum, completed in 1987, doubled its size to 30,000 square feet with this new entrance facade. Photo by Norman Mead

Far right: "Old Dutch," a colorful figure in the Mesa area in the 1940s and 1950s, came to town every two months or so with his mule, cart, and dog. Just one of the many semi-anonymous characters who devoted their lives to searching for the treasures of the Superstition Mountains, "Old Dutch" added to the flavor of those decades. *Courtesy, Mesa Southwest Museum Collections*

Below: This terrain along the Apache Trail outside Mesa resembles mountainous areas in China. Due to the similarity and locale, the movie *Burma Road* was filmed on location here. During the filming the Hollywood set designers transformed this steel-girder bridge into a rickety, bamboo structure that was blown up through special effects in the movie. *Courtesy, Norman Mead Collection*

in the *Tribune,* indicates that while times may change, many of the key issues do not. The list included:

National advertising, home building, new industries, conventions, trade promotion, control of soliciting, promotions of Highways 60-70-80, Christmas decorations, promotion of Mesa on road signs, resurrection of the Little Theater, stopping Southern Pacific trains in Mesa, Pepper Street widening, and Mesa Airport promotion.

One community issue about which there was little concern during the 1950s was the performance of the daily town newspaper. The *Daily Tribune,* having gone to a daily format in 1949, won acclaim from the community and from its peers. Among the stories featured on the front page of a typical issue in 1950 were reports on the second annual County Fair opened by Governor Dan Garvey; a photo of a young Mesa resident named Bobby Gurtler pulling a rabbit out of a hat; and a banner headline reading "Flying

Saucers Are Spaceships From Another Planet."

In the headline story, Navy Commodore Robert McLaughlin, in White Sands, New Mexico, claimed that "space men" would regularly "buzz" the installation, and was quoted as flatly stating that they were indeed "space ships from another planet." Sightings of UFOs soared in Mesa and throughout the Southwest as a result.

Meanwhile the career of young Bobby Gurtler, under the tutelage of Mark Barker, was picking up steam. He ultimately changed his name to Andre Kohl, and by the 1980s this Mesa lad had risen to become one of the most famous magicians in the world.

Similarly, the *Daily Tribune* would continue to rise in the world of modern journalism. Soon after its conversion to daily operation, it was sold by long-time owner-publisher Charles Mitten to a partnership, with seasoned Los Angeles newspaperman David Calvert, and eventually his son Ward Calvert, taking over as publisher.

Movie cameras were becoming commonplace around Mesa, so it wasn't earthshaking news when a cameraman on a high boom spent two days above Main Street, filming the arrival of the Oakland Oaks baseball team into Mesa. Lodging at the old El Portal, which had by this

The Oakland A's and the Chicago Cubs have both made Mesa their winter homes. Winter ball games are played at the Hohokam ball park in central Mesa to sell-out crowds, and are sponsored by the Hohokams, a civic organization. Courtesy, Norman Mead Collection

zona and the Southwest, both from the U.S. and allied nations. Despite the ongoing Korean War, citizens were more interested now in peacetime pursuits, and Mesa's energies were once again focused internally.

Cosmetic changes were in order. By the late 1950s, aware of the city's appeal to Eastern vacationers and "snowbirds," winter visitors who arrive each November and depart in the spring, the town began to spruce things up. The Chamber of Commerce, in conjunction with the Planning Commission, pushed the city to cover all unsightly irrigation ditches in the downtown area, so that visitors would have the proper impression of the fair city of Mesa.

Members of this committee illustrate the still-dominant presence of the original pioneer families in local politics: while it was chaired by Albert Gurtler, it included such familiar names as Virgil Crismon, Paul Pomeroy, and Innes Robson, as well as new community leaders like D.C. Aepli, Evans Blewett, Joe Lindbom, H.D. Miller, Zeb Pearce, J.E. Shelley, Dr. R.F. Anderson, Mary Strauch, Martin Young, and Neil Winterton. They were largely responsible for many beautification efforts that were instigated in Mesa during this period of "spring cleaning."

In 1951 new home construction hit the two-million dollar mark. Major contractors were making their presence known, like Joe Farnsworth, Jr., who built 80 new homes in Mesa that year. Less than a century before, that number would have doubled the number of dwellings in the original town center square mile.

The public schools were also experiencing tremendous growth during this time. Leadership roles were taken by educators Harvey Taylor and Rulon T. Shepherd in combining the Mesa school systems into one unified district. Both these men played significant roles in the cultural arenas of Mesa. Shepherd repeatedly won acclaim for his annual musical variety shows, and was rewarded by having the Westwood High School auditorium named in his honor. Although Taylor was best known for his administrative skills as an educator, his strong support of both local sports and the arts led to the naming of Taylor Field, which served as Mesa's main venue for large outdoor events for more than twenty years.

New shopping areas were on the rise, and Mesa was attracting retail business like never

time reopened as the Maricopa Inn, the team was captured on film by the cameras of TeleNews, with the resulting footage to be distributed to movie theaters and that new-fangled household necessity, television. The townsfolk took it all in stride.

The 1950s were a time of rapid growth and prosperity not just for Mesa, but for most of the nation as well. Williams Air Force Base was one of only a handful of U.S. military air bases not put into mothballs following the war. "Willie," as it was referred to by the townspeople, continued to bring a constant stream of servicemen to Ari-

JACOB WALTZ
The Dutchman's Legacy

▼ ▼ ▼

The tale of Jacob Waltz, the legendary "Lost Dutchman," and his hidden mine just east of Mesa in the Superstition Mountains has been the subject of dozens of books. The stories surrounding this legend comprise the most widely known chapter in Mesa's past. Many purport to have solved the secret location of his fabulous claims; still more present the information as mere fiction, skeptical that the mine will ever be located.

What is known is this: that a German—not Dutch—miner named Jacob Waltz came to America in 1839, at the age of 29, and was soon lured west by tales of vast riches. He pursued a career as a miner and prospector in the central Arizona region from the early 1860s up until his death in 1891.

He didn't set out to be a miner; he originally planned to homestead in the new settlement of Phoenix, and actually made an attempt at farming. This, however, proved not to be where his talents were, and he soon took to the mountains with his pack-laden burro.

He roamed the Superstitions for the better part of two decades, and apparently was not unsuccessful. He was reported to have regularly sold small amounts of his gold in Florence, around the Goldfield area, and in Mesa. In an interview with Superstition mountaineer James Colten, an unidentified Mesa resident recounted her memories of Jacob Waltz visiting her parents' store when she was a little girl:

The skin of his face was parched dry from the desert sun and was as hard as leather. His beard was almost snow-white and somewhat stained by tobacco below his chin. His hands were coarse and calloused revealing many decades of hard work. He no longer stood erect, for his age was now showing. His clothes were dusty and torn but were neatly in place. The only reason I noticed him was he looked like my aging father. No one at first paid him any attention until he went to pay for his supplies. In his wrinkled hand was a small cowhide poke. He loosened the strings and poured onto the counter yellow gold in a matrix of white quartz.

The legend of the Lost Dutchman's mine has brought thousands in search of the fabled treasure. These unidentified prospectors were captured by the camera of Walter J. Lubken, in about 1910. Courtesy, Norman Mead Collection

After gathering his supplies, he left as quietly as he came.

It was not the variety of gold that Waltz possessed, nor the sheer quantity of it, that was worthy of legend. It was the fact that the source of his riches remained a complete mystery for the remainder of his life, and has still not been explained. Try as he might, no man was ever successful in trailing Waltz to his mine. Waltz would always elude his followers. Although Waltz liked to give cryptic clues regarding the mine's location, especially in his dying years, he carried the secret to his grave.

In their book *Superstition Mountain: A Ride Through Time,* authors James Swanson and Tom Kollenborn proposed four possible solutions to the mystery of Waltz' gold supply:

Jacob Waltz was working the Peralta family mines. The Peraltas were a family of rich Mexican miners whose holdings in the Superstition Mountains were incredibly vast during the eighteenth century. This theory purports that Waltz and a cohort murdered two ancestors of the Peraltas and took over their mine. A series of stone maps, allegedly revealing the location of these Peralta family mines, were discovered in 1949 and are on permanent display in the Mesa Southwest Museum.

Jacob Waltz "high-graded" ore from another mine. It has been suspected that Waltz may have visited or worked for another mine, such as the Vulture Mine in Wickenberg, and made off with high-grade ore which he then processed at his camp in the Superstitions. This hypothesis has little documentation to support it.

Jacob Waltz found remnants of gold that had already been mined. It is possible that Waltz found remnants of some old Mexican *arrastras,* or grinding stones used to crush ore, and began an intense search of the area immediately around the stones for gold. Through a methodical search Waltz could have obtained a significant amount of gold had he been lucky enough to stumble on to such a set-up.

Jacob Waltz discovered the hidden treasure of the Jesuits. It was commonly believed that Jesuit priests, when fleeing the Spanish Inquisition in the sixteenth century, took shelter in the Superstitions with the vast treasures they had amassed. This was perhaps the most romantic of the Waltz theories, and tales of the Jesuits' riches have been magnified greatly throughout time.

Many have gone in search of Waltz' mysterious mine, and all have returned unsuccessful. Some have not returned at all, adding to the legend. Waltz, who died after contracting pneumonia during the great flood of 1891, was the only one with the answers, and chances are good that wherever he is, he is having a good laugh at our expense.

The cowboy with the quickest time wins in calf-roping. However, it's not that simple; he has to rope the calf, jump off while the horse keeps the rope tension tight, flip the calf over on its back, grip the tie in his mouth, and tie the calf's legs. Courtesy, Norman Mead Collection

before, as the J.C. Penney and Safeway chains each opened stores. Mesa stores were finally allowed to remain open on Sundays when the state Superior Court ruled Mesa's Sunday closure ordinance unconstitutional. Most establishments took advantage of this decision to add an extra day to their schedule, although most downtown establishments still remain closed Sundays to this day.

As retail stores moved into Mesa, sheepherding faded out of the city's economy. Mesa had been a popular wintertime grazing area for many flocks of Arizona sheep for more than 50 years, and Mesa's successful sheep ranchers included Larkin Fitch, Dwight Patterson, and Clifford Dobson. But with continued development of what was previously grazing land, there were fewer and fewer places for the sheep to feed. Basque sheepherders could still occasionally be seen leading their flocks across Mesa's narrow suspension bridge over the Salt toward summer pasture in the White Mountains of northern Arizona each springtime. Sheepherder's Park in north Mesa was dedicated in 1984 in recognition of this unique chapter in Mesa history.

It was the pigskin, and not the sheepskin, that was attracting attention to Mesa's high schools during the 1950s. One local high school football phenomenon was Mesa High School's "Whizzer" White, who, according to spectators, would frequently run the ball 50 yards the wrong way to avoid a tackle before changing direction and charging downfield for a touchdown. His agility and lightning speed attracted scouts from major colleges nationwide, but he elected to stay at home and go to Arizona State University. The ASU Bulldogs, as they were then called, rose to national recognition during White's collegiate career, and he is generally acknowledged as the school's first bona fide football star.

History often has a way of repeating itself. Westwood High School opened in 1962 as Mesa's second public high school. In the fall of 1968 a controversy arose over the coach's choice for a starting quarterback. The team favored a senior player, Steve Huish, while the coach went with a relatively untested junior. Huish was bigger and stronger, and although the junior had a better arm, he tended to be a little tackle-shy, and threw the ball away more often. The question arose: did he play because he was the better player, or because his father had been a famous football star?

The answer turned out to be the former. That junior quarterback, Danny White, son of

"Whizzer" White, set a slew of records at Westwood High before continuing on through a brilliant career that culminated in his becoming the starting quarterback for the NFL Dallas Cowboys.

Mesa's other colorful athletes included the Mesa High School all-girl Rabbettes. An unusual drill team, the Rabbettes performed on horseback with trick riding and roping maneuvers. This group of Wild West cheerleaders was featured on national television, and was a mainstay of the county fair.

Mesa's athletic glories during the 1950s were sometimes dimmed by an occasional scandal that would garner national attention. One 1952 headline screamed, "BOND SET FOR SIX WIVES OF MESA MAN," raising once again the controversial

Right: This children's version of bull riding is just one of the events held annually in Mesa at the Arizona Junior Rodeo. Courtesy, Norman Mead Collection

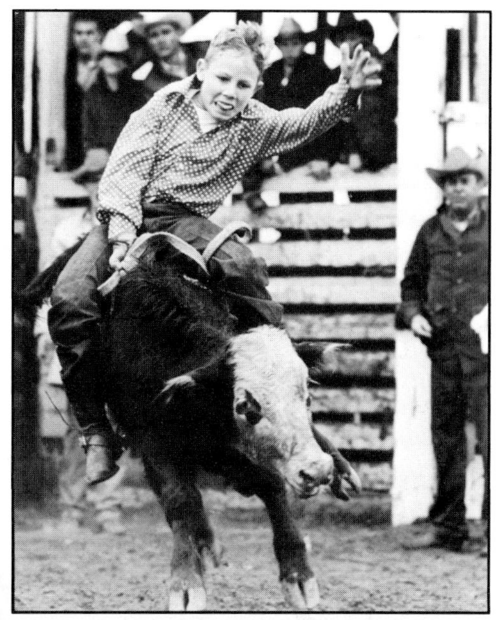

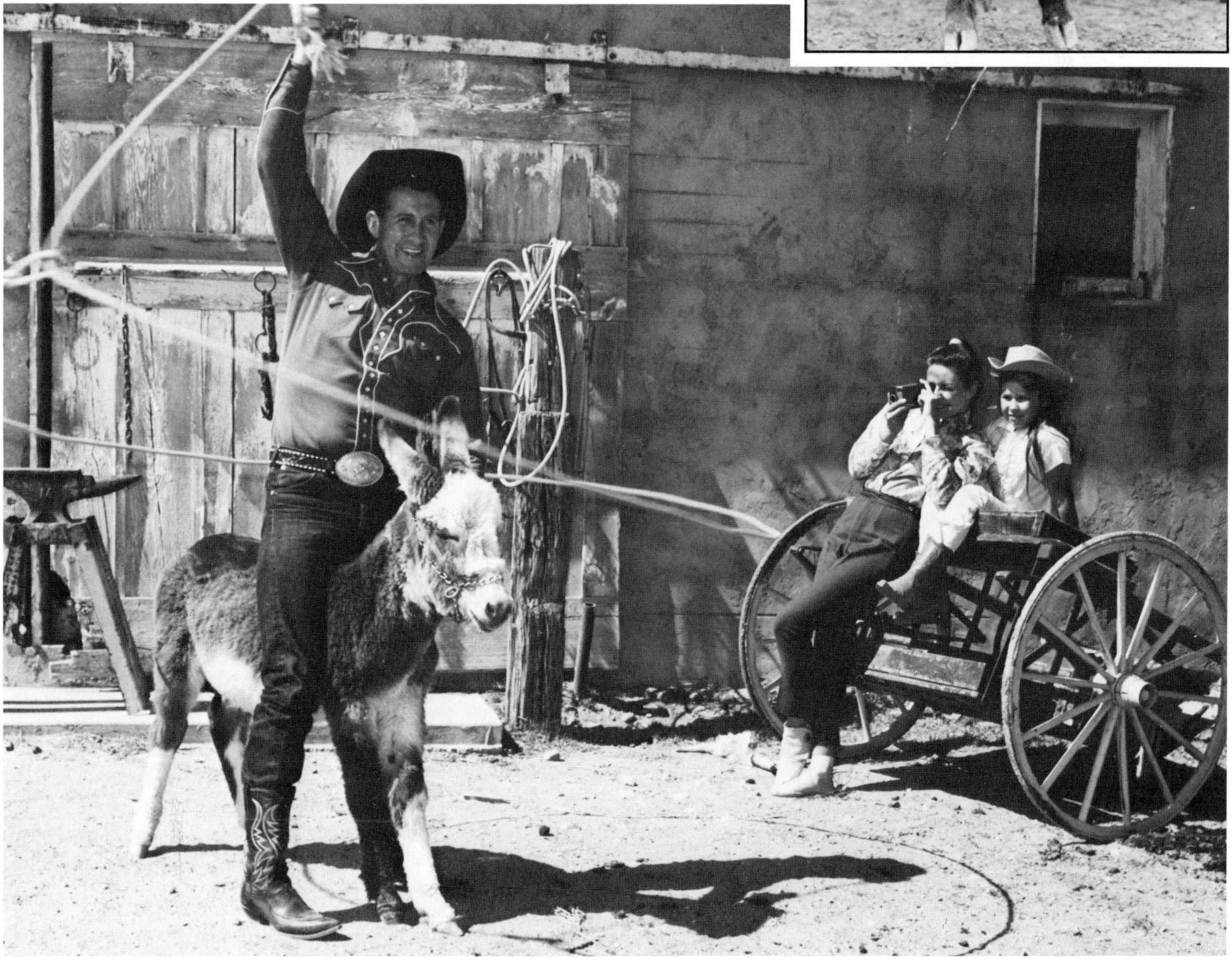

Below: Trick roping was a favorite at Mesa's nearby dude ranches of the 1930s, 1940s, and 1950s. King's Ranch and Red Mountain Ranch were two of the better-known guest ranches. Even today there are resorts in the greater Mesa area that are carrying on part of the old tradition—resorts such as Gold Canyon Ranch. Courtesy, Norman Mead Collection

Amphibious cars hit the beaches at Mesa's nearby Saguaro Lake. The boats, reminiscent of the 1957 Chevy, and the boys in their flat top and duck tail haircuts, vividly evoke the era of the 1950s. Courtesy, Norman Mead Collection

the event attracted riders from throughout the West. A prime tourist attraction for Mesa, the rodeo was sponsored by Mesa's 20-30 service club, with proceeds going to benefit the Arizona Boys Ranch..

A more outrageous event brought a return to the days of the ostrich, when Mesa presented, as part of the county fair, a series of ostrich races. The return of these huge birds to the region spurred great interest. Even Mesa's Chief of Police Marion Trowbridge got into the act, posing next to an ostrich with his ticket book, "sure there is something on the books ag'in it."

In 1958 the fair scored a major coup and received national recognition when it lassoed one of the top teen idols of the day, Ricky Nelson, to perform. The committees behind this annual event were constantly planning new means of making each year's fair bigger and better than the one before, and the signing of Nelson brought hordes of bobby-soxers to an event that was normally reserved for the 4-H crowd.

While Mesa was becoming acknowledged as one of the premier festival sites in all of Arizona, historic preservation efforts in the city were also picking up steam. Frank Midvale, owner of the property containing the Mesa Grande Ruins, tried to interest the city in the ruins as a tourist attraction. The Mesa Historical and Archaeological Society was formed for the purpose of getting a city museum built on that site. With the snowballing success of the tourism industry, the county fairs, "Rawhide Days," and assorted rodeos, Mesa still had its biggest days ahead.

But in 1959 a catastrophe struck: the Mesa Civic Center burned to the ground.

"SOARING FLAMES DESTROY MESA CIVIC CENTER BUILDING," read the headlines. In the newspaper photographs, a forlorn and stoic Mayor J.E. "Bert" Brown and Parks Director Maurice Bateman, who had overseen the management of the facility, seemed to reflect the loss that Mesa had suffered. It was a major blow to the town that had finally begun to see the tangible rewards of tourism and promotion, bringing a new economic era for the east valley. There was talk of replacing the structure, but the money was not there. A new community center was finally constructed in the late 1970s.

The 1960s, 1970s, and 1980s are too recent to accommodate critical historical reflection, and

issue of polygamy. Police were once again on the hunt for an accused polygamist, George Merrill Dutson, some 60 years after the practice had been removed from Mormon church doctrine. The incident outraged the American public, and triggered some anti-Mormon sentiments across the country.

However, it outraged the local members of the Church of Jesus Christ of Latter-day Saints even more, and the members of this multiple marriage were quickly excommunicated from the church. The six pleaded innocent to charges of "open and notorious cohabitation and adultery," but were eventually convicted.

The *Tribune*'s straightforward coverage of that story and others resulted in an award from the Arizona Press Association for Best Daily Newspaper of 1952. The *Tribune* deftly balanced reporting of sensitive stories such as this with finely crafted feature writing, including coverage of recreational activities such as the World Championship Junior Rodeo, held each year in Mesa.

While the award for that year's best All-Around Cowboy went to Bobby Hall of Phoenix,

are better left to the next generation of historians to evaluate. Mesa's recent history, which could fill a volume in its own right, has been capsulized very briefly in the conclusion of this chapter. Mesa during the 1960s and 1970s was generally thought of as a nice bedroom community with good schools and wide streets. It was Phoenix that picked up the ball during this time and expanded its economic base, while Mesa pursued a somewhat lower profile. It was acknowledged by all as "a great place to live," but not heavily advertised as such. Scottsdale, which had played a secondary role for so many years, picked up the gauntlet and ran with it. They developed a wide variety of tourist attractions and cultural opportunities, including the "Parada Del Sol" rodeo and parade, and their claim of being "the west's most western town" was now not disputed even by Mesa's old-timers.

The "Rawhide Roundup" disappeared, the Rabbettes hung up their lassoes, the rodeos were discontinued, and other such "Old West" events were relegated to the rear sections of the daily paper. For two decades, Mesa's long-cultivated image as a fun-filled Old West town was sublimated in favor of creating a business environment conducive to growth and development.

This was a resounding economic success for the city. John Naisbitt, in his book *The Year Ahead: 1986,* listed Mesa among "The Ten Best Places to Start a Business," and stated, "If one word were used to describe Mesa's business climate, that word would be 'dynamic.' The population is well-educated and the labor force highly skilled. Industry has been moving to Mesa, attracted by its excellent climate and well-managed growth." More than 6,000 new businesses started up in Mesa during a 10-year period. Naisbitt cited Mesa's strongest selling points as friendly and cooperative local officials, man-power, training, and nearby educational facilities—Arizona State University and Mesa Community College, among others.

But in recent years, Mesa has strived to remember its roots. The catalyst was the city's widespread centennial celebration in 1977, resulting in several new developments linking Mesa to its past. The Mesa Southwest Museum was opened in the fall of that year, and within a 10-year period grew to become the second-ranked museum in the state.

The construction and unveiling of Mesa's Centennial Hall and community amphitheater in 1978 once again provided a first-rate meeting and concert facility, and further stimulated a revival of the town center area. It was expanded in 1987. The formation of the Mesa Convention & Visitors Bureau in 1984 provided an entity devoted solely to bringing major conventions and events to Mesa. An annual fall Pow Wow, cosponsored by the museum and the Convention & Visitors Bureau, draws Indian participants from throughout the Western United States. This has given Mesa a new annual tourist event, drawing more than 30,000 spectators during its first four years.

Expansion is still constant, showing no signs of slowing down. The town's geographic size increased from 24 square miles in 1970 to more than 100 square miles by the mid-1980s. Meanwhile the city government is currently funding a rejuvenation of the *original* town center square mile, the square mile that *was* Mesa for so many years. This plan includes preservation of the 1895 Joel Sirrine House, development of a historic walking tour, and the stimulation of new business and retail development in the area. Mesa still has its cowboys, and the Cadillacs that were commonplace on Mesa streets during the "go-go" years of the 1950s have been replaced today by Mercedes, Corvettes, and BMWs.

Is Mesa ready for another new era of growth and achievement in the 1990s? Only time will tell.

Trying to relive the facts and fantasies of the lost Dutchman, many miners have searched for his famous mine. Even today, between Mesa and the Superstitions, one can still see some of these "characters" at different commercial establishments. Courtesy, Norman Mead Collection

CHAPTER 7

PARTNERS IN PROGRESS

For eons the fertile Valley of the Sun had lain ripe for the husbandman. All the ingredients were there: kindly climate, fruitful soil, untamed water. The only thing absent was the catalytic intellect and brawn of man.

Mesa's first farmers, the Hohokam, saw the promise and, limited only by their primitive technology, tapped the moody Salt River with an incomparable system of canals. Mother Valley rewarded them for about two millennia before their civilization mysteriously vanished about the time of Columbus.

The industrious Mormon pioneers of the late 1870s broadened and extended the parched Hohokam canal beds in order to feed the patchwork quilt of farms and pastures that began to characterize Mesa and its environs. Growth was slow in this little farming and cattle-raising community during its first 33 years, due in part to an unruly Salt, which was soon to be bridled.

In 1911 the population surged for the first time from the original 79 settlers to 1,700 in the aftermath of the newly completed Roosevelt Dam—by far, Mesa's greatest milestone. The dam was a monument to the resolve of the local landowners who put up their precious lots as collateral on the federal construction loan. Their reward was a tamed river and a reliable water supply, the source of riotous agricultural development during the next 40 years.

The succinct four "Cs"—cotton, citrus, cattle, and climate—soon became Mesa's hallmark. To this list you may add a fifth "C," Canadians, an alliterative construct for tourism, or "Snow Birds," who seasonally migrated southward to bask in the valley's benign winter sunshine.

World War II brought a large influx of temporary residents into the East Valley, clustering at Williams Air Force Base and Falcon Field. Many of these ex-military either heralded Mesa's charms abroad or returned after the war.

By 1950 the population had swelled to about 17,000. Concurrently, the town reached its second and third milestones—the development of refrigerated air conditioning and the passage of Arizona's new right-to-work law. While the cooler summers attracted more residents, the new "enabling" legislation began to attract industry.

The next 30 years saw Mesa's population double each decade, with the largest 10-year jump occurring in 1980, spurred on by the energy crisis of the mid-1970s. And with the construction of the fourth milestone, Superstition Freeway, Mesa became a large bedroom community as well as a commercial and industrial hub.

By 1980 Mesa's population had reached 162,000; as of 1987 more than 280,000 people had been calling it home, making it the third-largest city in Arizona and the second-fastest growth city in the nation.

Once solely agrarian, it now supports a growing and diverse industrial base and counts tourism as its third major industry, with 600,000 winter visitors in the East Valley annually, spending more than $200 million in Mesa alone.

However, the real story of Mesa lies in the craft, industry, and courage of its citizens, past and present. The histories of some of these citizens, chronicled on the following pages, have helped make this book possible

Mule-team freighters at Government Wells, the first stage stop outside Mesa en route to Roosevelt Dam (the only place where water and a change of horses were available). Freighters usually made the trip in three to five days: the stage could make it in two. Courtesy, Norman Mead

Mesa Southwest Museum and Guild

Within a thick-walled adobe building in historic downtown Mesa resides a treasure trove—a time warp into the enigma of prehistory and the romance of early exploration, settlement, and growth.

While the Mesa Southwest Museum chronicles the past, its building is a cameo of Mesa's own evolution and of the individuals who propelled it.

Originally the building was constructed by the WPA in 1937 to house City Hall. As government grew, it also berthed the firehouse, police station, courthouse, library, and East County offices.

During this civic expansion phase a community-wide movement took shape to start a Mesa museum, spearheaded by a few determined members of the community. One, the late Mitzi Zipf, reporter and columnist for the *Mesa Tribune,* popularized the museum's cause in print and regularly attended city council meetings to champion it.

Another, the late Harriet McCarter, was the daughter of Mesa pioneer physician Ralph Palmer, better known as the "doctor on horseback" and a former mayor of Mesa. Harriet was for many years the secretary and behind-the-scenes "mover" of the Mesa Historical and Archaeological Society.

After a long gestation period, the Mesa Museum (its original name) was born in May 1977. An integral part of the city from the outset, it occupied 3,000 square feet of space on the south end of Old City Hall.

Three months earlier the city had hired its first museum director, Mesa-born Tray C. Mead, an Arizona State University graduate and avocational archaeologist. With a strong scholastic background in southwestern history and archaeology, Mead worked with local civic organizations and area influentials

The Mesa Southwest Museum as it looks today. More than 200,000 visitors tour this municipally operated facility each year, ranking it among the most attended museums in the state.

to create a program to build a regionally recognized institution.

Once he installed the first exhibit, Mead took steps with the aid of McCarter and Zipf to form the Mesa Southwest Museum Guild. In recognition of their unique contributions the guild later named its acquisition fund after these two extraordinary women.

The first president of the Mesa Southwest Museum Guild was Sally Orrantia, a descendant of the Ramon Mendoza family, prominent Mexican-American pioneers who settled in the area in 1893. Orrantia's appointment helped establish the museum's tradition of incorporating important contributions of diverse southwestern cultures into its programs. An example of this special focus was the exhibit on the work of Pima Indian author and poetess Anna Moore Shaw. Born in territorial Arizona in 1898, Shaw made special contributions that helped form a bond between the Pima Indian community and the museum.

If there is one word that characterizes the museum in its first decade, it is "growth." From its original 3,000 square feet of space as a cohabitant of the Old City Hall building, it now solely occupies the entire 30,000-square-foot building, enhanced by two new additions, and covers an entire city block. The museum guild's growth and special contributions have been equally dramatic during this period.

In its first year about 12,000 people viewed its exhibits; 10 years later more than one million had passed through its portals—a current average attendance of 200,000-plus per year. It is second only to the Heard Museum of Phoenix as the most visited in Arizona.

The nation's bicentennial celebration provided the spark for further growth. As a special bicentennial project, the Mesa school system built a little adobe schoolhouse, a replica of Mesa's first permanent school. Located beside the museum building and on its property, it was dedicated to the city in a ceremony presided over by then-First Lady Betty Ford.

Mead started with only one professional staff assistant. Today he lists more than a dozen full-time staffers.

Members of the first Mesa Museum Guild board of officers pose in front of the newly opened Mesa Museum of History and Archaeology in 1978. The facility changed its name to the Mesa Southwest Museum in 1985.

During these first 10 years the museum's collection has grown from a few items to more than 30,000, stored in a special humidity- and temperature-controlled vault eight feet by two stories high. The cache includes an estimated $5 million in rare artifacts ranging from prehistoric stone statues to fine oil paintings by contemporary artists. These are continually rotated into the museum's changing exhibitions.

From the outset Mead implemented a rotating exhibition program with special receptions hosted by the guild—a primary reason for the museum's uncanny popularity. It was the first museum west of the Mississippi to feature Jupiter and its Moons, a major Smithsonian scientific exhibit chronicling NASA's *Voyager I* mission. The museum also regularly curates its own major shows, ranging from displays of prehistoric and historic native cultures to contemporary national and international art exhibitions.

The museum is equally well known for its permanent, hands-on exhibitions. A visitor can pan for gold in a stream in the courtyard, lock himself into an authentic 1880s territorial jail, or tickle the ivories on a nineteenth-century parlor organ.

The guild and museum are not only chroniclers of the region's rich, romantic past, they also have perked popular pride and interest in the traditional arts, crafts, and cultures of the area, such as tatting, quilting, and blacksmithing. To sustain this thrust, the museum has maintained a close affiliation with the artists and craftspersons in the area. It also sponsors archaeological explorations in the region and has recently acquired the spectacular 5.6-acre Mesa Grande Ruins—the most important Hohokam Indian archaeological site in Arizona.

Sired by the community, and keeper of its cultural heritage, the Mesa Southwest Museum and Guild are prominent exemplars of the city's vision, vitality, and growth.

STAPLEY WHOLESALE, INC.

Three generations of Stapleys — Thyrle H Stapley (seated), A.T. "Fred" Stapley (right), and John G. "Jack" Stapley.

"The fruit doesn't fall far from the tree," especially in the case of A.T. "Fred" Stapley, chairman of the board of one of the biggest plumbing wholesale companies in Arizona and the nation.

Fred's grandfather, O.S. Stapley, arrived in Mesa with the first wave of Mormon pioneers in 1878, and soon saw the need for a farm products and hardware supply company in the valley. So, 17 years before Arizona gained statehood, he began the O.S. Stapley Company, one of Arizona's great pioneer businesses, with $250.

In 1925 T.H Stapley, Fred's father, founded Arizona Hardware, a division of the O.S. Stapley Company and wholesaler to the Stapley retail outlets, valley subcontractors, and other retail stores.

Fred spent the majority of his business career at the Arizona Hardware Company. Like his grandfather, he began at the bottom, unloading boxcars. He then moved up to outside sales, then credit manager, and general manager. During his career ascendance, Fred had a temporary reversal—descending into the briny deep during a hitch as a submariner with the U.S. Navy after the end of World War II.

At the age of 51 he decided to go out on his own as his grandfather O.S. had done 84 years before. In 1979 he founded Stapley Wholesale, Inc., in a rented, 6,800-square-foot building with no merchandise, no customers, and three employees. Fred's wife, Doris, answered the phones; his brother, Don, handled sales; and he made the deliveries.

The business was started at the right place but not at the right time—while Arizona was one of the nation's fastest-growing areas, the valley was beginning a four-year business recession.

The year after its inaugural, a fourth-generation Stapley joined the business. John G. "Jack" Stapley, Fred's son, signed on after six years of marketing experience with IBM. Now president of the company, Jack was instrumental in developing its aggressive marketing program that finally overcame the area's recessional vapor lock and propelled the firm to local and national notoriety.

In 1984 the trade magazine *Supply House Times* featured Stapley Wholesale for its record growth from zero to $11 million in five years. In 1986 *The Wholesaler* named the company to its Top 100 list of national wholesalers doing more than $10 million in annual sales.

In fewer than eight years Fred and his son have built an organization that is a major force in Arizona's plumbing industry. Today Stapley Wholesale, Inc., employs 42 people in its own $2.4-million, 75,000-square-foot facility on South Pasadena Street in Mesa. The Stapley penchant for success is still as evident as it was at the turn of the century when patriarch O.S. established the business ground rules—"stock tight, sell low, and turn like crazy."

Jack and Fred Stapley at the firm's 75,000-square-foot warehouse, located on South Pasadena Street.

SEMFLEX, INC.

Robert and Christine Thiele, owners of Semflex, a multimillion-dollar microwave-component manufacturer.

Robert and Christine Thiele first "incorporated" at the altar in Orange County, California, in 1972. Eight years later the handsome young couple extended the contract to the "executive suite."

Unlike most, the Thieles' personal relationship doesn't end after morning coffee and begin anew after the 5 p.m. whistle. Theirs is a full-time union that has produced a son and daughter and a thriving multimillion-dollar microwave-component manufacturing business.

Both partners own and operate their eight-year-old high-tech company, with Bob as president/treasurer, and Chris as vice-president/secretary.

Their sleek, 23,000-square-foot, state-of-the-art building is situated on only 1.5 acres of their 4.2-acre parcel. The remaining land is slated for an additional, 65,000-square-foot, tight-security facility a few years down the road. Inside the facility is an array of more than $2 million worth of custom-crafted electronic test stations, computer-driven lathes that cut to within .0001 of an inch, and busy, white-smocked engineers, draftsmen, and technicians in an immaculate, hospital-like milieu. From all this comes products that are no thicker than knitter's yarn—but worth their weight in gold.

The firm employs 63 personnel, 45 of whom are professionals, and a sales force that covers the United States, Europe, Asia, and the Middle East.

All this didn't happen by fiat; it evolved from the couple's toil and dreams. The view from their first "executive suite" didn't command the grand sweep of the East Valley and Red Mountain a league away. Instead it overlooked the cluttered kitchen table and garage floor.

Bob began his career during a four-year hitch in the U.S. Air Force as a jet engine mechanic. After his discharge in 1971 he returned to his native Orange County, where he met and married Chris. He was majoring

Semflex, Inc.'s 23,000-square-foot corporate headquarters in Mesa is situated on only 1.5 acres of the firm's 4.2-acre parcel. Another facility is currently being planned for construction on the site.

in business at Cal-Fullerton before they wed, but because of his strong scientific bent, Bob left academia and was promptly employed by the Aeronics Corporation of America as a junior-grade electromechanical engineer. It was there that he became involved with the microwave-component business.

When Americon purchased Aeronics Bob went with the firm to Santa Clara, where he worked with sophisticated electronic cabling as operations manager for a 30-person electronics service department. When Omni-Spectra bought out Americon, Bob was put in charge of one of its divisions and moved to Tempe in the latter part of 1978.

An impending division move to chilly New Hampshire was too much for the warm-blooded Southern California couple. So Bob and Chris chose to change their careers and enjoy the dependable sunshine of the East Valley.

They decided to go into business for themselves, Bob having seen a void in the quick-reaction, customized, microwave-component market. They borrowed a how-to book from the library on starting a small business and took their 72-page proposal to 12 area banks. Only one approved their loan application—but for one-third of what they requested. The couple had asked for $50,000, but got only $17,000. Supplemented by $10,000 of their personal savings, they started design, production, and mechanical work in their kitchen and garage. That was the start of their "survival phase," according to Bob.

In November 1980 they incorporated as Semflex, Inc., an acronym for semi-rigid and flexible (cable). They leased a 1,900-square-foot office in Tempe and began design and production in mid-1981 with four of Bob's associates from Omni-Spectra. Sales topped $192,000 that first half-year. Chris was inventory controller, financial manager, and receptionist, while Bob handled purchasing, engineering, sales, and "janitorial services." The couple remembers how they'd drop off the kids at the nursery in the morning, pick them up at night, and return with them to the shop, where they would work until midnight. Bob recalls "working seven days a week during our critical survival period in the early 1980s. We were fast-food junkies in those days." On an average, they doubled sales each year from 1981 to 1985.

With the aid of the Mesa Industrial Development Authority and a local bank they financed construction of their new corporate headquarters on McDowell Road, just east of Falcon Field. The building was started in

A Semflex employee operates a fluorescent X-ray coating thickness gauge for nondestructive, noncontracting measurements of coatings, which include gold, nickel, and silver.

The Thieles took care to set up a capable facility that includes more than $2 million worth of high-tech test stations and equipment, as well as engineers, craftsmen, and technicians.

November 1984, and in April of the following year they moved in and expanded their select work force to its current level.

The rest is a story of customized engineering, rigid controls, tick-tight production schedules, reputation marketing, and prudent management. The firm's ability to meet a special part problem of any of its 70-odd corporate clients in the military and space industries with on-schedule, quick-response, quality-engineered microwave products has helped position Semflex as a leading supplier of high-performance microwave cable assemblies and components. "They look to us to design a specialized cable or component to fit a particular need or system," Bob explains.

So much for the esoteric side of the aisle. Until recently it was exclusively Chris' management skills that ran Semflex. "She is the realist, the overseer, and our long- and short-range planner," Bob lovingly admits. Their computer-based Material Requirement Planning System tracks costs and time for each minute stage of a component's production. This has been a boon for bid and delivery estimates. As an added safeguard, the couple does not permit any one customer to control more than 25 percent of their backlog orders. This spares Semflex the vulnerability of big-client dependency.

What does the future hold for Semflex, Inc.? Sales should hit $4.7 million in 1988 and are expected to reach $6.5 million in the next two years. Says Bob, "We're going to continue to grow and build our reputation for quality, service, and problem solving." What else would one expect from the dynamic duo?

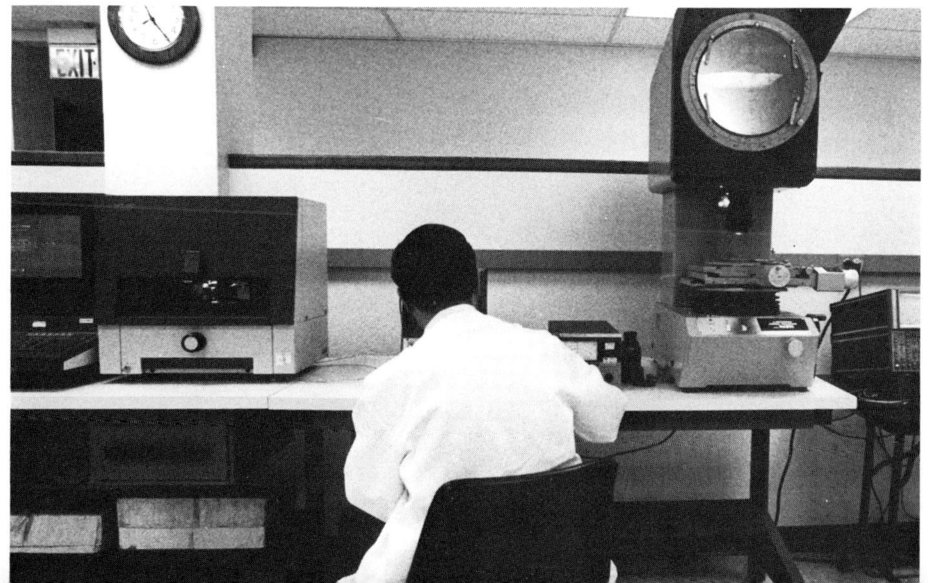

McConaghie/Batt & Associates

Like his Mormon brethren a century before him, Darryl McConaghie left Utah for the Valley of the Sun with his family, a dream, a willingness to risk, and little else.

McConaghie earned his baccalaureate degree in landscape architecture from Utah State University in 1975 after serving four years in the United States Air Force. Following graduation he and his family headed south to Mesa to start a new life. There, after a four-year stint with a prominent Mesa landscape and architectural planning firm, he struck out on his own.

McConaghie began his new firm in 1979 on a virtual shoestring budget in a 64-square-foot room in the basement of the La Officina building with $7.50 in his jeans' pocket and paid the rent by bartering landscape maintenance services with the landlord.

Cordell Batt, a fellow alumnus of McConaghie's, earned his degree in landscape architecture in 1977 and joined McConaghie as a full partner in 1981. To round out the team and service their burgeoning business, the partners brought Wendy Scofield on board as an associate in 1984. Scofield broadened the organization's expertise with her newly acquired degree in ornamental horticulture from Arizona State University.

The firm's eight-year existence is a microcosmic mirror image of Mesa's growth. By 1987 a total of 374 projects had been completed, with more in the hopper. Many of these have had a noticeable effect on Mesa's development and beautification throughout its dynamic renaissance.

Some examples of this phase are the Sirrine Street/Centennial Way conversion, along with the Ramada Renaissance Hotel, the Centennial Retail Center, and the Centennial Hall expansion. Other representative projects include landscape design for a five-mile stretch of the Outer Loop Highway and Red Mountain Expressway, and a large number of public schools, churches, and branch buildings of four major Arizona-based banks.

McConaghie's skill and professionalism are best exemplified by his appointments as trustee for the Desert Botanical Garden of Phoenix, as landscape consultant for the City of Mesa, and as a member of the Mesa Design Review Advisory Board.

In 1987 the City of Mesa bestowed four Superior Design awards on the firm for its work on the United Bank Plaza, The Arizona Bank Building, the Centennial Retail Center, and the Dobson Medical Office Building.

McConaghie and Batt are registered landscape architects in the State of Arizona, and all three principals of the firm are members of the Arizona Society of Landscape Architects.

The firm's professional reputation was duly recognized by the Mormon Church, which designated it as the landscape design review consultant for the five-state southwest area.

Like the City of Mesa, McConaghie/Batt & Associates has come a long way since its humble beginnings.

The principals of McConaghie/Batt & Associates: Cordell Batt (left), Darryl McConaghie (seated), and Wendy Scofield. The firm's eight-year growth has paralleled that of Mesa.

CRISMON'S FLOWERS

To Charles Crismon, his store at 25 East Main is more than a flower shop; it is part of Mesa's history and an indirect link with some of its original settlers.

A florist and historian, Crismon is enamored of his city's past. A devout Mormon for whom family ties and lineage are of a theological as well as secular nature, he devotes much of his spare time to chronicling the city's first families. Therefore, it is doubly understandable that he proudly stresses his descendance from Charles Crismon, Sr., and Francis Pomeroy, patriarchs of two of Mesa's four founding families back in 1878.

His father, Virgil, was born in 1909 in Lehi, five miles north of old Mesa. The elder Crismon grew up on his father's farm and in 1930 graduated from Mesa High. Virgil's schooling at Brigham Young University was abruptly terminated when he lost his hard-earned savings in a string of banks that had been toppled by the Great Depression.

A year after his marriage to Helen Hathcock in 1936, the young couple moved to Salt Lake City, where Virgil learned the florist business. In the autumn of 1938 he returned to Mesa and opened the city's first local flower shop at 10 North Macdonald.

Nine years later the Crismons built a larger shop at 25 East Main Street. Charles, the youngest of Virgil's five children, was born in a house that once stood just behind this shop. He recalls nostalgically, "Just think, in the early 1900s our store would have stood on pastureland owned by my great-grandfather Pomeroy, and only one block from the center of town."

Before he passed away in 1985, Virgil left his mark on Mesa in many ways. He was elected to the Mesa City Council in 1948 and became mayor two years later. Following his tenure as mayor he was named Mesa Man of the Year, and appointed to a 22-year post on the Maricopa County Planning and Zoning Commission. While serving as a commissioner, he was also a member of the Arizona Development Board from 1964 to 1969, and president and co-founder of the East Mesa Area Development Association.

Virgil's nonpolitical activities were likewise legion. A leader in his church for decades, he was appointed Bishop of the Latter-day Saints 10th Ward in Mesa from 1963 to 1969. He was a Rotarian and longtime scout leader, as well as a two-term director of the Mesa Chamber of Commerce and its 1960-1961 president.

It is little wonder then that Charles Crismon had resisted the city's attempts to remove him from his present location in order to make way for an eight-story office building—the centerpiece of Mesa's 10-acre downtown "superblock." Instead he has struck a tentative trade with the development company that will allow him to remain in that same general locale and fronting on Main Street. Says Crismon, "Our roots are too deep here to just cash out and walk away."

Virgil Crismon (below left) learned the florist business in Salt Lake City in 1937, and the following year he relocated to Mesa, establishing the first local flower shop. Like his father, Virgil, Charles Crismon (below right) now serves Mesa's floral needs at Crismon's Flowers.

COURY ENTERPRISES

When Tony Coury crossed the United States-Mexican border in 1924, he was 13 years old, all alone, and unable to speak English. One phase of his epic was ending, and a new one was about to begin.

He was born in 1911 in Morenci, Arizona, to Lebanese parents seeking the promise of the new land. But the promise proved elusive. So, when Tony was two years old, they returned to Lebanon.

In 1924 he and his father, Messih, sailed for America to start the quest anew. They would make it this time, and then send for the rest of the family. However, when they arrived at the border only Tony, a United States citizen, was allowed to cross. Plagued by the painful dilemma, Messih finally sent Tony across—with the couple's last $10—and ruefully returned to his family in Lebanon. Speaking only Arabic and French, and with no formal education, the intrepid youth meandered to Miami, Arizona, with only five dollars left.

Pete Mansour, a dry goods store owner who, fortunately, spoke Arabic and English, took him under his wing. Coury earned his keep working in Pete's store and peddling the slower-moving dry goods out of a battered black suitcase to the local Mexican mining families. In the process he learned Spanish as well as English.

Enterprising and compassionate, young Coury bought an old Durrant for $11 in order to expand his territory, offering customers who couldn't pay the full amount the option of an installment plan. A visionary even in his mid-teens, he saw "a better opportunity for business" in the Valley of the Sun. So, four years after his arrival in Miami, he headed west with a new Durrant and settled in Mesa.

A self-taught mechanic by then, he started Tony's Car Market at 215 East Main—a combination wrecking yard and used-car lot. He also specialized in car repair by hiring a mechanic for a dollar a day, and husbanded his resources, in part, by sleeping in the back of his shop.

Not one to let up, Coury still peddled dry goods house to house in the evenings out of the same beat-up old suitcase. It was during one of his evening sales sorties that he met—and soon fell in love with—a customer's daughter, Carmen Celaya.

Coury's business focus changed when, at the urging of his mechanic, he laid down his wrench, showered, put on his "Sunday clothes," and concentrated on selling automobiles. In 1935 he opened a Nash dealership; a year later he married Carmen; and in the late 1930s he started a Desoto-Plymouth agency.

Things shifted to high gear in 1953, when he opened a Buick agency, now his only automobile proprietorship, at 525 West Main, three blocks from his first car market. In just a few years the new enterprise grew to become one of the largest volume dealerships in Buick's four-state, Los Angeles zone. Shortly thereafter, Coury was named to its Dealer Council Board. Since 1978 Coury Buick has been among the top 10 of Buick's 102 dealers in the Los Angeles zone, and since 1983 it has been a member of Buick's nationwide Select 60. In 1986 Coury Buick was rated number one in customer satisfaction among Buick's 3,300 dealerships across the country.

It's been said that, "The real measure of a man starts with the size of his heart." In 1935—the year before his marriage to Carmen—Coury had scraped enough money together to send for his parents, his three brothers, and his sister, whom he helped settle in Mesa. Leonille, Coury's eldest daughter, remembers her father saying, "Always buy from people in town, even if it costs more. They're our neighbors." It was that sense of family and community that characterized Tony Coury's life even more so than his tenacity and entrepreneurial success.

"I'm a workhorse, not a show horse," he would reiterate. And community workhorse he was. A devout Catholic, he helped organize the drive to build the first Catholic parish church in Mesa and later spurred the campaign for construction of the replacement church and school, Queen of Peace. For Tony and Carmen Coury's boundless work for Catholic Social Services and countless other charitable causes, they both received their church's highest lay award, The Order of the Holy Sepulcher of Jerusalem, from Pope Paul VI. Ecumenical as well, Coury was "glad to support all denominations."

A community activist, too, he helped organize the Mesa Elks Lodge, the Mesa Country Club, and was among the first members of the Mesa Chamber of Commerce and Lions Club. He also served on the Mesa Civic Center Committee and the Mesa Lutheran Hospital Advisory Board.

"If someone needs help, call me. But get someone else to be president," was Tony's rather modest position. And help he did—loaning money to his extended family and to his friends so that they could embark on their own business careers.

Tony Jr. is now president and chairman of the board of Tony Coury Buick, for which he has garnered additional kudos. Albert "Butch" is a lawyer and a successful developer, heading Coury Development, Inc. William is president and owner of the Hilton Pavilion, a 262-room, four-star luxury hotel in Mesa's new commercial hub. Leonille Recker is a successful career and personnel consultant for individuals and organizations. Carolyn Brehany is a special assistant for Coury Development, and Antionette Chucri is, like her father, a community activist, as well as a busy wife and mother.

In the words of Bishop Thomas O'Brien, who officiated at Tony Coury's requiem in 1985, "Integrity, humility, decency, honesty came naturally to him somehow. He seemed to know what it (life) was all about."

To this, one can add that Coury was quick-aged, but truly a mellow vintage, and he never ate the seed corn. His compassionate stewardship produced bounty for family, friends, and community, and left Mesa the richer for it.

THE ARIZONA REPUBLIC AND PHOENIX GAZETTE

The *Arizona Gazette* began covering the news in the little territorial village of Phoenix in the fall of 1880, three years before Mesa City was incorporated and 11 years before its first newspaper was published.

Ten years after the *Gazette's* debut, *The Arizona Republican* started up its press in the year-old territorial capital, and in 1899 purchased the area's Republican Party rival paper, *The Phoenix Daily Herald*—the Valley's first afternoon newspaper. By 1920 *The Republican* had become Arizona's largest circulation newspaper—and it still is.

In 1928 the *Arizona Gazette* became the *Phoenix Evening Gazette.* The *Republican* changed its name to *The Arizona Republic* in 1930—the same year it combined publication with its biggest rival, the *Phoenix Evening Gazette.*

In 1946 both papers were purchased by the late Eugene C. Pulliam of Indianapolis,

News articles are written at the downtown facility of Phoenix Newspapers (above), then transmitted 15 miles by microwave to the $63-million production facility in Mesa (left), located at Mesa Drive and Baseline.

one of the founders of The Society of Professional Journalists, Sigma Delta Chi. A year later Pulliam broke ground for the *Republic* and *Gazette* main building on East Van Buren in Phoenix. To this day it remains the home of the newspapers' editorial, advertising, and business offices, and of some of its production facilities. Though published jointly by Phoenix Newspapers Inc., both publications have maintained separate and highly competitive editorial operations.

As the Valley's population expanded, especially eastward, and local communities developed sharper identities, Phoenix Newspapers Inc. saw the opportunity to fill a growing need for more area news and advertising coverage, and late in 1979 the *Republic* and *Gazette* began their first weekly community news editions for the residents of Mesa-Tempe. Local news and advertising for those sections is handled at the *Republic* and *Gazette's* Southeast Valley Bureau located in Mesa.

To keep pace with the dynamic growth in Mesa and Tempe, Phoenix Newspapers Inc. from 1982 to 1987 built and expanded a $63-million satellite production facility on a 10-acre site at Mesa Drive and Baseline. The 67,000-square-foot complex contains three high-speed presses, each capable of printing 58,000 newspapers per hour. The *Republic's* East Valley daily editions and predate sections are all printed there. All composition is still done at the newspapers' Van Buren building and transmitted by microwave to the Mesa facility 15 miles away. Additional satellite plants are in the planning stages for other Valley areas.

The corporation's more than 2,500 full-time and 700 part-time employees, along with its president, Eugene S. Pulliam, have kept the *Republic* and the *Gazette* Arizona's largest and most influential newspapers.

MESA COMMUNITY COLLEGE

Mesa Community College, the state's largest single-campus, two-year college, with an enrollment of nearly 20,000 students and more than 400 faculty and staff, is proud to call Mesa and the dynamic East Valley home.

MCC had its beginning in 1963 as an extension of Phoenix College with 330 students, 11 instructors, and an energetic dean, Dr. John Riggs. Its headquarters was in the former LDS church, now a restaurant at Main and Extension, with some classes in nearby office buildings.

In April 1965 the governing board of the county junior college district officially created Mesa Community College to serve the growing East Valley. A 160-acre parcel of land was purchased at the corner of Southern and Dobson, an area formerly used for cotton growing and sheep ranching.

Construction of the original buildings began in September 1965. Ground-breaking ceremonies were held October 15. Classes began at the new site on September 14, 1966, with a total of 2,053 students. Dedication ceremonies were held October 30.

In 1964 Mesa Community College, then an affiliate of Phoenix College, was located at Main Street and Extension.

From an initial enrollment of 330 students in 1963, Mesa Community College, now located at Southern and Dobson, boasts nearly 20,000 students.

Dr. Riggs served as MCC's first president until 1974. He was succeeded by Dr. Helena Howe. Theo Heap was president from 1978 to 1984, and Dr. Wallace A. Simpson became the college's fourth president in February 1984.

Dr. Simpson believes that "a community college education is a positive force in our society. Its objective is to offer growth to all people of the community in an encouraging setting. The effect of having adults, young adults, senior citizens, persons who are in the work force, and people with various ethnic, racial, and religious backgrounds together is an exciting chemistry that stimulates growth for both faculty and students. A community college is an extraordinary educational institution that fulfills the hopes of all people."

Surprisingly, the college has an international flavor with more than 600 students representing more than 75 countries. Recently the college established a Native American Center to work with the institution's growing population of Native American students. The Adult Re-Entry Center gives specialized assistance and counseling to adults who are returning to education after an extended absence. Two campus fitness centers, one exclusively for handicapped students, rival the most up-to-date health spas, and both are staffed by certified fitness instructors.

MCC's course offerings run the gamut from the academics to occupational programs to "fun" noncredit courses in its Lifelong Learning Program. The college offers two-year associate degrees in arts, general studies, and applied sciences; registered and licensed practical nursing programs; and associate degrees and certificates in a host of occupational skills.

The college has continued to grow and now has its own extension campus to serve the growing Southeast Valley—the Chandler-Gilbert Community College Center at 2626 East Pecos Road in Chandler with an enrollment of some 2,500 students.

From a small extension campus to the flagship of the Maricopa College District, Mesa Community College continues to be a key player in the educational and business growth and development of Mesa and the entire East Valley.

FIESTA MALL

Fiesta Mall is yet another example of the phenomenal growth of Mesa and the East Valley of the Sun during the past decade.

Rising out of land that once knew the sound of farm machinery and the bleating of sheep, the mall was completed late in 1979 by Homart Development Co., a major Chicago-based commercial real estate developer and a member of the Sears Financial Network.

Throughout Mesa's early history ribbons of steel funneled its growth. In the second semester of the twentieth century, it is bands of asphalt and concrete.

The Fiesta Mall retail center is the happy consequence of the city's location, sitting in a vortex of accelerating demographic density and serviced by a high-capacity road network. Bounded on the south by the Superstition Freeway, on the east by Alma School Road, and on the north by Southern Avenue, the center provides ready access for its abundant clientele.

This area, some two miles southwest of downtown Mesa, is fast becoming the city's commercial hub. The growth of this hub is due in large part to the mall, which has acted as a lure for the modern, 16-story Western Savings building, the Hilton Pavilion Hotel, and scores of new mercantile buildings and restaurants, with more hotel and commercial-retail buildings in progress.

Fiesta Mall's success is reflected in its eight-year growth statistics, which show little sign of slackening. Its 4 major department stores, more than 140 specialty stores, 2 major restaurants, and 12 fast-food emporia drew more than 8 million shoppers during its inaugural year and more than 15 million in 1986. The complex also boasts a sizable list of merchants waiting in the wings.

Fiesta Mall is owned by Homart Development Co. and Westcoast Estates. Homart is the major commercial real estate development arm of the Coldwell Banker Real Estate group, a member of the Sears Financial Network. Westcoast Estates is a general partnership of which Grosvenor International is the managing partner. Grosvenor is headquartered in Vancouver, with area operations in the United States, Canada, and Australia.

Fiesta Mall has had a decided impact on the economy of the city and surrounding area, with its enterprises employing more than 2,000 people, and supplying in excess of $2 million in annual tax revenues to the City of Mesa. It also provides commercial and retail spillover to the scores of peripheral enterprises that have sprung up around it.

In 1986 Fiesta Mall enjoyed the distinction of being first in sales per square foot, first in shopping preference, and second in pedestrian traffic volume in Arizona. In fact, the success story of Fiesta Mall says "volumes" about Mesa's business and residential growth in the state during the past decade.

Fiesta Mall boasts 4 major department stores, more than 140 specialty stores, 2 major restaurants, and 12 fast-food outlets. Its clientele has increased from 8 million shoppers during its first year to more than 15 million in 1986.

THE HAWS COMPANIES

Walter Haws was born in Colonia Juarez in 1894 to American Mormon settlers. With Pancho Villa's depredations against Americans in Mexico, Walter and his family were forced to flee to the United States in 1912.

He married Maude Nuttall and tried his hand at dairying, mining, and farming before the couple and their two infant children made the bumpy, six-day, 140-mile trek from Pima, Arizona, to Mesa by horse-drawn wagon in 1915.

After another round of mining and aborted efforts at ranching and cotton farming, he doggedly turned to carpentry and helped build the Mormon temple in 1924. Finally, he took his first temporary job as a truant officer with the Mesa schools; the job lasted 37 years.

Haws started Mesa's first flower delivery service in 1930, when he began ordering flowers from a shop in Phoenix for local funerals and special occasions. Four years later "Hooky Haws" was selling plants from his backyard nursery on his 2.5-acre lot.

By the mid-1950s Haws' nursery was no longer just an after-hours hobby. With his son Don he stepped up the landscaping and maintenance operations, and by the mid-1960s, with his son Lyman, he began a full-service flower business. Over the years the nursery has sold hundreds of thousands of plants, shrubs, and mulberry trees that greened and shaded the East Valley's growing communities.

Haws' youngest son, Henry, returned to the family business after earning his degree in landscape architecture at Cal Poly Pomona in 1960 and working for two years as a landscape architect with the State of California. Henry Haws & Associates (HHA) was born in the back of the nursery sales room in 1962, with Henry doubling as nursery assistant during his company's early years.

Like his father, operating on more than one front was quite normal for him. Henry began 14 years of public service in 1968 with his election to the Maricopa County Board of Supervisors, where he served for 10 years, followed by two terms in the Arizona House of Representatives.

Throughout his public life Henry successfully managed his corporation. After beefing up his landscape architectural staff to meet the growth in the valley, he added civil engineering and surveying to the corporation's landscape architecture business in 1984. By 1987 there were 15 professionals on staff.

With his mind as agile as a quiz kid's, the 93-year-old Haws retired in 1984, thus ending his 50 years in the nursery and floral business.

Henry's corporate entities now include Haws Inc., a florist operation with two shops—on South Mesa Drive and on East Brown near Horne—and HHA Inc., his civil engineering, surveying, and landscape architecture firm.

Henry Haws' contributions mantle the entire valley—his projects of note too numerous to list. He and Walter, the indefatigable duo, have added to the greenery and scenery of the East Valley for more than 60 years, and have helped to soften, texture, and beautify its growing urban sprawl.

Walter P. Haws, who started the nursery that became The Haws Companies, retired in 1984, ending a 50-year career in the nursery and floral business.

Henry Haws, who has served on the Maricopa County Board of Supervisors and in the Arizona House of Representatives, has spearheaded the growth of The Haws Companies into a versatile firm.

Morea-Hall Engineering, Inc.

Since its incorporation eight years ago, Morea-Hall Engineering, Inc., has completed a staggering 1,380 projects, half of which are located in the Mesa area.

Much of its exponential growth was due in part to its "Mesa connection" and its close association with Mesa-based architectural firms.

During Harold Hall's previous employ in 1974, he was involved in a future use and development study of nearly 120 buildings in a four-mile tract in historic downtown Mesa. Since then the firm has engineered such structures as the 12-story Ramada Renaissance Hotel, the four-story United Bank building on Mesa Drive, the two-story Arizona Bank building on Macdonald Street, the Sousa Elementary School, and additions to the Mesa Southwest Museum, YMCA, and Centennial Hall. In all, structural engineering has accounted for about 100 buildings in the Mesa area, running the gamut from office buildings to schools, churches, shopping centers, police and fire stations, and the Champlin Fighter Museum at Falcon Field.

Hall's favorite was the Ramada Renaissance Hotel. It was a fast-track project where construction ran hand in hand with the design of the building—kind of an engineering "hip shoot." According to Hall it is the first staggered-truss building in Arizona.

Hall is the scion of a long line of builders in Illinois, and virtually teethed on a two-by-four. He achieved part of his boyhood dream when he received his BSCE from Arizona State University in 1971 and became a registered civil and structural engineer in Arizona and five other states.

Claudia Morea's family was in ranching and insurance back in Wyoming. She earned her BSCE in 1970 from the University of Wyoming, and is a registered civil and sanitary engineer and land surveyor in Arizona.

Hall was associated with a prominent local consulting engineering firm for eight years before incorporating with Morea in 1980. Morea spent the early portion of her professional career working with the State of Arizona as an environmental engineer prior to their partnership.

The firm started with six professionals.

Today it has 24, including its other officer, William Ware, a registered structural engineer.

Morea-Hall Engineering has specialized in surveying and site development, largely in the Mesa area, for a passel of new housing tracts, shopping centers, and elementary and high schools. Some of the more recent have been the 94-acre Red Mountain High School, the Sun Valley Plaza and Mesa Shores shopping centers, the Mesa Lutheran Hospital expansion, and Val Vista Greens and Four Peaks Estates.

Behind many of the new buildings punctuating Mesa's landscape were hundreds of thousands of man/machine hours spent by Morea-Hall's engineers, draftsmen, and computers before even one lump of soil was disturbed.

One of Morea-Hall Engineering's projects in Mesa was the Ramada Renaissance Hotel, shown here during construction. Erection of the specially designed steel trusses was completed in just 18 days.

ABLE STEEL FABRICATORS, INC.

Charles "Chuck" Clark, Jr., the 34-year-old president of Able Steel Fabricators, Inc., hit the ground running when he arrived in Mesa from Ohio with his dad, "Jim," in January 1975.

Eight months later the pair bought Russell's Welding Shop on South Country Club Road. Though Chuck knew little about welding, he got Russell to teach him as part of the deal.

Under the aegis of Able Welding and Fabricating, "able to do anything," they started in ornamental iron, trailer hitches, general welding repairs, and some subcontracted construction work on grain sheds. "But there were no bucks in it."

Thirty-one months after touchdown in Mesa the father-and-son team bought the 20,000-square-foot Evans Steel fabricating plant and incorporated as Able Steel Company. So, with 20 employees and four trucks, they began erecting steel roofing and interior walls for mini-storage warehouses around the valley. The fabrication and building jobs got progressively larger, and soon the pair was involved in structural steel fabrication and construction of more substantial buildings, such as JCPenney at Westbridge Mall, the Val Vista Fire Station, and additions to the Motorola building at Broadway and Alma School Road.

Using November 1980 as a benchmark, they decided to fabricate heavier structural

The current home of Able Steel Fabricators, Inc. From a small, two-man welding shop in 1976, Able Steel has grown into Arizona's second-largest steel fabricator, with a fabrication plant of 50,000 square feet.

steel for larger, more profitable buildings. In perfect character, Chuck and Jim went for broke.

They borrowed the capital and bought a five-punch CNC beam line. The 180-foot by 30-foot monster was a "piece of equipment in search of a home," so in December 1980 they bought 10 acres in northern Mesa off Greenfield Road; built a two-story, 6,000-square-foot office building and a 30,000-square-foot fabrication plant; bought

additional processing machinery; and increased their work force to 50—6 years and 11 months after touchdown.

The years 1981 to 1984 were inauspicious. Interest rates climbed, and construction slumped valleywide. But the partners hung on like pit bulls, gradually subcontracting their erection business and concentrating solely on fabrication. By 1984 the light glimmered through the tunnel and it's been bright ever since.

From 1982 to 1988 the firm completed 370 building projects. Its 1986-1987 sales were close to $9 million, with $12 million booked in orders so far in the first eight months of 1987-1988. Three project managers are inundated with a current order backlog of 120 days. One of the firm's current projects is the Arizona State University stadium expansion, a six-story athletic facility at the end of Sun Devil Stadium.

From a $15,000 investment in a small, two-man welding shop in 1976, Able Steel Fabricators, Inc., has grown into the second-largest steel fabricator in Arizona, with 95 employees and markets in California and New Mexico and throughout Arizona. Now that's hitting the ground running.

ASU's athletic administration building and loge roof containing 860 tons of structural steel.

ALUMI-COVER AWNING COMPANY, INC.

Arizona always seemed to have beckoned Milt Roberts. In his late teens and early twenties he had left his native East Texas on three occasions during the Depression to work in the copper mines around Globe and Miami. But the tug of Texas always won out. Then, in 1960, he and his wife, Cathryn, and their three teenage boys left for good and settled in Mesa.

For the next six years Roberts sold mobile homes. Adventurous and independent since youth, he finally decided to strike out on his own and started a retail aluminum

awning company on East Main.

Two years later, in January 1968, he took the final plunge. With $5,000 in savings, he incorporated and began manufacturing his own aluminum trailer and home-exterior accessory products in a 10,000-square-foot rented building on Second Avenue and Country Club Road.

It was pure pioneering—virgin territory with no real competition around yet. He purchased one roll former to shape the aluminum sheets, hiring three laborers and a salesman while he doubled as foreman and salesman. Cathryn, his Girl Friday, kept the office humming.

By 1971 business was booming. Roberts bought his second roll former (no small investment), moved to a 20,000-square-foot

building just inside the Mesa city limits on the south bank of the Salt River, opened a warehouse in Tucson, and persuaded his oldest son, Ken, to join the corporation. As Ken tells it, "I didn't want to leave my job with Motorola, but my dad needed help." Today Ken readily admits that it was the smartest decision he ever made.

A year after Ken came on board the company's facilities were expanded to 30,000 square feet, and two years later to 40,000 square feet of space. In 1983 Milt retired for health reasons at 70 years of age and Ken became president.

Today, 20 years after incorporation, Alumi-Cover Awning Company, Inc., has eight roll formers going full bore, two more warehouses—one in Surprise, Arizona (just outside Sun City), and one in Albuquerque, New Mexico, and a seven-state market area. In 1968 the firm only operated in Mesa and the East Valley. Today it markets to retailers throughout Arizona, New Mexico, Utah, Nevada, Kansas, southern Colorado, and West Texas.

One other thing has changed as well—it is no longer virgin territory. There are now four direct wholesalers in the valley, but the firm's production has not lost a beat.

Alumi-Cover Awning Company's tenfold growth in 20 years is not only a testimonial to the daring and vision of its founder; it is also indicative of the enormous expansion of the mobile-home community, particularly in the East Valley where the firm does nearly 50 percent of its business.

When Milt Roberts (left) incorporated and began manufacturing aluminum trailer and home-exterior accessory products, he had one roll former and doubled as foreman and salesman. His wife, Cathryn (below), kept the office running smoothly. Today, with eight roll formers and two additional warehouses in two states, Alumi-Cover markets to retailers in seven states throughout the Midwest and Southwest.

MINING CAMP RESTAURANT & TRADING POST

If you stand quietly just outside the Mining Camp Restaurant a little after dusk you just might hear the taunt of the Dutchman or an Apache war whoop drifting down from Syphon Draw in the Superstition Mountains a quarter-mile to the east.

The rough-sawn Ponderosa pine restaurant sits on a gently sloping rise near the base of the sheer, deep-etched Superstition Escarpments, which brood hauntingly over the sprawling Valley of the Sun. Apache Junction lies a few miles to the southwest, and the historic Apache Trail is less than one mile away.

The 27-year-old restaurant complex is said to be on the site of the 1848 Paralta mining expedition massacre waged by avenging Apaches. It is also the place where the mill for the defunct Palmer Mine once stood, its tailings still visible at the entrance to Syphon Draw.

The compound consists of the restaurant, modeled after a mining-camp cook shanty, and five mock buildings—a hotel, barn, assay office, jail, and bathhouse.

The real story, however, is not its lore; or its lip-smacking, family-style fare, served to more than 140,000 patrons each year; nor is it the authentic interior, replete with historic mining and area memorabilia. It is Vinton Fugate, the 40-year-old proprietor.

If corporate-bound, Fugate would have insisted on starting in the mail room. But he chose a different setting in which to launch his career, and decided to learn the business from suds to spuds.

At the age of 13 he began as a dishwasher at the brand-new Mining Camp while still in school. He continued on a part-time basis through high school and two years of college. From "pot-walloper" he graduated to mopping floors and busing tables, and then cooked for 13 years. He "loves the business" and couldn't think of anything else he would rather do.

The three Cordalis brothers—Ken, Tom, and Jack—who founded the Mining Camp, took a liking to Fugate. After Ken's fatal auto accident and Tom's departure for Colorado, Jack Cordalis recognized Fugate's skill, drive, and savvy, and took him in as a partner in 1981 on a "sweat equity" arrangement.

In 1984 Jack Cordalis retired, and Fugate purchased Jack's holdings and became full owner; the restaurant has since been completely renovated. The gift shop was doubled in size, the kitchen revamped, and all five of the outbuildings constructed.

Because the restaurant was always closed during the three slow summer months, it lost money during those months due to its built-in, fixed costs. Fugate bit the bullet and opened year-round, beefed up his marketing program, and finally put the business in the black all year long. In three years he doubled his gross. The restaurant has a 400-seat capacity and serves up to 1,800 Sunday dinners every week.

Fugate believes that "Hard work and loving it gave me luck." You can look him up; he is in the book—*The 100 Best Restaurants in Arizona.*

The menacing Superstition Mountains provide an appropriate backdrop for the Mining Camp Restaurant.

CHANDLER READY MIX

Ron Perkins is carved from the same tough mettle as his Utah-born Mormon grandparents who pioneered Arizona long before the turn of the century.

Born and raised in the rugged Arizona high country surrounding Snowflake-Taylor, this inveterate outdoorsman worked as a logger and general handyman and gandy dancer for the Apache Railroad in that area until the Korean War, in which he served in the Marine Corps. Finding "insufficient compensation" in railroading upon his return, he left for the more prosperous East Valley in 1957.

There he learned the concrete trade during the two years he worked for a cement contractor. Then he and Dewain Connolly bit the bullet and launched Connolly and Perkins Cement Contractors, Inc.

Perkins sold out in 1963 and started Ronald R. Perkins Cement Contractor, Inc.; in 1971 he began Chandler Ready Mix with Ray Wright as a partner, purchasing Wright's share in 1982. Wanting to concentrate on "something more than just contracting," Perkins relinquished the older company to his son in 1975, leaving him free to focus on the supply aspect of the industry.

One hard and set way to measure growth in a community is to chart the development of the concrete industry. According to Perkins, "99.9 percent of all construction, including premanufactured homes, use concrete."

Perkins' company, "one of the smallest in the area," is a microcosm of the East Valley boom. When it started on East Baseline Road in Mesa, for example, Perkins had eight employees, five mixer trucks, a used batch plant, one front-end loader, a belly dump truck, and a trailer.

Today the firm has grown more than sevenfold. Its more than $5 million in equipment comprises 34 mixer trucks, 3 new computerized batch plants, and 6 belly dump trucks and trailers. His 100 employees operate the four-acre site on East Baseline, and Perkins' new 32-acre aggregate crushing plant, Aztec Materials, Inc., was started in 1978 at East Lehi Road and the Salt River bed.

In the beginning Chandler Ready Mix had only four competitors in the East Valley; today the competition has doubled, with some of the world's largest cement companies solidly ensconced, having taken over a number of independents in the process.

During the past 16 years Perkins' firm has prospered in the face of tough competition, business recessions in the valley in 1974 to 1975 and 1982 to 1983, and tight money at "six points over prime" from 1973 to 1978. Of all the independent ready mix companies that began when his did, Perkins' is the only one that hasn't gone belly up or been taken over.

Dogged determination and the willingness to risk all is what one would expect from an ex-Marine and outdoorsman whose idea of relaxation is big-game hunting on the North American continent. A huge Kodiak bear—one among his trophies—attests to that.

Since Chandler Ready Mix began, it has grown sevenfold to include a fleet of 34 mixer trucks and 6 belly dump trucks, as well as 3 new computerized batch plants.

THE ARIZONA GOLF RESORT AND CONFERENCE CENTER

The Arizona Golf Resort and Conference Center is the opulent offspring of three previous recreational facilities—Apache and Golden Hills country clubs, and the latter's successor, Golden Hills Golf Resort.

It was Jack Lake and his capable right-hand lady, Carolyn Denton, who, in less than 10 years, transformed an also-ran resort into a premier mecca for out-of-town vacationers, national and international business groups, and recreation-loving locals.

Lake was managing all of Western Savings' properties when it first acquired title on the foreclosed Apache Country Club in 1967. By the time he left Western 10 years later, he had seen the facility go through two teetering transitions.

A finance major with an MBA from the University of Utah and 15 years' experience in the banking and development industry, Lake saw promise in the 135-acre Golden Hills Resort if it was given a large infusion of venture capital, tasteful remodeling, a new thrust, aggressive marketing, and careful orchestration by deft management. He also needed faith, and the grit to risk it on a calculated roll.

To his credit, risk it he did in 1978. "Before I bought the resort you could break your leg on the 14th fairway and starve to death before someone came by." Laughingly, he adds that, "On one occasion, the

In 1983 Jack Lake rebuilt all 18 greens on the resort's golf course, converting them into some of the best in the valley.

coffee shop's one-day's gross was $1.31."

But Lake stuck with it, even though it took two years for the ink to blacken. In 1980 he hired Carolyn Denton as general manager. A charming, efficient, English lady with more than 20 years of resort management experience on three continents, Denton has a list of credits that reads like a jaunt through a travel agency's brochures.

With the Superstition Freeway about to terminate close by, Lake took the final calculated plunge and implemented his five-year redevelopment plan in 1982.

In 1983 he rebuilt all 18 greens on the course, turning them into "some of the best in the entire valley." Next he began gutting and refurbishing every one of the resort's 132 units. In 1986 he constructed a 10,000-square-foot conference center with its 320-seat banquet facility, and in 1987 culminated his $4-million revamp by gutting and remodeling the entire clubhouse and creating a charming rendezvous for discriminating diners and nightlifers—Annabelle's Restaurant and Lounge.

Today the Arizona Golf Resort and Conference Center is the sole high-quality, full-service destination resort in Mesa. Lake and Denton have artfully transformed this charming oasis into a popular vacation spot and conference center with championship golf, tennis, swimming, and spas, as well as nightly dining and weekday happy hours, both replete with live entertainment.

Mesa and the East Valley have profited greatly from Jack Lake's vision, taste, and commitment.

The front entrance to the Arizona Golf Resort and Conference Center. In 10 years Jack Lake and Carolyn Denton transformed this also-ran resort into a popular center for vacationers and businesspeople.

SOUTHWEST PROPERTIES, INC.

How do you make a mountain out of a molehill when there's no molehill in the first place? You take a pinch of treasury green, add 10 parts vision, and mix with equal parts of skill, risk, and confidence.

Seventeen-year-old Clifford Wolfswinkel, devastatingly poor when he arrived in Mesa 40 years ago, put an end to his abject condition several years later with the above recipe.

Clarence, Clifford's father, was plagued by asthma and left Hull, Iowa, for Mesa in 1948 with his wife and sons. There he ran a gas station, as he did back in Iowa, where Clifford, his eldest son, worked for him until the Korean War called him away.

In 1953 he returned to Mesa and opened a pet shop with his wife of three years, Eleanor Mae. According to Mae, Clifford's long-term goal was "to put $10,000 in the bank." And he did. He then invested it, against the family's advice, in 3,200 acres of desert between Phoenix and Tucson, and reaped a huge profit from the sale of his sand and cactus holdings, which became part of Arizona City. That was the start of Wolfswinkel's "mountain."

After the Arizona City windfall he founded Southwest Properties in 1958, and

Southwest Properties will bring Mesa into the twenty-first century with development of the huge Fiesta Center, at Southern Avenue and Alma School Road. The Fiesta Center will spring from the same site first settled by the Wolfswinkels 40 years ago.

Clifford Wolfswinkel, who founded Southwest Properties in 1958. Today the firm is a diversified developer with dealings in five states throughout the West, Southwest, and Midwest.

began buying and selling land throughout the state. Clifford was particularly optimistic about the East Valley. Mae remembers him saying in the early 1960s that he could drive down any road in Mesa, and anywhere he threw his hat would be a "good buy." As a visionary with a sixth sense for land values, he had few peers—his hundreds of millions of dollars in successful land transactions attest to that.

It was with the sale of his approximately 2,000-acre tract in Mesa to General Motors for "a couple of million" that Clifford "really felt successful for the first time," according to his daughter, Penny Essel, president of Southwest Properties.

Since 1958 Clifford Wolfswinkel has played a pivotal role in the valley's development, and in the early 1960s began developing large tracts statewide, as well as in Colorado and California. In the early 1980s he began acquiring and operating farmland in Iowa, Minnesota, North Dakota, and Michigan.

Today Southwest Properties, Inc., is a diversified developer of more than 42,000 acres of residential, commercial, retail, recreational, and mixed-use properties throughout the West, Southwest, and Midwest. Through its affiliate companies—Windmills West, Inc., and Windmill Farms, Inc.—it farms approximately 25,000 acres in Arizona and four other states.

Since Clifford Wolfswinkel's untimely death in January 1988, his children have taken the tiller, captained by his daughter, Penny. David is vice-president of Southwest, Kathy is president of Windmills West, and Clifford's three younger brothers, whom he got started in business, have gone on to build their own realty "mountains."

McDonnell Douglas Helicopter Company

November 1, 1986, was a historic day for both Mesa and McDonnell Douglas Helicopter Company.

The banner occasion was the formal opening of the helicopter company's new Arizona headquarters. The ceremonies also marked the completion of the 1.3-million-square-foot addition to the firm's existing 570,000-square-foot assembly and flight test center. The $300-million, 13-building complex is the newest and most advanced helicopter facility in the free world.

Gathered for the auspicious event were Arizona's principal federal legislators, its governor, moguls of Arizona's and Mesa's governments, the company's president, the chairman of McDonnell Douglas Corporation (McDonnell Douglas Helicopter's parent company), and thousands of employees and guests.

But the real story was not in the massive assemblage of concrete, steel, and electronics rising out of desert land controlled by the Apache Indians a long time ago. Nor

McDonnell Douglas Helicopter Company's recently completed headquarters facility at Mesa. The light helicopter assembly, delivery, and flight test center is at the lower left.

was it the gathering of dignitaries at the inaugural. Rather, it was the firm's commitment to shape its future in Mesa—the vibrant heart of Arizona. "We found an attractive business environment and put our substance on the line and in a big way," said Sanford McDonnell, former chairman of McDonnell Douglas Corporation.

The foundation for this dynamic company was laid, not in Mesa, but in California back in 1934. That's when Howard Hughes, driven by a passion to build the world's fastest raceplane, started the aircraft division of the Hughes Tool Company, which evolved into Hughes Helicopters, Inc.

After developing a series of unique helicopters, from the Flying Crane in 1952, through the OH-6 of Vietnam fame, to today's juggernaut—the AH-64 Apache attack helicopter—Hughes relocated Apache assembly and flight test operations to Mesa.

In early 1983 Hughes began production operations at its newly built Apache Assembly and Flight Test Center, fittingly within view of the Superstitions—a sacred Apache mountain range. In 1984 Hughes Helicopters, Inc., became a subsidiary of the McDonnell Douglas Corporation, and the following year became the McDonnell Douglas Helicopter Company.

William P. Brown, president of McDonnell Douglas Helicopter Company.

McDonnell Douglas was no neophyte in rotorcraft design, having been involved in development of a number of different helicopters during the 1940s and 1950s. Although none of its rotorcraft ever went into production, the company's first helicopter was airborne in 1944—eight years before Hughes' first "chopper" lifted skyward. The firm's

Reno Johnson, Sr., chairman of the White Mountain Apache tribe (right), presents a Medal of Valor to William P. Brown for the contribution of the Apache attack helicopter (in the background) to national defense.

McDonnell Aircraft unit decided to concentrate on jet fighters and spacecraft after losing the Army's OH-6 light observation helicopter contract to Hughes Helicopters in the 1960s, but is involved in vertical lift today with the successful AV-8B Harrier II vertical takeoff fighter.

Shortly after joining the McDonnell Douglas family, the helicopter company began to confront a pressing need for expansion and decided this could be done most effectively in Arizona. Thus was launched the 1.3-million-square-foot facility expansion program in Mesa. Today all headquarters functions and helicopter design, assembly, and flight test work are done in Mesa, along with ordnance engineering assembly and testing. The company's California facility near Los Angeles International Airport serves as the central machining center.

The AH-64 helicopter is the firm's leading program. The Apache is the most potent combat helicopter in the free world, and the only attack helicopter capable of operations at night and in adverse weather. The U.S. Army plans to buy as many as 1,000 twin-engine Apaches through the mid-1990s as a primary defense against the Warsaw Pact's superior armor concentrations in Europe.

McDonnell Douglas also relocated its light helicopter assembly and flight test and ordnance operations to Mesa in 1987. Its popular MD 500 helicopters, currently flown in many countries worldwide, are among the fastest, quietest, and most agile light commercial and military helicopters in service today. The company has produced more than 4,000 of its OH-6A/MD 500 series light helicopters. The firm's 25mm Chain Gun ® cannon is the primary weapon on the Army's Bradley Fighting Vehicle.

What of the future? McDonnell Douglas, in concert with Bell Helicopter Textron and other high-tech corporations, leads the SuperTeam designing a new-generation helicopter to fulfill the U.S. Army's LHX light attack/armed reconnaissance requirements. SuperTeam design work is under way in the company's 640,000-square-foot Engineering and Advanced Development Center at the Mesa complex.

Mesa's new corporate citizen has more than kept the promises it made to both city and state before it arrived on the scene, and the community has profited conspicuously from the helicopter company's presence.

The facility has become a "magnet for commerce," with thousands of its foreign and domestic visitors stimulating the economy and spreading the news abroad about the attractions of Mesa and the valley. The firm's presence has also generated considerable peripheral business for a large number of local corporations.

McDonnell's more than 5,000 Arizona employees, a large percentage of whom were hired locally, funnel a lion's share of their combined annual $180 million in pay to local merchants, governments, and charities. The company's annual economic impact on the Valley of the Sun is nearly one billion dollars (using a standard multiplier of three).

The philosophy behind this success, says president William P. Brown, is dedication to total quality work and customer service.

When one adds the human factor to McDonnell's Mesa equation, its corporate presence becomes even more impressive. The company's labor force of highly skilled engineers and upper-level technicians enriches the area's labor base, and the thousands of volunteer hours donated each year by its employees to local civic, charitable, religious, and social causes has enhanced Mesa's quality quotient. Add also the company-based test pilots, credited with locating missing persons and assisting downed civilian pilots during their flight missions.

The arrival of the McDonnell Douglas Helicopter Company and the return of the vaunted "Apache" to its ancient preserve have added a vertical thrust to Mesa's economy and community.

DESERT SAMARITAN HOSPITAL & HEALTH CENTER

Health care in Mesa, though slow in unfolding, has come a long way since pioneer physician Ralph Palmer, the "doctor on horseback," made "house calls only" during the first 20 years of the twentieth century.

Forty-five years would elapse before Mesa's founding families and the next two generations would have their first health care facility. In fact, no hospital existed in the entire East Valley until 1921. It was then that expanded health care became a close-knit family and community affair—a relationship that has prevailed to the present.

In 1921 a group of public-spirited citizens from Mesa bargained for the 12-room LeSueur home sitting on two acres at East Main and Hibbert. However, the fund-raising campaign was terminated by the cotton crash of 1922, and the balance of the mortgage on the newly constructed nurses' residence and the LeSueur home came due.

The community accepted the challenge. Mrs. LeSueur donated half of her home to the hospital, and the Mesa Women's Club and city council paid the balance of the mort-

In 1973 ground was broken for Desert Samaritan Hospital & Health Center. Today "Desert Sam" has evolved into a full-service medical center at the cutting edge of rapidly changing medical technology.

The LeSueur home functioned as Mesa's first hospital in 1921. The city leased the building to the hospital for one dollar per year.

gage. The city, now sole owner of the site, then leased it to the hospital for one dollar per year. The East Valley had its first 12-room hospital, with an operating and emergency room upstairs and 12 beds downstairs.

In 1923 Southside District Hospital was formed as a not-for-profit corporation with a seven-member board from Mesa, Tempe, Chandler, and Gilbert. Its first administra-

tors were Lois and John Hansen. Lois, an R.N., was nurse, cook, and cleaning woman, while John maintained the facility and tended the hospital's cow and chickens.

The community continued its foster

The 37-bed Mesa Southside District Hospital succeeded the old LeSueur home in 1933. By 1956 the hospital had grown to 103 beds, and had 139 full-time and 41 part-time employees and a 73-member medical staff.

role. The Mormon Church made several contributions when Southside's doors were about to close, and the townspeople and civic groups donated everything from food to a coffee pot to a cooking range. The patients came from all over the East Valley and from the construction sites on the Salt River, where three dams were being built from 1923 to 1930.

In 1933 the old LeSueur home was replaced by a new 37-bed hospital built by WPA workers with federal, city, and hospital funds. By 1956 the 103-bed facility had 139 full-time and 41 part-time employees, and a 73-member medical staff; by mid-year it was fully accredited.

By 1965, after five stages of uncoordinated growth, Southside was in dire need of modernization and expansion to meet the giant strides made in technology and the relentless press of population.

After more than two years of careful evaluation and extended negotiations, Southside merged with Good Samaritan Hospital of Phoenix on August 2, 1968, in order to provide the resources needed to build a new hospital for East Valley residents. Both institutions shared a history of long-term community service, not-for-profit status, financial stability, hospital accreditation, and community board organization.

The community remained solidly behind its future hospital, with more than 400 people participating in the numerous planning sessions held throughout the area. Seventy-seven Mesa and Tempe physicians lent their support to the new hospital, as did the mayors of both cities, the local newspapers, civic groups, and businesses. Samaritan Health Service was formed, and the acquisition of land began.

The strong bond between Mesa residents and the hospital was demonstrated when the Dobsons, an old-time Mesa family and "grateful patients" of the old Southside Hospital, donated a "set piece"—24 acres at the epicenter of Dobson Road and the Superstition Freeway. Fifty-eight acres were then purchased to round out the 82-acre parcel.

Ground was broken in 1970. Three years later, on April 15, Desert Samaritan Hospital & Health Center admitted its first patients. "Desert Sam" cost $18.8 million with a cost per square foot at the national average.

Today Desert Sam has evolved into a full-service medical center at the cutting edge of rapidly changing medical technology. It boasts a staff of more than 1,400 nurses, allied health professionals, and support personnel, and more than 700 physicians representing 45 medical specialties. This fine staff treats patients from Mesa, Tempe, Chandler, Gilbert, Apache Junction, and Ahwatukee.

The legitimate heir to Mesa's first hospital, Desert Sam still enjoys the same special relationship with its community that its predecessor had for 67 years. The only change has been in its size and its new, state-of-the-art, full-service treatment facilities.

Recent statistics speak for themselves. In 1986 the hospital's 343 private rooms had the highest occupancy in Arizona; its obstetricians delivered nearly 5,000 spanking-new Arizonans in each of the past three years in its 16 labor/delivery/recovery rooms and four surgical delivery suites; more than 60 percent of its surgery is done on an outpatient basis in its 13 modern surgical suites; and more than 35,000 patients are treated each year in its emergency department. In addition, Desert Sam enjoys an amazing 98-percent aided and unaided name recognition.

Desert Sam was the first hospital in the East Valley to employ a radiation oncology unit, a full-body CAT scanner, a cardiac catheterization lab, a magnetic resonance imaging unit, and to perform open-heart surgery.

A pacesetter still, Desert Samaritan Hospital & Health Center has maintained its position as a health care leader in the East Valley since the old LeSueur home was converted in 1923.

CHAMPLIN FIGHTER MUSEUM

The U.S. Navy Grumman F6F-3 Hellcat was flown during World War II. It is one of the Champlin Fighter Museum's 27 historic aircraft.

During World War II Falcon Field, Mesa's municipal airport, hosted contingents of British and U.S. Army air cadets. Before hostilities ended, 1,380 British and 116 Americans had received their wings and fought together in the skies above England and in the liberation of Europe and the Far East.

Today the field hosts the Champlin Fighter Museum, home to the world's largest collection of historic fighter aircraft.

Arizona businessman and the museum's owner, Doug Champlin, has assembled 27 original or perfect-flying replicas of history's most famous fighter aircraft, now on view in two of the field's renovated World War II hangars. More aircraft exhibits are planned.

Champlin opened his unique museum in January 1981 to house antique fighter aircraft that he began collecting as an avocation in 1969 back in his hometown of Enid, Oklahoma. It was there that this third-generation Champlin oil scion and history major from Cal-Berkeley learned to fly and became enamored of the lore and valor of a bygone age.

About a dozen aircraft were in Champlin's collection when he moved his museum to Mesa. Since then he has enlarged his rare inventory, which ranges from World War I fighter planes flown by the Red Baron—Manfred von Richthofen—and American fly-

ing aces Captain Eddie Rickenbacker and Lieutenant Frank Luke, Jr., to the fighters piloted by World War II aces Majors Dick Bong and Joe Foss of the United States, and the more recent types of planes flown in both the Korean and Vietnam wars.

In 1983 the museum became the official home of the American Fighter Aces Association, which includes some 500 American fighter pilots, each of whom has at least five confirmed enemy aircraft victories to his credit.

This rare breed of solo warriors meets biannually at the Champlin Fighter Museum to renew common bonds and relive fading memories. The meetings have been attended by some foreign aces who have joined their fellow knights of the sky in a brotherhood reserved for former battle heroes, regardless of their nationality.

The museum also hosts banquets for unit reunions and corporate functions, as well as visits by enthusiast groups and foreign and U.S. military brass.

Of special interest for the history buff is the Aces Gallery, which features about 500 large photographs of these heroes of the skies complete with accompanying biographical notes and personal wartime memorabilia of some Allied and enemy aces as well. These intimate cameos, heightened by more than 50 specially commissioned paintings of World War II aircraft in combat settings, are housed in a new building connected to the two hangars.

The J. Curtis Earl machine gun collection, displayed in a 3,500-square-foot addition to the four-building complex, is the largest of its kind west of the Mississippi and contains some original nineteenth-century machine guns, and aircraft and ground automatics from the World War I, World War II, Korea, and Vietnam eras.

This ultimate showcase of fighter aviation history is open to the public seven days a week from 10 a.m. to 5 p.m.

A museum prize—a Soviet MIG-17 (left) flown in Vietnam—shown with a USAF F-86, flown in Korea.

SALT RIVER PROJECT

Long before they thought of shelter, Mesa's Mormon pioneers first began recarving the ancient Hohokam canal network and tying it to the Salt River.

But, like the Hohokam before them, they soon were held hostage by the moody Salt River, which frequently either rampaged or trickled, racking or parching their vulnerable farms and pastures.

A persistent drought through the end of the nineteenth century was the final affront that coalesced the valley's residents. A "Committee of Nine" was formed to seek ways and means of capitalizing on national legislation, then being drafted in Washington, D.C. Mesa residents W.H. Wallace and C.S. "Jack" Steward were members of the committee that was instrumental in gaining local acceptance and unity, which resulted in Theodore Roosevelt Dam being funded through the National Reclamation Act of 1902. Roosevelt Dam, located 70 miles up the Salt River, stored precious life-giving water for residents' needs, both then and now.

It was truly the vision and courage of Mesa's early settlers and the other valley landowners who ensured the passage and success of the new federal legislation by pledging their land as financial backing. The act only provided federal loans for reclama-

One of Mesa's new, all-electric subdivisions that has been developed in the past few years is supplied with the Salt River Project's low-cost electricity.

tion projects in the area. But to become eligible for these funds, Mesa and other valley farmers had to jointly pledge their land as collateral before a federal loan was approved to finance the Roosevelt Dam. With the help of the Committee of Nine, the local residents formed the Salt River Valley Water Users' Association in 1903. But that was just the first step. The federal legislators also asked for a guaranteed distribution system. The huge dam would be virtually worthless without a means of delivering water. Mesa, again showing foresight and unity, was one of the first cities to sell its canal system.

The world's largest masonry dam, Roosevelt was completed in 1911, six years after

it was begun. It was the first of six on the Salt and Verde rivers that currently provide the water resources for the Salt River Project's intricate, 1,300-mile delivery system, which irrigates 238,000 acres of agricultural land with over a million acre feet of water annually.

In 1917 the Salt River Valley Water Users' Association took over operation of the system from the U.S Reclamaition Service. Today Salt River Project (SRP) is governed by locally elected boards and councils.

A spin-off of the SRP's irrigation projects was the hydroelectric generating units on the four dams along the Salt, which power the valley's growth. As the demands of population and commerce grew, SRP augmented its electric power base with primarily coal-fired generation, supplemented by hydro, oil, gas, and nuclear power.

Since the early 1900s the Salt River Project has been a major stimulant in Mesa's growth and commerce and is carefully planning well into the twenty-first century to ensure the adequate supply of its two precious staples—water and power.

Mesa's substantial population growth is characterized by this myriad of cars in the 1930s. Water and power supplied by the Salt River Project enabled Mesa to meet the needs of its rapidly growing population. Courtesy, Mesa Southwest Museum Collections

ZEB PEARCE COMPANIES

Patriarch Zebulon Pearce might well have been a Mississippi businessman or pedagogue if his father Jesse's lungs could have weathered the delta's humidity. Instead the Pearces left Baldwyn in 1877 for the drier, therapeutic air of Salt Lake City when Zeb was just 10 weeks old.

When he was three the family headed southwest to Saint George, Utah, and then tacked southeastward in a wagon train, fording the Colorado at Lee's Ferry and traversing the wild Arizona Territory to the high country around Taylor-Snowflake. Finally, in 1881, they reverse-tacked southwestward down the Mogollon Rim to a new pioneer community long before it was officially known as Mesa.

Like his father before him Jesse tilled the soil, acquiring a 160-acre homestead parcel at what is now the northwest corner of Country Club and Main. But unlike his father young Zeb opted for higher education, graduating from the Arizona State Normal School at Tempe (now ASU) in 1899. Later he studied mining engineering at the University of Arizona, but was forced to interrupt his studies and return home in 1903 to manage his ailing father's homestead. Shortly thereafter he married Rachel Leebrick.

After their marriage Pearce taught at Magma and Alma schools and Mesa High, and then decided to change roles from math teacher to merchant—a fortuitous choice that would affect the Pearce clan to this day. In 1911 Zeb Pearce purchased Guy Attaway's half-share in the produce business co-owned by L.B. Johnson. Three years later the partnership was incorporated as the Johnson Pearce Produce Company. And so began what is the oldest extant business in Mesa.

In 1919 the partnership began a farm and home-specialty enterprise, incorporating it as the Mesa Seed & Feed Company. Both operations were moved to a former livery stable at 151-155 West Main Street—the continuous location of Zeb Pearce's enterprises for the past 69 years. The combine expanded its produce business to Phoenix, and in 1926 Mesa Seed & Feed and Johnson Pearce Produce reincorporated as the Johnson Pearce Commercial Company.

The new organization built warehouses, refrigeration facilities, and a transportation network to support its extensive farm produce business. It was these updated facilities—and the repeal of Prohibition in 1933—that led to the firm's final development phase.

Literally days after the federal government legalized the sale of alcoholic beverages, the Adolph Coors Brewing Company sought a central Arizona distributor. The Johnson Pearce Commercial Company, headed by Pearce, landed the franchise be-

Zebulon Pearce studied engineering, taught mathematics, and co-owned the Mesa Seed & Feed Company before distributing beverages, a vocation he began shortly after the end of Prohibition.

cause it had ammonia-cooled food lockers that could store the unpasteurized draught beer, which required refrigeration.

Four years later Pearce purchased the shares of his partner, C.M. Johnson, and in 1943 changed its charter to Zeb Pearce and Sons—a partnership of Zeb and his sons, Arthur L., Ralph Norman, Charles R., and J. Phillip, who sold his shares to the corporation in 1958.

Through the years it has spun off all of its produce and seed-feed interests, and now operates solely in the beverage and mineral water markets. Before Zeb passed away in 1969 at the age of 92, he turned the helm over to his three sons.

Today two generations of Pearces own and operate the Zeb Pearce Companies. Zeb's sons Arthur, Norman, and Charles are directors, and grandsons Arthur L. Pearce II and Norman D. Pearce are president and vice-president, respectively.

The younger management team now charts the activities of the firm's four subordinate corporations—Pearce and Sons Distributors, Zeb Pearce and Sons Wholesale Liquors, Pearce Distributing Company, and Central Truck and Equipment Company.

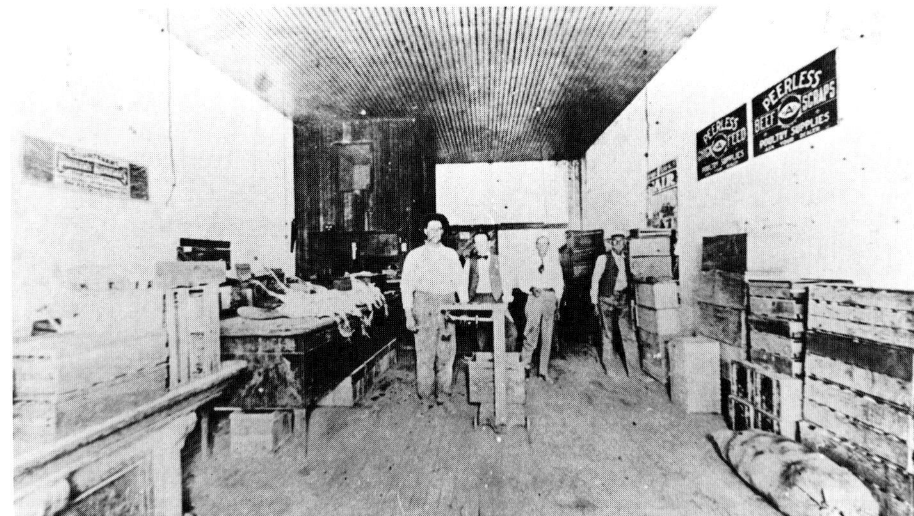

The interior of Johnson Pearce Produce Company at its original location. Pictured among two unidentified men are Charlie Johnson (left) and Zeb Pearce (second from right). Photo circa 1915

First United Methodist Church, and the ASU Sun Angel Foundation. Countless other charitable and service institutions benefited from his largess over the years.

Zeb's sons and grandsons have followed his civic-minded lead. His son R. Norman was a member of the Mesa City Council for 12 years and a major contributor to the University of Arizona Department of Medical Research. Arthur L. was one of the founders of the Arizona Zoological Society, and his son, Arthur L. II, is a member of its board of directors.

The Pearce family has established student loan funds at Mesa Community College and ASU, and two awards for excellence in teaching at ASU's College of Liberal Arts in memory of its alumnus and alumna, Zebulon and Rachel Pearce.

Deeply rooted in tough and resourceful pioneer stock, and steeped in 77 years of business tradition, the present generation of Pearces is ably advancing the family enterprises into the twenty-first century.

The firm is the oldest and second-largest Coors distributor in the nation, and Heileman Brewery's fourth-largest distributor. Coors constitutes 70 percent of its sales and Heileman's 20 percent. The company markets to 87 percent of Arizona's population and enjoys a 20-percent share of the entire Arizona beer market, which is the fourth-largest per-capita consumer of beer in the nation.

From its corporate offices at 155 West Main, the firm manages more than 316,000 square feet of warehouse, office, and refrigerated storage space in Mesa, Phoenix, Glendale, Tucson, and Safford, and its 270 employees distribute its several lines to more than 5,700 retailers in central and southern Arizona.

The Pearce family interests range far beyond their conglomerate. Zeb was on the Mesa School Board for years and served on the Mesa City Council for 12 years, capping his political career as mayor from 1944 to 1946. Pearce's interests were of a philanthropic nature as well. He was a major donor to the Mesa Lutheran Hospital, the Mesa

Two generations of the Pearce family keep the Coors flowing in central Arizona. At top (left to right) are Chuck, Norman, and Art Pearce; below (left to right) are Bob, Norman D., and Art II.

In 1919 Johnson Pearce incorporated a farm and home specialty store called the Mesa Seed & Feed Company at 129 West Main. This photograph was taken during the town's cotton festival.

BIESEMEYER MANUFACTURING CORPORATION

"Build a better mousetrap, and the world will beat a path to your door—if you package it attractively and market it aggressively."

Biesemeyer Manufacturing Corporation doesn't make mousetraps. But it does make something as simple and straightforward—and infinitely more reliable.

The company's uncanny success rests on its completed maxim, and the fateful symbiosis of a genius inventor-craftsman, Bill Biesemeyer, and a dynamic marketer-manager, Roger Thompson.

Biesemeyer had been a maker of quality cabinets and an award-winning boat builder. His knowledge of woodworking and woodworkers' needs led him to his initial invention—that quintessential woodworkers' tool—the T-Square® saw fence system.

Biesemeyer took the simple, commonplace, and ancient carpenter's T-Square and transformed it into a totally reliable guide for table saw users to cut wood precisely in a fraction of the time. And, like the mousetrap, it only has two moving parts.

Thompson had spent 20 years as a management and marketing executive virtually consumed with streamlining organizations and maximizing sales for such firms as Sears, Talley Industries, and Fotomat Corporation.

Owners of Biesemeyer Manufacturing Corporation (left to right): Roger and Victoria Thompson, and Joan and Bill Biesemeyer.

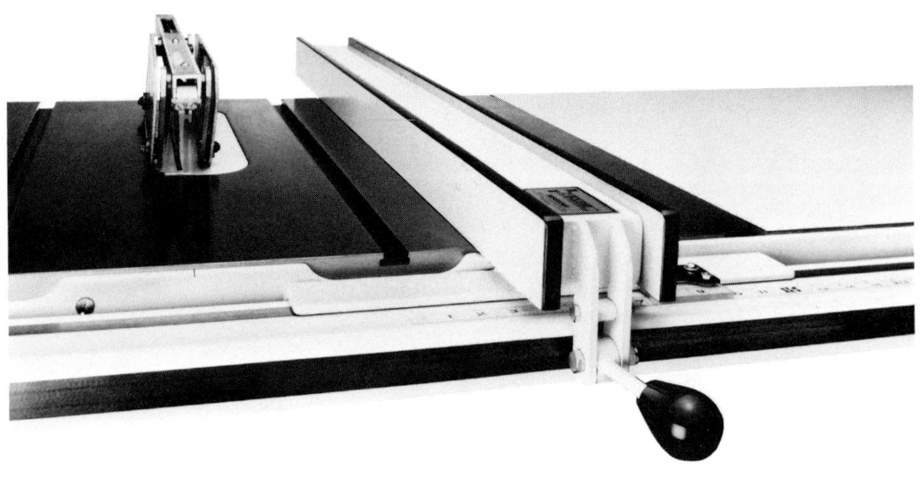

The award-winning T-Square® saw fence system—the flagship product of the company.

One fateful day in the spring of 1980 Thompson visited Biesemeyer at the small cubicle the latter was renting in a machine shop in Phoenix. Hampered by a lack of cash, equipment, and space, Biesemeyer was still turning out small numbers of this unique, quality product and personally selling them to the local market while Joan, his wife, did the bookkeeping in their home.

After Thompson and Biesemeyer decided to join forces, they located the new T-Square Tool Company in a 5,000-square-foot suite on South Alma School Road in Mesa. Thompson remembers Biesemeyer ironically saying, "It's too large; we'll never fill it up."

Just a few weeks away from that historic merger were two of the industry's major trade shows—three weeks apart. The first was in Atlanta, the second in Louisville. With no displays or graphics it was madcap time putting the act together. The Biesemeyer T-Square show was born out of two display suitcases and played to a standing-room-only crowd from a 10-foot by 10-foot booth. The rest is history.

No one at either show had ever seen

the product. "The people went nuts over it." The booths, manned by Thompson and his wife, Victoria, were jammed with customers and dealers. Thompson believes that, "If those shows hadn't come along when they did, we would have had a more difficult time getting started," and he returned from Atlanta with a backlog exceeding 500 orders. Three weeks later he repeated the blitz and came away with orders for another 500 systems. And he had signed up an army of dealers in the process. The two shows had given their company a substantial jolt of capital when they needed it most. With this, Joan expanded her critical role as controller of the financially growing company.

Six months after moving in, the corporation rented an adjacent 5,000 square feet of space—10,000 square feet in all—and the "roll" continued.

Less than a year later Thompson entered the T-Square® saw fence system in the International Challengers Award competition. The majority of the 180 entries were highly sophisticated machines. Biesemeyer's product, however, had only two moving parts and cost only $299. After overcoming their disbelief, the judges awarded the firm first prize. Biesemeyer Manufacturing was still on a roll.

The company then began manufacturing and marketing a variety of labor- and money-saving products to service the large array of woodworking saws on the market.

One of the keys to Biesemeyer Manufacturing's fabulous success is its market focus on the small, labor-intensive, one- to 10-man shops, which constitute 80 percent of the total woodworking industry.

Four years after incorporation, *Inc.,* "the magazine for growing companies," published its annual list of the 500 fastest-growing private businesses in the United States. Biesemeyer Manufacturing placed 113th. That edition also featured Biesemeyer and Thompson in a section entitled, "Private Lives."

A year later they did it again—only better. This time *Inc.* listed the firm as the 57th fastest-growing company nationwide, with a growth rate 3,243 percent over its base five years before.

In 1986 the Mesa Chamber of Commerce singled out Biesemeyer Manufactur-

The company's high standard of quality is apparent in this view of a small area of the manufacturing facility.

ing for yet another kudo as the first recipient of the Mesa Growth Company of the Year Award. The following year the chamber included the firm in a 15-minute Mesa-area promotional film along with such fast company as McDonnell Douglas and Talley Industries.

Back in 1984 Biesemeyer Manufacturing purchased the 80,000-square-foot industrial park where it had previously rented space, and two years later purchased another 70,000-square-foot industrial park across the street. These properties contain four buildings on seven acres.

Neither partner has even considered slowing the pace; the unabated growth of Biesemeyer Manufacturing is ample evidence of that.

The future is bright for the eight-year-old firm that now manufactures and markets a line of 18 precision woodworking tools, with more on the way. And it hasn't nicked the market yet, even though to date the company has sold more than 100,000 saw fence systems. The T-Square® saw fence system is now considered the industry standard, and the firm's worldwide market is serviced by a huge army of retailers and 50 employees in its Mesa complex.

The key to the partners' success? Biesemeyer will tell you it's "always keeping the end-user in mind by providing him with the quality products he really needs at a price he can afford."

But even a casual observer would opine that the real key to the success of Biesemeyer Manufacturing Corporation is symbiosis—the teaming of an inventive genius with a marketing firebrand.

Skill and harmony abound among the operations and management staff.

SOUTHWEST AMBULANCE, INC.

Southwest Ambulance's Central Dispatch Information System handles approximately 180 calls per day throughout Maricopa County.

When Bob Ramsey was a Boy Scout in Phoenix during the mid-1950s, he became so imbued with the importance of emergency medical care that he started the First Response Patrol in his troop. He and his fellow scouts learned first aid techniques and responded to calls for emergency help from anywhere in their neighborhood. As a result, he was featured in *Boy's Life.*

Although he went on to major in history and Asian studies at Arizona State University and to work, after graduation, in mixed-media and advertising, Ramsey never lost his fascination with emergency health care. It was not surprising, therefore, that in 1982 he founded Southwest Ambulance, Inc., currently Arizona's largest private company in its field.

Ramsey, president and chief operating officer of the corporation, has earned an enviable reputation as an innovator in the several industries with which he has been associated. Ramsey's wife, Jenny Norton, is a representative to the state legislature from Tempe.

In the mid-1960s he started one of the first mixed-media companies in Arizona, became vice-president/marketing in the Paddock Pools organization in 1975, served as a solar energy consultant, and worked with Arizona's Indians in establishing a newspaper, building a solar school, and organizing emergency medical services. Moving on to the Ambulance Industry in the late 1970s Ramsey advanced rapidly to the title of executive vice-president of the firm KORDS-PMT. He soon broke away to establish the first privately owned non-stop transcontinental air ambulance service, which afforded an easy segue to starting his own emergency ground transportation firm.

The impact of Southwest Ambulance and its president on the emergency medical transportation industry in Arizona has been little short of spectacular. Ramsey has brought about exciting changes and established such programs as specialized training for emergency vehicle drivers, less expensive medical transportation for those who do not require all the facilities of an ambulance, courses for paramedics and emergency care technicians, billing preparation for other ambulance services (the City of Phoenix is one), and consulting help for HMOs and other medical organizations.

"This is a sunrise industry," Ramsey declares. "Prehospital services are just emerging as vital components of total health care, and we have only begun to explore the possibilities."

One of those possibilities is in cost containment, a field that has intrigued Ramsey for years. At least a partial solution is Southwest's new ambulette service, which uses "medi-cabs" and "medi-coaches" to transport patients who do not require full ambulance service.

Another is the innovative Southwest Ambulance instructional program, called Evade. Not only ambulance drivers but also firemen, police officers, and other drivers of emergency vehicles come to Southwest's Mesa, Arizona, school for instruction, and to nearby field sites for practical driving problems.

The company's standard ambulance service is kept at high levels, too. Forty ambulances operate from 21 stations in Phoenix, other Maricopa County cities, and in Pinal County. In 95 to 98 percent of all cases, they average only 3.5 minutes in response time.

Southwest has franchises for exclusive ambulance service in Tempe, Chandler, Glendale, Casa Grande, and North San Diego County, and it shares services with other companies in most other communities of central Arizona. Its headquarters is at South 40th and LaSalle streets near the border dividing Phoenix and Tempe.

To respond without delay to calls for help from its many service areas, Southwest Ambulance has a staff of 250, including drivers, paramedics, instructors, office personnel, mechanics, and many other specialists. "We are operating a private business," observes Ramsey, "but you can be sure we all consider ourselves in partnership with the public sector. We are on full alert 24 hours a day, seven days a week, and lives hang on the state of our readiness and proficiency."

A timely response to this accident in Mesa typifies Southwest Ambulance's high level of service.

BILL JOHNSON'S RESTAURANTS, INC.

Bill Johnson was born in Oklahoma in 1916. He worked in the Oklahoma oil fields, among other places, during the 1930s. Eventually, the economic choke of the Dust Bowl turned Johnson's gaze westward. In 1941 he and his wife, Gene, moved to California in quest of the dream that brought so many of his compatriots there in the late 1930s.

Bill went to work in a Long Beach shipyard and Gene worked as a waitress. In 1943 Bill had a chance to purchase a small, seven-stool hot dog stand outside the shipyard. He seized the opportunity, and in 1944 he opened his first full-service restaurant in Compton, California. He called it Harrell's Cafe, after his daughter, Harrell Dean "Dena." It featured barbeque-type food crowned with Gene's special-recipe barbeque sauce. During the early 1950s Bill and Gene opened two more restaurants in Comp-

Bill Johnson, founder of the Big Apple Restaurants, at the Big Apple radio studio. Photo circa 1956

ton and Buena Park, both called Gene's Barbeque. Bill Johnson became a celebrity in the Los Angeles area by broadcasting live radio shows on KXLA seven nights a week from his restaurant in Compton.

As successful as his restaurants in California were, Bill's dream was to live in the Valley of the Sun and run a chain of western-style eateries there. He opened his first Big Apple restaurant on East Van Buren in 1956. He continued his live radio broadcasts on KPHO. Bill's dynamic personality and flamboyant style set the Big Apple apart from the more conventional eating establishments in Phoenix. Its innovative western atmosphere and Gene's one-of-a-kind barbeque sauce made it an immediate success. Although it specialized in barbeque, it was a full-service restaurant featuring extensive breakfast, lunch, and dinner menus.

In 1966 Bill Johnson passed away; however, his legacy lives on through the efforts of Gene and their four children: Dena, Rudy, Johnny, and Sherry. Eight years later the family began the Big Apple expansion phase. Today there are three more Big Apples—two in Phoenix and one in Mesa. A fifth is scheduled for Chandler in later 1988. From an original staff of 20, the company now employs more than 400 people. Future plans include

Big Apple Mesa, at 950 East Main, shares the western theme integral to all Bill Johnson's Restaurants.

nine additional family-owned units through 1993, as well as a national franchise package. The new Chandler Big Apple will serve as the franchise prototype. Like all of Bill Johnson's Big Apples, the franchise theme is western, complete with pistol-packing waitresses, sawdust-covered floors, and numerous antiques and authentic relics of the Old West.

The really fascinating facet of the Johnson restaurants' success story, however, is its barbeque sauce. In the beginning customers would bring their empty bottles and jugs into the Big Apple on Van Buren for some of Gene's great-tasting sauce. In 1972 the Johnson family rented the Cahill's Prickly Pear Jelly Company facilities to run their first commercial batch of 71 cases. Gene cooked the sauce, and the kids bottled and cased it. A year later they ran more than 2,000 cases. By 1987 their California bottling agent produced 230,000 cases of Bill Johnson's Big Apple Barbeque Sauce, Arizona's largest-selling barbeque sauce, carried in all major grocery chains throughout Arizona and eight other states.

CITY OF MESA

The historic Joel E. Sirrine house was completely restored and furnished with items from the late 1890s.

In the summer of 1883, five years after first settling on the "large mesa" in the East Valley, the residents of newly incorporated Mesa City officially began the business of governance, electing their first mayor, three councilmen, a marshal, assessor, treasurer, recorder, and poundmaster to administer its one square mile. First on the council's agenda included the naming of streets, purchasing an "iron jail cage," regulating saloons, and "building foot bridges across certain canals."

Surely, its first mayor, Scottish immigrant A.F. Macdonald, never dreamed that from such pedestrian beginnings would emerge one of the nation's fastest-growing municipalities, doubling in geographic size every 10 years since the 1930s.

Today Mesa's efficient governmental infrastructure nurtures a vibrant politico-economic enclave in the East Valley with a host of quality services.

Mesa's crime-protection system has come a long way since the city's first marshal, Wellington Richins, patrolled its dusty streets. Today there are more than 550 personnel in the Mesa Police Department, operating out of its headquarters and two substations, with two more in the offing. From its first volunteer company in 1898, Mesa's Fire Department has grown by 250 opera-

tives working out of 12 station houses, with two more in development.

The city owns and operates a municipal airport at Falcon Field, a cemetery, and an electric utility service for seven square miles of its core at rates below those of neighboring cities.

The Public Works Department maintains more than 800 miles of city roads and operates the potable water supply that flows from the Central Arizona Project and from Mesa's deep artesian wells. To ensure future water resources, the city has purchased the water rights on 12,000 acres of Pinal County farmland, runs a water conservation office to heighten public water conservation awareness, and grants tax rebates for low water usage.

On the qualitative side, Mesa operates 42 city parks, a three-branch library system, a civic center—replete with exhibits and indoor concert facilities—an outdoor amphitheater, an art gallery, the Mesa Southwest Museum, a theater and museum for youth, and subsidizes some of the Mesa Symphony's concerts. The three routes of the city's Sunrunner Bus System, as well as its Dial-A-Ride vans and sedans for the elderly and handicapped, service the city's 107 square miles and interconnect with the Regional Public Transportation Authority buses.

All these services exist with no city property tax, a one-percent city sales tax, eight employees per 1,000 residents, and a 1988-1989 budget of $248 million for its 284,000 citizens.

Mesa—a city riding high in the saddle with a caring, trail-wise government at the reins.

Even with the explosive growth of the past few decades, Mesa offers a dynamic blend of new construction and open fields, which are still farmed today.

BROADWAY SOUTHWEST

Broadway Southwest's history began in 1895, when merchandiser Sam Korrick opened The New York Store in Phoenix. This small retail outlet was equipped to meet the needs of frontier Phoenix, offering everything from corsets to cowboy hats.

As business boomed, Sam Korrick renamed the store Korrick's and opened a second valley outlet in what is now the Chris-Town Mall. Not surprisingly, the rapidly growing Phoenix market—and Korrick's thriving business—soon caught the attention of the California-based Broadway-Hale Corporation, the largest department store operation in the Southwest.

In 1961 the Broadway-Hale Corporation purchased Korrick's. The company sought greater market share by expanding and renovating its store in Chris-Town, and building four new Broadway stores in the Valley.

By 1979 Broadway-Hale Corporation merged and became Carter Hawley Hale, with Broadway stores in Southern California, southern Nevada, New Mexico, and Arizona.

In order to compete more effectively in the rapidly growing areas of the Southwest, the stores in Nevada, New Mexico, and Arizona became known as Broadway Southwest, with their own operating division in Mesa.

Broadway Southwest corporate headquarters is located in Mesa, , occupying the entire top floor of its 206,000-square-foot store in Mesa's Fiesta Mall. From there it manages the operations of seven Broadway stores in Arizona, two in Nevada, and one each in New Mexico and Colorado. Currently, 652 of Broadway Southwest's 14,000 associates across four states are employed at its Fiesta Mall facility.

"The growing city of Mesa has provided Broadway Southwest with a strong foundation for future growth and earnings," comments Broadway Southwest president and chief executive officer Martin M. Kalkstein.

To demonstrate the area's above-average growth rate, five of Broadway Southwest's 11 stores are located in the valley, with Mesa's Fiesta Mall store leading the others in both sales volume and profitability.

Much of Broadway Southwest's success in Mesa, as well as the other markets, is attributed to meeting the growing demands of its target clientele. The customer is more sophisticated and contemporary than that of eight years ago, when the Mesa store first opened. This group has a higher demand for quality and style, standards that Broadway Southwest never has difficulty in meeting.

To be even more responsive to today's customer, the stores offer a number of specialized services. Discounts and exclusive benefits are available to the growing population of citizens age 55 and older, in addition to a time-saving shopping plan that serves the busy life-style of career men and women.

Plans to develop additional stores in the East Valley indicate the area's potential for growth and sales—and with it, the hopes that Broadway Southwest will grow and prosper there as it has elsewhere in the Southwest.

Broadway Southwest's corporate headquarters occupies the entire top floor of Mesa's Fiesta Mall store.

DOBSON RANCH INN AND RESORT

The history of the Dobson Ranch Inn and Resort doesn't begin with its opening in 1979. It starts in Ontario, Canada, in 1886, when William Wesley "W.W." Dobson left that province and homesteaded 160 acres near Alma School and Baseline. This endeavor was to become one of the valley's great land and cattle empires and would make the Dobson name one of the best-known in Mesa.

Ironically, it was Wesley's brother, John, who became the bigger land and cattle owner. Just 17 when he arrived in Mesa with his brother, John worked the elder Wesley's homestead from sunup to sundown for a dollar a day plus board. Forsaking formal schooling, John managed to save enough of his wages to lease-purchase 80 acres from his brother and farm on his own.

When the Roosevelt Dam began to take shape, John began expanding his holdings, and by the late 1930s had built one of the largest ranches in the valley. He wound up with more than 4,000 acres of ranchland in Mesa and Chandler, and about 60,000 acres of rangeland east of Mesa and in the White Mountains.

Running his cattle out of the high country in the fall, fattening some 20,000 head each year on his feed lots along Baseline, John became a major cattle feeder and sheep rancher. As his children came of age they either became partners in their father's business or received land of their own. When John retired in 1941, his son, Cliff, took over the Baseline Cattle Company, and when the elder Dobson died in 1949, Cliff entered into a partnership with his brother-in-law, Dwight Patterson, and continued to expand the Dobson holdings under the aegis of the Baseline Cattle Company and Sheep-springs Sheep Company.

Many of the biggest development projects in southwest Mesa erupted from Dobson's and Patterson's spread. The boom was triggered by the construction of the Supersti-tion Freeway, which cut through part of the Dobson Ranch. The first sonic wave was felt in 1963, when the 160-acre Mesa Community College was constructed on part of Dobson's cattle and sheep grazing land on Southern and Dobson, and in 1970 the Desert Samaritan Hospital was erected on 24 acres donated by Cliff Dobson and his wife.

That same year Dobson and Patterson sold most of their remaining 3,000 acres to Continental Homes, which sold 107 of those acres for Fiesta Mall and used the remainder for its huge Dobson Ranch development—an integrated community of homes, apartments, shopping centers, lakes, and a golf course. Cliff, who died that year, didn't live to see the massive developments become a reality.

Dwight Patterson realized the value of

In the midst of what was once 4,000 acres of ranchland in Mesa and Chandler stands the 10-acre Dobson Ranch Inn.

a resort hotel on his 10-acre site on Dobson and Superstition Freeway—dead in the middle of Mesa's rapidly developing commercial hub—and formed a partnership to build the Dobson Ranch Inn.

In 1977 Lee Roy Kellis, Raymond L. Flynn, and Robert O. Cummins joined with Patterson to construct and promote a resort hotel. A joint venture was then created with 20 additional Mesa community members, and the entire project capitalized from within with no debt service.

The Dobson Inn was completed in 1979 and became the first quality resort hotel in Mesa. Its 212 executive rooms consist of 12 two-room executive suites and 38 executive kings, an oversized heated pool and spa, a fitness center, and complete conference, meeting, and banquet facilities that accommodate up to 450 people. This design of the resort reflects Spanish, Indian, and Old West influences, and is interspersed with wide expanses of greenery. For the discriminating linkster there is the 18-hole championship Dobson Golf Course, just three minutes away.

Dale Anderson, a member of the partnership, subleased part of the site adjoining the resort hotel to build The Other Place, one of the valley's quality dining establishments. The restaurant includes optional outdoor patio dining around cozy beehive fireplaces, and the Charro Lounge, which features nightly dancing.

The inn comes alive from late February to early April, when the Milwaukee Brewers check into the 63 rooms reserved for them annually at their spring-training headquarters. The Brewers are part of an eight-team Cactus League centered in Arizona, primarily in the East Valley and Scottsdale. Most of the remaining rooms are booked well in advance by their rabid fans, who combine a vacation getaway in luxury surroundings with team togetherness at the hotel and the nearby 7,500-seat Compadre Stadium. For two weeks during the team's training two Milwaukee radio stations broadcast local color and team tidbits back home from the inn's lobby and poolside.

Much of the huge economic impact (estimated at $45 million) of the four major-league teams training in the Mesa area stems from the efforts of Dwight Patterson, regarded in the valley as the Father of the Cactus League. It was Patterson who, in the early 1950s, attracted the Cubs and the teams that followed to the benefits of Arizona spring baseball. And it's Patterson who is the point of contact for those interested in exploring further Cactus League expansion.

From one of the largest cattle and farming enterprises in the East Valley has sprung

Dwight Patterson of the Baseline Cattle Company helped develop the Dobson Ranch Inn and is responsible for attracting the Chicago Cubs and other Cactus League baseball teams to the Mesa area as their spring-training grounds.

the hub of Mesa's latter-day commercial activity—and one of the favorite vacation spots for East Valley visitors and baseball groupies alike—The Dobson Ranch Inn and Resort.

BEST WESTERN MEZONA MOTOR HOTEL

For nearly 85 years the corner of Main and Morris has been a rendezvous for recreating Mesans and out-of-towners—first, in the early days, as a social center, and, more recently, as a prominent hotel.

Frank Vance was in his family's bakery business before he decided to host Mesa recreational events. In about 1908 he enlisted his neighbor, W.A. Burton, a part-time builder and the town undertaker, to build Vance Auditorium on the vacant lot on the corner of Main and Morris.

Completed appropriately on Valentine's Day 1908, Vance Auditorium soon became the biggest social gathering place in Mesa. The stucco-on-wood building had a seating capacity of 2,500, with banquet facilities in the basement. The structure hosted basketball games, roller-skating parties, and dances. The auditorium was also the scene of most of the town's cultural fare—plays, lectures, exhibits, and the newest rage, the silent films made before Mesa's first movie house was built. A strict Mormon, Vance would not allow drinking or smoking in his establishment, and, as a result, its popularity soon began to wane.

The auditorium's competitor for youthful attention was the Rendezvous on Center and Second streets, where the management held dances three nights a week, and drinking and smoking codes were only laxly enforced.

In about 1920 the Maricopa Stake of the Church of Jesus Christ of Latter-day Saints was looking for a proper location where its youth—and the youth of the area—could socialize in a more structured and wholesome environment. Vance donated the auditorium to the Maricopa Stake, which subsequently remodeled it.

The Mutual Improvement Association (MIA) of each of the four Mesa wards in the stake began sponsoring a weekly, Friday-night dance at the Vance, which was renamed the Mezona in about 1925. Van Brinton, a local insurance man, and William Gollaher, a plumber and part-time saxophonist, teamed up to run the Mezona for the stake. Gollaher would hire Francis Gilbert's dance band, "the best in Arizona," for the Friday-night dances, and in short order, the Mezona began to enjoy areawide popularity because of the variety of programs the management offered and the equitable way in which the dances were run.

Brinton and Gollaher also scheduled exhibits, banquets, commencements, civic meetings, local contests, visiting lecturers, and the annual Mesa Citrus Show, and the Stake Decoration Committee regularly staged three-act plays there.

The Great Depression didn't dampen the Mezona's popularity one iota. In fact, attendance perked, turning the establishment into *the* Friday-night hangout for many of the valley's youth. Brinton introduced a budget system to encourage attendance, charging 10 cents for admission and a nickel a dance (a jitney dance). For a dollar a couple could dance all night. A family could buy a budget booklet for the whole year for $25, and a individual could purchase an annual booklet for $15. Brinton even permitted barter for those without cash; no one was ever turned away for lack of money. If they were broke they were given tickets, or he would trade tickets for cigarettes to take the "nails" out of circulation.

According to Dilworth Brinton, Van's son, who later took over as Mezona manager, "There was little else for the youngsters to do on a Friday evening when basketball wasn't in season except take in a cowboy movie at the Nile or go dancing at the Mez-

The old Mezona building, erected in 1908 by Frank Vance as a social center, served Mesa as a cultural center and dance hall until it was closed for structural reasons in 1970.

ona. Why, the whole family would come on Friday night." Dilworth remembers, "Even the Baptists danced in Mesa . . . because parents would rather have their children at a wholesome place such as the Mezona on a Friday night than sparking down on the canal banks."

The Mezona was remodeled again in 1948 with funds from Salt Lake City, and the LDS Church took title. Entertainment interests changed after World War II, and in 1970 the City of Mesa condemned the building as structurally unsound and obsolete. So ended, according to Brinton, "the most important social and recreational activity center in Mesa between 1926 and 1946."

In 1972 Bob Cummins, Ray Flynn, and Lee Roy Kellis, local businessmen and developers of numerous hotel properties in California and Arizona, put together a joint venture with 21 East Valley professional and business partners and leased the 4.5-acre Mezona property from another group of investors that had purchased the property from the LDS Church.

In 1973 their corporation, Appollo-Mezona, Inc., opened the 140-room Mezona Motor Hotel. Another investment group, Goldmar Incorporated, subleased the remainder of the Mezona property adjacent to the hotel and built two restaurants to complement the hotel—the Figg Tree (now the House Of Yee), and the Humpty Dumpty Coffee Shop.

The Mezona was, at the time, the largest hotel in Mesa. It is now one of the largest downtown hotels in the city, just three blocks from the historic center of town. Once the stopping-off place for most of the prominent sojourners visiting Mesa, the Best Western Mezona Motor Hotel is today the spring-training headquarters for the Chicago Cubs.

In 1973 Appollo-Mezona, Inc., a group of local businessmen and hotel developers, opened the 140-room Mezona Motor Hotel where the old Mezona building once stood.

During the Cactus League season, when the "Cubbies" are in town, the packed hotel bustles with excitement generated by the ballplayers, their families, and the Midwest FANatics, who seasonally reserve rooms at the Mezona. During the summer months the Tokyo Yomiuri Giants baseball team calls the Mezona home.

In addition to its spacious, well-appointed rooms, the hotel provides room service, a secluded patio pool, and meeting facilities. Most importantly, Best Western Mezona Motor Hotel is located within easy walking distance of Mesa's historical points of interest and its new cultural and civic activity centers.

MESA TRIBUNE

In 1977 the *Mesa Tribune* became part of Cox Enterprises Inc. The Tribune Newspapers recently won the 1987 Society of Newspaper Design's Gold Award for overall design, outranking many larger newspapers nationwide.

It was 13 years after Mesa's founding before the city had a newspaper of its own. Then, in 1891, two local lawyers started the four-page *Evening Weekly Free Press,* filled with equal portions of Mesa happenings and syndicated material. But it wasn't until 1901 that the paper went daily.

For the next 67 years Mesa's newspaper alternated between daily and weekly publication with a succession of owners and name changes. It became the *Mesa Daily Tribune* in 1913 and reached its full growth in 1958, when it went to a six-day publication schedule and added a color cartoon section to its Saturday edition.

In July 1977 a new day dawned for Mesa and the entire East Valley when Cox Enterprises, Inc., headquartered in Atlanta, Georgia, purchased the *Mesa Tribune.* Cox Enterprises, Inc., owns 19 newspapers, 8 television stations, 11 radio stations, a cable division, and auto auctions.

Within a year after purchasing the afternoon *Mesa Tribune*, a Sunday edition was launched; two years later the daily became a morning publication. The *Tempe Daily News* was acquired at that time, forming Cox Arizona Publications, Inc. Concurrently the management of the newspapers began encouraging the concept of an East Valley community among readers, and the papers took an aggressive editorial stance on the East Valley's important issues.

With the acquisition of the *Chandler Arizonan* in 1983, all three Tribune newspapers were in place. They moved quickly to fill the East Valley's news and advertising needs.

In November 1986 the papers were redesigned. The name "Tribune" was added to the *Chandler Arizonan* and the *Tempe Daily News.* The "new" Tribune Newspapers subsequently won the 1987 Society of Newspaper Design's international competition. Of the 7,034 entrants, the *Tribune* was the only newspaper in any circulation category to earn the Gold Award for overall design, winning out over such formidable competitors as the *Seattle Times* and the *New York Times.*

In the 11 years since it became part of Cox Newspapers, the *Mesa Tribune* has become a sophisticated, complete mini-metro. The Tribune Newspapers' new, state-of-the-art printing plant is capable of turning out 96-page editions for all three papers, which during the past two years have increased circulation by 43 percent to 76,000, making them some of the fastest-growing newspapers in the country.

Tribune reporter Deena Higgs types a story on a Crosfield Video Display Terminal, while fellow reporter Lawn Griffiths looks on.

LANDMARK RESTAURANT

The Landmark Restaurant has been an integral part of Mesa's development since the turn of the century.

Its main building was dedicated in 1911 as the Latter-Day Saints Alma Ward Church. The two other "landmark" structures on the site were built to accommodate some of the church's social activities. A combination recreation hall and cultural center was built in 1925, with a concrete patio between the hall and church for Thursday-evening dances. Fifteen years later the ward erected a small building next door for its Boy Scout troop.

In 1937 a section was added to the church's front entrance on Main, relocating the entrance to Extension. The remodeling enhanced the basement and included the addition of street-level rooms for church dinners and additional activities.

In the mid-1950s the ward was moved to more modern facilities and the complex was sold to an insurance agency. Later the site became the headquarters and temporary campus of Mesa Community College. In 1971 the main building was converted, operating as the Schoolhouse Restaurant until the end of the decade.

It was then that a successful young restaurateur from Concord, New Hampshire, turned the structure into a charming and popular landmark for East Valley dining.

Don Ellis and his wife, Candy, couldn't resist the "lure of the area," and moved to the valley in 1979 after selling the second of a pair of successful dining establishments in Concord. Don had spent nearly 20 years in the food and beverage business, and diligently searched the valley for the "right property," purchasing the Schoolhouse Restaurant in the latter part of 1981.

Though that restaurant had deteriorated in its later years, "its possibilities and potential charm were enormous."

What followed, according to Don, was a classic example of "sweat, guts, and stubbornness"—and family solidarity. While Don ran the business, Candy, Don's mother, father, brother, and sister-in-law turned a major face-lifting project into a family affair as they repaired, remodeled, and redecorated the restaurant inside and out. The two other buildings were repaired and refurbished, and the patio flagstoned and covered, turning them into an attractive and busy banquet complex.

Ellis has transformed an also-ran bistro into a popular dining spot for locals and "snowbirds" alike. The main dining room has a quiet, comfortable, old-fashioned congeniality, excellent midwestern- and New England-style fare, and "probably the largest salad bar you will ever see."

How popular is it? Through word of mouth Don's summer clientele is now triple that of his winter trade when he first opened the establishment six years ago.

For some of the older diners the Landmark Restaurant is pure nostalgia, as they reminisce about the times they spent there on campus or at church functions.

The building that now houses the Landmark Restaurant was dedicated as a Mormon church in 1911. The structure also served Mesa Community College and housed the Schoolhouse Restaurant. Below is the restaurant as it appeared in 1937.

The original train depot was located near what is now the corner of University and Center. The depot was at the track's end on a spur line that went through Tempe to Phoenix. It was this spur line that made Mesa the important end-point and key stop in the freighting of supplies to the Roosevelt Dam construction site. Courtesy, Mesa Southwest Collections

P ATRONS
▼ ▼ ▼

The following individuals, companies, and organizations have made a valuable commitment to the quality of this publication. Windsor Publications and the Mesa Southwest Museum and Guild gratefully acknowledge their participation in *Mesa: Beneath the Shadows of the Superstitions.*

Able Steel Fabricators, Inc.*
Alumi-Cover Awning Company, Inc.*
The Arizona Golf Resort and Conference
   Center*
The Arizona Republic and Phoenix Gazette*
Best Western Mezona Motor Hotel*
Biesemeyer Manufacturing Corporation*
Broadway Southwest*
Builders Guild, Inc.
Champlin Fighter Museum*
Chandler Ready Mix*
City of Mesa*
Coury Enterprises*
Crismon's Flowers*
Desert Samaritan Hospital & Health Center*

Dobson Ranch Inn and Resort*
Fiesta Mall*
The Haws Companies*
Bill Johnson's Restaurants, Inc.*
Landmark Restaurant*
McConaghie/Batt & Associates*
McDonnell Douglas Helicopter Company*
Mesa Community College*
Mesa Tribune*
Mining Camp Restaurant & Trading Post*
Morea-Hall Engineering, Inc.*
Zeb Pearce Companies*
Salt River Project*
Semflex, Inc.*
Southwest Ambulance, Inc.*
Southwest Properties, Inc.*
Stapley Wholesale, Inc.*

*Partners in Progress of *Mesa: Beneath the Shadows of the Superstitions.* The histories of these companies and organizations appear in Chapter 7, beginning on page 112.

The students of North Elementary School in Mesa turned out in a big way for a photographer who traveled the circuit around 1914. Courtesy, Mesa Southwest Museum

BIBLIOGRAPHY
▼ ▼ ▼

Publications

Haury, Emil. *The Hohokam.* Tucson: University of Arizona Press, 1978.

Laird, Linda, and Jones, Robert. *City of Mesa Historical Survey.* Mesa: Mesa Southwest Museum, 1984.

Martin, Douglas D. *Arizona Chronology.* Tucson: University of Arizona Press, 1966.

Merrill, Earl. *One Hundred Echoes from Mesa's Past.* Mesa: W. Earl Merrill, 1975.

Merrill, Earl. *One Hundred Footprints on Forgotten Trails.* Mesa: Mrs. W. Earl Merrill, 1978.

Merrill, Earl. *One Hundred Yesterdays.* Mesa: Mrs. W. Earl Merrill, 1978.

Mesa Tribune. 1898-present.

Our Town: Mesa Arizona, 1878-1978. Mesa: Mesa Public Schools, 1978.

Roots to Blossoms: History of Mesa Civic Organizations. Mesa: Mesa Centennial Committee, 1978.

Archives

Church of Jesus Christ of Latter-Day Saints Geneological Library, 464 E. First Avenue, Mesa, Arizona.

Mesa Southwest Museum, 53 N. Macdonald Mesa, Arizona. Features the largest community repository of historical photos, papers, notes, and oral histories of past and present Mesa residents.

Mesa Public Library, 64 E. First Avenue, Mesa, Arizona.

Oral Histories

Mark Barker, promoter and entertainer
Dilworth Brinton, local historian and columnist
Walter Zipf, long-time Mesa resident, and daily newspaper columnist with *Mesa Tribune*